The Revd. Dr. Eric Gallagher and
Dr. Stanley Worrall are distinguished
Methodists who have themselves taken
part in many of the critical and interesting
incidents which they record. Dr. Gallagher
has been President of the Methodist
Church in Ireland and Dr. Worrall
Headmaster of the Methodist College,
Belfast. Both are widely respected in
ecumenical circles.

CHRISTIANS IN ULSTER
1968–1980

CHRISTIANS
IN ULSTER
1968–1980

ERIC GALLAGHER

AND

STANLEY WORRALL

Oxford New York Toronto Melbourne
OXFORD UNIVERSITY PRESS · 1982

Oxford University Press, Walton Street, Oxford OX2 6DP
London Glasgow New York Toronto
Delhi Bombay Calcutta Madras Karachi
Kuala Lumpur Singapore Hong Kong Tokyo
Nairobi Dar es Salaam Cape Town
Melbourne Auckland
and associate companies in
Beirut Berlin Ibadan Mexico City

Published in the United States by
Oxford University Press, New York

British Library Cataloguing in Publication Data
Gallagher, Eric
Christians in Ulster 1968–1980
1. Northern Ireland—Politics and government
2. Christianity—Northern Ireland
3. Northern Ireland—History—1969.
I. Title   II. Worrall, Stanley
941.60824   DA990.U46
ISBN 0–19–213237–7

Library of Congress Cataloging in Publication Data
Gallagher, Eric, 1913–
    Christians in Ulster, 1968–1980.
    Bibliography: p.
    Includes index.
    1. Northern Ireland—Church history.
    2. Northern Ireland—History—1969–
    3. Ireland—Church history.
    4. Ireland—History—1922–
    I. Worrall, A. S.   II. Title.
    BR797.N67G34   274.16'0826   82-2126
    ISBN 0-19-213237-7   AACR2

Typeset by Oxprint Ltd, Oxford
and Printed in Great Britain
at the University Press, Oxford
by Eric Buckley
Printer to the University

Almighty God, in whose hands lies the
destiny of men and nations. Let not
the hopes of men perish, nor the
sacrifices of men be in vain.

O holy and life-giving Spirit, enable
us by your grace to root out from our
common life the bitterness of ancient
wrongs and the thirst to avenge the
betrayals of long ago. Save us from
the tyranny of History and set us free
in a new obedience to serve each other
in the present hour.

Accepting the redemption wrought for
us, we believe that all our sins of
yesterday are covered by your mercy;
grant us therefore grace and courage
to give and to receive the forgiveness
which alone can heal today's wounds.
Draw us, O Lord, towards loving kindness and guide us into the way of peace.

North Oxford Churches' Lent Booklet

Preface

This book is an attempt to examine objectively the record of the Irish Churches during the present troubles in Northern Ireland. We have ourselves been closely concerned in many of the events described. Our own point of view is manifest in what we have written, but our aim has been to state the facts as fairly as possible. The book is not written to prove a case, but to provide, as far as we can within a limited compass, the evidence on which a judgement can be based. We have not, however, sought to conceal our own conclusions.

In the nature of things much of what has been said and done by or in the name of the Churches has borne the character of response to events deriving from the political turmoil and the illegal violence. Hence in chapters 3 to 8 the main narrative thread is provided by the public events rather than by church initiatives. In chapters 9 to 11 we are concerned with matters more directly under the control of the Churches and can accordingly make the development of church policy itself the main theme. The first two chapters set the scene and the last attempts to offer some reflections. Our narrative ends at the close of 1980, but we have been able as the book went through the press to refer briefly to some happenings in 1981 that seemed to us particularly relevant to our theme.

We are indebted to many in Northern Ireland who have supplemented our researches with interviews and who have read parts of the text and made valuable suggestions. In particular Mr David Gallagher, of the Methodist College Political Science Department, has materially helped our research, and Miss Esther Fyffe has, in an honorary capacity, typed the whole work. We are also grateful to the Oxford University Press which commissioned the work and whose editorial staff have been extremely helpful with advice and guidance.

R.D.E.G.
A.S.W.

Contents

Abbreviations

ACAS	Arbitration and Conciliation Advisory Service, an agency of the British Department of Employment for resolving industrial disputes
BBC	British Broadcasting Corporation
BCC	British Council of Churches
CRA	Civil Rights Association (= NICRA)
CUE	Christian Understanding Everywhere
DUP	Democratic Unionist Party
FoR	Fellowship of Reconciliation
ICC	Irish Council of Churches
ICTU	Irish Congress of Trade Unions
IRA	Irish Republican Army
LAW	Loyalist Association of Workers
NICRA	Northern Ireland Civil Rights Association (= CRA)
NILP	Northern Ireland Labour Party
NIMMA	Northern Ireland Mixed Marriages Association
NUM	New Ulster Movement
NUU	New University of Ulster
OUP	Official Unionist Party
PACE	Protestant and Catholic Encounter
PCR	Programme to Combat Racism
RTE	Radio Telefis Eireann (Broadcasting service in the Republic)
RUC	Royal Ulster Constabulary
SDLP	Social Democratic and Labour Party
UDA	Ulster Defence Association
UPNI	Unionist Party of Northern Ireland
UTV	Ulster Television
UUUC	United Ulster Unionist Council
UVF	Ulster Volunteer Force
UWC	Ulster Workers' Council
VUP	Vanguard Unionist Party
WCC	World Council of Churches

Prologue

The room was a single sitting-room above a mainly one-storey hotel; the stairs came up directly into the room. The eight of us sat in silence as a good deal of uneasy shuffling was heard at the foot of the stairs. The first thing to appear above the floor line was the muzzle of a sub-machine gun, followed a moment later by the tense face of the policeman holding it. When he saw no guns covering him he advanced more confidently, and soon the room was full of policemen. The officer in charge demanded our names. 'Arthur Butler, Bishop of Connor.' 'Harry Morton, General Secretary of the British Council of Churches.' 'Jack Weir, Clerk of the Presbyterian General Assembly.' 'Eric Gallagher, former President of the Methodist Church in Ireland.' 'Arthur McArthur, of the British Council of Churches.' 'Ralph Baxter, Secretary of the Irish Council of Churches.' 'Bill Arlow, his assistant.' 'Stanley Worrall, retired headmaster of Methodist College.'

Blank bewilderment and disbelief! Downstairs they had found Rory O'Brady, President of Provisional Sinn Fein, reading by the fire. He was not on the wanted list and is reputed to have said 'You will find the men you are looking for upstairs.' But in fact the men they wanted had fled some hours before. 'How can you prove that you are the people you say you are? Give us numbers and we will telephone your homes.' Eventually the Special Branch were satisfied of our identity, and no arrests were made. 'We shall leave a guard on the house tonight and you may leave in the morning.'

Thus came to a premature end the attempt of Protestant churchmen from Northern Ireland to halt the campaign of violence that had then been carried on by the Provisional IRA for nearly five years. The place was Smyth's Hotel, Feakle, and the date 10 December 1974. That morning we had spent three and a half hours in what diplomatic correspondents call 'a frank exchange of views'. Eric Gallagher and Jack Weir had made a powerful appeal on humanitarian grounds, and had also explained very clearly why the campaign of terrorism would not succeed. Six years later their argument has lost none of its force. The Provisional leaders had expounded, courteously and clearly, their aim of a federal Ireland; they had sought to justify their 'military' methods; and they had expressed their one requirement for 'peace'—an unequivocal, but undated, commitment by the British government to withdraw finally from Ireland. It had been agreed that each side would spend the afternoon reflecting on what had been said and that we would meet again at tea-time.

Then, as we lunched in the hotel dining-room, came the news that disrupted these plans. 'Our man in Dublin Castle', as they significantly described him, had sent warning that the authorities knew of the gathering and that the Special Branch was about to leave Dublin on the long journey to the County Clare. It would be convenient, they said, for four of the seven representatives to leave immediately. Three, who were not liable to arrest, would remain to hear the outcome of our private deliberations in the afternoon. So Rory O'Brady, Billy McKee, and Seamus Loughran were the only ones still present—when the police had come and for the most part gone—to receive the document we had prepared. What might have happened if we could have discussed this at first hand with the 'military' chiefs, David O'Connell, Seamus Twomey, and others, whom we had met in the morning, will never be known.

Meanwhile our encounter with them was very quickly made public. The morning after our return home we heard our names read out to the world on the eight o'clock news, and the whole secret enterprise was revealed. Then began the torrent of abuse and the quieter assurances of support and gratitude. The whole issue of how the Churches, and how Christians, should act in a time of conflict had been brought into the open. At the same time, quite independently, the same question was raised in a different form by a joint appeal from the official leaders of the main Churches for a new approach on the part of the general public: to 'pray, think, speak, and act for peace'.

The full story of what took us to Feakle in December 1974 and of the not inconsiderable outcome of the meeting must await its proper place in the narrative that follows; but the questions it raised must be posed at the outset. Any attempt to assess the performance of the Churches in Northern Ireland during the troubles must start from some conception of the role the Churches might properly be expected to play.

What then is the yardstick by which the achievement of the Churches in Northern Ireland during the crisis of the 1970s can be measured? What is the role that might ideally have been expected for them? Suppose for a moment that the Churches could be disentangled from the aspirations of those participating in the conflict and could act with integrity as units of the Body of Christ, what would then constitute a proper fulfilment of their mission in the situation? Would it be to act as agents of compassion to a suffering population? In that case it would be fair to judge the Churches by the intensity of their effort to relieve suffering and to compare them, favourably or unfavourably, with other agencies of welfare, voluntary or statutory. That organized Christianity has a 'Good Samaritan' role at any time of abnormal human distress will be generally accepted, but if its response is exhausted by that kind of activity, it is offering a palliative rather than a cure.

Should the Churches then have furnished a blueprint for a renewed society and have actively pursued its realization? That would have meant advancing a specific social and political programme and being judged by the persistence and skill of their efforts to achieve its fulfilment. The comparison of effectiveness would then be with the political parties, and the 'success' or 'failure' of the Churches could be measured by the degree to which the 'Christian' programme of reform and constitutional restructuring prevailed over rival proposals. But in so far as the conflict arises from the simultaneous advancement of mutually incompatible programmes of restructuring, there is nothing very salutary or distinctive about adding yet another to the schemes that give content to the debate.

There is committed to the disciples of Christ a ministry of reconciliation. Does this mean that the Churches should constitute a kind of ACAS, exercising a shuttle diplomacy between parties in conflict, seeking to expand the common ground and dissuade from the more extreme positions, until eventually a working compromise is reached? Perhaps this is to get nearer to the proper role for the Christian Churches. But the ministry of reconciliation is part of a more fundamental ministry. The gospel is not simply one of human reasonableness but of 'salvation'. The Church is called to proclaim to men the reality of God, and to promote the fulfilment of individual and social life which God's grace in Christ makes possible. Reconciliation between groups in conflict is more than a pragmatic accommodation; it is the attainment of a higher synthesis made possible by common acceptance of a destiny transcending the sectional interests that have led to the conflict.

It is by that kind of criterion that the Churches have to be judged, by the effectiveness of their witness to and promotion of that kind of fulfilment, both for individuals caught up in the crisis and for the society in which they are placed. It is easy from a position outside the situation to dismiss the Churches in Northern Ireland as having manifestly failed in this mission. To do so without the closer examination of their actions which this study is intended to make possible would be unfair. But more important still must be the recognition that the Churches in Northern Ireland are themselves part of the problem. Put crudely, they have to save themselves before they can save society; progress in the first part of the requirement is itself to be reckoned on the credit side of grace. So before we study the record of these Churches during the 'troubles' of our time, we must face briefly the historical factors that have entangled the Churches in the political issues at stake.

1 Divided Country—Divided Province

The unhappy story of relations between Ireland and England goes back to the twelfth century, but the religious element first entered into it at the time of the Reformation. In Ireland, as in England, the Reformation was formally accomplished by acts of Parliament, passed at the instance of the Tudor monarchs. By these the sovereign was made the ultimate authority in Church as well as in state, and the use was ordered in all the churches of the Bible in English and Cranmer's English liturgy. In England these changes were accompanied by energetic preaching of the reformed doctrines, and the services, being in the vernacular of the people, were accepted gladly. In Ireland neither of these conditions obtained: the higher clergy conformed to the new order and held on to the cathedrals, parish churches, and endowments; the people never abandoned the traditional faith. Most of them spoke Irish, yet no serious attempt was made to provide the new Prayer Book or the Bible in Irish. Services in English meant even less to the common people than services in Latin. So Ireland, unlike England, proved a ready field for the Jesuit missionaries of the Counter-Reformation and became a country in which the religion of the people was not the religion of the state, a situation without parallel in post-Reformation Europe; and religion was added to the grievances of the Irish against English rule.[1]

Then into the north of Ireland came settlers, all of them Protestant. Lands of rebel noblemen were confiscated by the Crown; lands of bankrupt families were bought up by private adventurers: in both cases the Irish inhabitants were dispossessed of their tenancies and either driven to less fertile land in the bogs and mountains or retained by the new settlers as landless labourers. Such were the 'plantations' of Ulster in the early seventeenth century, and such the origin of the two communities still at bitter variance in Northern Ireland.[2] The settlers and their descendants have as long a right of possession as any people of Anglo-Saxon descent in North America. No doubt the two populations would long ago have been assimilated to one another, if it had not been for the difference of religion. By discouraging intermarriage, this had kept them apart through the centuries, maintaining a conflict of interest which is economic and political in character but given permanence and emotional depth by the religious element in it. Scots were a majority among the settlers, and were Presbyterian in outlook. Eventually these dissented from the established Church, and their descendants constitute the largest single Protestant denomination in Northern Ireland today.

The visitor to modern Belfast will not go far before he sees somewhere or other an inscription advising him to 'Remember 1690'. That was the year of Protestant victory, but no less important to folk memory is the year of Protestant calamity. In 1641 the dispossessed rebelled and massacred many of those who had settled on their lands a generation before.[3] The Protestants have been on their guard ever since. The word 'bawn', common in place names, means a fortified farm, and one can still be seen not far from Carrickfergus with curtain wall and corner towers encompassing the milking-sheds and farm machinery of today. It shows vividly how the settlers for a long time lived. Cromwell, taking England's revenge for 1641, sacked Drogheda and sent Catholic landowners to 'Hell or Connaught'.[4] Then he settled many of his discharged soldiers on yet more Irish land. The part played by land in Ireland's long conflicts is reflected in Belfast today, where intimidation of people, forcing them out of their homes is a common form of violence. The people who do it are descended from peasants who came into the city during the industrial revolution, bringing with them ancestral rivalries for the possession of land.

But what of 1690, which we are urged to remember? Whenever Britain has been endangered by continental powers she has feared that advantage would be taken of Irish disaffection. James II had been deposed by Parliament, but the Catholic Irish[5] supported him, and his ally Louis XIV sent 7,000 troops to Ireland. Until the arrival of William III, who still rides in triumph on the gable-ends and the Orange banners of Ulster, the danger to the northern Protestants was acute. This campaign, in which the English and the settlers together cleared Ireland of the Catholic King and the foreign army, brought to an end in harsh penal laws such toleration as the Roman Catholic Church had received in the seventeenth century. It also provided the iconography of Ulster Protestantism with its most enduring images. The geography of the struggle in 1689–90 drew attention to the difference between 'planted' Ulster and the rest of Ireland and thus sowed the seeds of the eventual partition. It was Londonderry,[6] with its special relationship with the city of London, that stood for weeks as the bastion of Protestantism and English rule against armies drawn from the southern parts to uphold the claim of the Catholic King. It was at Carrickfergus, on Belfast Lough, that William III landed, and his conquest of the country proceeded from the north southwards and not from the traditional English strong-hold of Dublin and the Pale. The Boyne, at which the decisive and much commemorated battle was fought, although many miles to the south of the modern border, stands in the minds of Ulstermen as a kind of geographico-theological symbol of division.

And so when, two centuries later, the campaign was mounted for Irish Home Rule, the opposition to that measure found its main support in Ulster. By this time Catholics were fully 'emancipated' and could play a full part in public life. But by the Act of Union (1801) the old Irish Parliament had been abolished and Irish members formed a relatively small element in the Parliament of the United Kingdom at Westminster. So long as that was so, Ireland would be governed mainly in the Protestant interest and in the economic interests of the larger island. Discontent had been greatly intensified by disastrous famine in the 1840s, which a distant government had done little to alleviate. Fenian[7] violence and the obstructive tactics of the Irish party in the House of Commons forced attention on Ireland's problems.

Acts to disestablish the Church of Ireland and to buy out the landlords helped to redress the most serious grievances, but many in Ireland sought Home Rule, or complete self-government in internal affairs. The Protestant descendants of the Ulster settlers saw that this would make them a minority and endanger their privileges. From the 1880s onward they cam-paigned to resist the proposals for Home Rule. The cry 'Home Rule is Rome Rule' reveals the substantial religious element in their fears.[8] The campaign was fostered by an organization known as the Orange Order, and it culminated in 1912–14 in the enrolling of volunteers, the illegal importation of arms, and preparations for the setting-up of a provisional government in Belfast. In September 1912 the Ulster Covenant, couched in religious phraseology reminiscent of the Scottish Covenant of the seventeenth century, but expressing a stark political content, was signed at a gigantic gathering outside Belfast City Hall and at church doors with the support, if not the leadership, of the clergy of the various Protestant denominations.[9] The threat of armed revolt forced the British government to enact Home Rule in a form that provided for the temporary exclusion of the six north-eastern counties. Before the act came into force the Great War of 1914 caused the postponement of its implementation.

Following the example of the Ulster Volunteer Force, Catholics in other parts of Ireland had by now enrolled in an Irish Volunteer Force, dedicated to securing the country's independence. A rebellion staged in Dublin at Easter 1916 proved abortive in the short run but seminal in its long-term effect. Regarded by the British as traitors in wartime, its leaders were executed and so became eventually symbolic martyrs of the modern Irish state. In the year of the rising the Ulster volunteers, who had enlisted to a man in the British Army on the outbreak of war, suffered fearful losses in the battle of the Somme. To this day the contrast between the 'traitors' of Dublin and the 'heroes' of the Somme stirs profound feelings in Ulster. People easily forget that most of the Irish volunteers, on the advice of their political leader, John Redmond, had also joined the British army.

We cannot here follow the details of the events which led in 1922 to the establishment of two states in Ireland, one enjoying 'dominion status' and in due course to become a republic outside the British Commonwealth, and the other remaining a part of the United Kingdom with its own parliament and government at Stormont, controlling its internal affairs.[10] A state with an overwhelming Catholic majority had been achieved by force of arms south of the new border; another state, with a Protestant majority, had come into being north of that border because of the threat of armed resistance to incorporation in an all-Ireland state. Whatever the legal bases—in the one case a treaty between the new state and Britain, in the other an act of the British Parliament[11]—the immediate reason for each state's existence lay in force, a truth never absent from the minds of those who seek to change or to maintain the arrangements made at that time. And on both sides, while the Churches had formally refrained from supporting the use of arms, ordinary men had been convinced that their action was in defence of their Faith.

When partition took place the Churches, influenced perhaps by the belief that it would prove temporary, did nothing to alter their structures to take account of the political border. This has had important consequences. Not only are all the Churches organized to this day on all-Ireland basis; but the border itself in places runs through a diocese, a presbytery, a circuit. Ministers are appointed, north and south, irrespective of their own origins. Clergy and laity meet in committee in Dublin and Belfast. The Roman Catholic Primate of all Ireland has his see in Northern Ireland, at St Patrick's city of Armagh, while the stipends of Anglican clergy, most of whom work in the north, are paid from an office in Dublin, which claims from the British exchequer tax rebate on subscriptions covenanted in Northern Ireland. Thus whatever part the Churches have played in fostering political division in Ireland, they continue, with the Rugby Union, the banks, and to some extent the trade unions, to testify to the existence of Ireland as an entity coextensive with the whole island.

The two Churches which claim continuity from the ancient Celtic Church of St Patrick, the Church of Ireland and the Roman Catholic Church, both maintain a diocesan and parochial organization covering the whole country. Presbyterian and Methodist congregations south of the border are widely scattered and, in some cases, united with each other. One Methodist minister in five and one Presbyterian minister in eleven serves in the Republic.[12] The Church of Ireland, however, has nearly as many parochial clergy there as in Northern Ireland, but serving much smaller congregations. Of the total population of the whole island, about 4,500,000, the Roman Catholic authorities reckon about 1,100,000 to be 'non-Catholics'.[13] The statistics of the Anglican, Presbyterian, and Methodist Churches claim about 800,000 as having some connection with them. The discrepancy comprises those whose church connection has totally lapsed—obviously a much smaller proportion of the population than in most Western countries—and of the membership of other denominations. These include four Churches which use the name Presbyterian: the Non-Subscribing Presbyterian Church, which does not accept the Westminster Confession and has links with unitarianism (about 4,000); the Reformed Presbyterian Church, which traces a lineal connection with the Scottish covenanters (about 4,000); the Evangelical Presbyterian Church, a tiny secession resulting from the refusal of the

Presbyterian Church to hound a 'heretic'; and the Free Presbyterian Church, that of Dr Paisley, founded in 1951, counting at the census of 1971 over 7,000 members and today considerably more. There are about 10,000 Congregationalists and 16,000 Baptists who, unlike their counterparts in Britain, hold aloof from ecumenical contacts. There are 16,000 Brethren, and considerable numbers in various evangelical societies and pentecostalist churches. Smaller numbers belong to the Society of Friends, the Salvation Army, and the Moravian and Lutheran Churches. Except for congregations in Dublin, the smaller denominations are confined to Northern Ireland.[14]

The Roman Catholic, Anglican, Presbyterian, and Methodist Churches are unofficially described as 'the four main Churches', and their chief officers, the Cardinal, the Primate, the Moderator, and the President, respectively as 'the four church leaders'. The main Protestant Churches with the Non-Subscribing Presbyterian, Moravian, and Lutheran Churches, the Society of Friends, and the Salvation Army are members of the Irish Council of Churches. This is an all-Ireland body and maintains relations with the Roman Catholic Hierarchy through the presence of Catholic observers and the work of some committees.

Some of the Protestant Churches, whose main weight of membership is in British territory, have joined the British Council of Churches, which has met on occasion not only in Belfast but in Dublin, to be greeted there, be it said, with the same courtesy and hospitality as have characterized the attitude of the southern authorities towards the Protestant Churches since partition.

It follows from the all-Ireland organization of the Churches that each denomination operates in two jurisdictions and must relate to the law of two states. This book is concerned with the record of the Irish Churches in Northern Ireland. Accordingly we shall deal with Church–State relations in the South only in so far as they affect the fears of northerners that the southern state is a Roman Catholic theocracy, to which they would be subjugated if Ireland were united.

It is important to grasp that no Church is established, in the English or Scottish manner, either north or south of the border.[15] In 1869 the Parliament of the United Kingdom not only disestablished the Church of Ireland but also, by payment of capital sums, ended its annual provision, the *Regium Donum*, to the Presbyterian clergy, and its subsidy paid since 1795 to the

Roman Catholic seminary at Maynooth, then known officially as the Royal College of St Patrick. The southern state in its Constitution of 1937 accorded a 'special position' to the Roman Catholic Church and 'recognition' to the other Churches;[16] but this distinction meant nothing in law, and the clauses in question have since been abrogated. The bishops and clergy have no special legal status or privileges, and the only state money to pass into church hands is in respect of specific services rendered by the Church, as in the maintenance of schools and hospitals. All denominations are on the same footing in this matter, but the massive employment of members of religious orders, who plough their state-subsidized salaries back into the institutions they serve, enables the Roman Catholic Church to derive more benefit *pro rata* for the pupils and patients from the monies received.

The clergy have no seats in the Senate and, as a matter of Church order, they do not seek election to the Dail. It is often contended, however, that they exercise a decisive influence behind the scenes. Non-Catholics point to the laws on censorship, contraception, and divorce as being the enactment of Catholic moral principles. In particular it was held that the Hierarchy prevented by open veto the introduction of a health scheme for mothers and children proposed by the Minister for Health, Dr Noel Browne, in the early 1950s.[17] Catholics reply that if ninety-five per cent of the population belongs to the Roman Catholic Church, it is clear that the great majority of legislators will be, and will represent, Catholics. It is therefore by virtue of their fidelity as Catholic laymen and not because they are unduly influenced on specific issues by the clergy that they enact laws reflecting Catholic moral principles. There is no doubt that since the crisis over the 'mother-and-child scheme' the bishops have sought to avoid the appearance of dictating to the state. The problems of conscience posed to a Catholic deputy, when measures are proposed in certain sensitive areas, are well illustrated by the action of Mr Liam Cosgrave when Prime Minister. He voted against a bill promoted by his own government to liberalize the law on contraception. Growing secularization, especially among the more articulate sections of the public, is undoubtedly creating a situation in which the minds of legislators will be more open to attitudes at present forbidden to Catholics by the Hierarchy, and changing Catholic attitudes in other countries will make this easier for them. It remains to be seen how far principles traditionally distinctive of

Roman Catholicism will continue to be enshrined in the secular law. There is little doubt that the present trend towards a position in which the Church would be expected to uphold its distinctive principles by its direct influence on its own members, without legal sanctions, would be at least accelerated in an all-Ireland state. Nevertheless Catholics would still comprise seventy-five per cent of the electorate, enough to explain the fears of northern Protestants.

Nor are those fears easily allayed in face of the steady erosion of Protestant population in the South. There was a sharp decline in the immediate aftermath of partition. A slower reduction in numbers has continued ever since. Emigration and losses due to the two world wars have had their effect. Intermarriage with Catholics of necessity becomes more frequent as Protestant numbers decline, and Catholic rules in this matter make it extremely likely that each such marriage means the loss of a Protestant family in the next generation. The enforcement in Ireland from 1908 onwards of the *Ne temere* decree put an end to the custom long tacitly accepted, at any rate among the middle classes, that the sons of a mixed marriage were brought up in their father's church, the daughters in their mother's. When, for all these reasons, the numbers in a locality become so small that a church must be closed, any remaining members can easily be lost. There is a vicious spiral of decline. In the North, the marriage rules operate in the same, not in the reverse direction, and so do the rules about contraception. Thus while the Protestant minority in the South gets smaller, the Catholic minority in the North gets larger, until the possibility of the Protestants becoming a minority in 'their own state' is no longer absurd.

Their small numbers would in any case have ensured that the southern Protestants would not constitute a danger to the integrity of the state comparable to that caused by the Catholic minority in the North. On the whole they have not, in fact, seen themselves as an aggrieved community. Opposition to laws enshrining distinctive Catholic moral principles has not come primarily from Protestants, let alone from the Protestant Churches, but rather from the literary and intellectual élite to whom church allegiance, if professed at all, is not paramount in their thinking. Divorce, contraception, and pornography are not causes likely to be taken up with enthusiasm by members of the non-Roman Churches in Ireland, which share with their Catholic neighbours a conservative and somewhat puritan approach to many things. Of course, the censorship made an ass of itself, as the law is said to do! But it is to be doubted whether many Protestant church members disapproved of it in principle. When radio and television came along the Protestant churches found themselves accorded a considerably larger share of time for religious broadcasting than their relative numerical strength entitled them to expect; and as the policy of the broadcasting agency was for long to get the Churches to devise the religious programmes, the latter had much more direct influence on the output than is the case with the BBC. It is their decline in numbers rather than their treatment by the state which alarms southern Protestants. This makes the burden of providing education for their children in a country where primary and secondary education, though now largely state-supported, is denominationally managed, increasingly heavy. It also means that churches in rural areas, if open at all, are heavily subsidized from central church funds, which means in the main from Northern Ireland. This decline in numbers, with all its sad consequences, the southern Protestants attribute in large part not to their standing within the state but, as we have seen, to the marriage rules of the Roman Catholic Church.

In considering the nature and evolution of the Northern Ireland state since 1920, it is important to bear in mind what was the point and purpose of partition. Protestants constituted about one-quarter of the population of the island. Having failed to keep the island in the Union, they had rescued, as it were, from the new, inevitably Catholic, regime, an area comprising one-sixth of the territory and one-third of the population. The rest of the island would now be controlled by 'the other kind'; but this part was 'their' part, 'their' share. It would be controlled by 'their kind'. When Lord Craigavan, Northern Ireland's first Prime Minister, spoke of 'a Protestant parliament for a Protestant people', he was not so much asserting an ascendancy over non-Protestants as claiming the Protestant share. If the only way to give Protestants a fair share in the government in Ireland was to give them a territorial share, so be it; but it must be clearly understood that they would control their share as completely as the Catholics would control theirs.[18] In judging the actions of the Ulster Protestants and of the Unionist governments it must in justice be recognized that that was how they understood the settlement. It was not their aim to promote a pluralistic state—that might have been appropriate to the island as a whole, but in circumstances of partition it was for them to maintain a Protestant state, the counterpart of the Catholic state south of the border. If a third of the population in the northern area was Catholic, that was just too bad. If the Catholics didn't like it, they could leave; but in practice most of them were economically better off in the North, and they knew it. So the argument went, and with some force, until in the 1970s the marked economic growth in the Republic began to bring in question the last assertion.

The boundary commission set up in the early 1920s might have done something to make the partition coincide more closely with the demographic reality; but whatever it might have done to make the old county boundaries look like a logical international frontier, nothing could have helped the roughly 150,000 Catholics in the Belfast area or the sizeable pockets in north Antrim and elsewhere. The plantations had not been systematic enough, and the lure of the industrial city in the nineteenth century had made things worse. It is said that in those days trains would arrive from the west, crowded with the younger sons of farmers; on walking out of the Great Northern Station they would turn, if Protestant, to the right, if Catholic, to the left, thus building up the sectarian strongholds of Sandy Row and the Falls Road respectively. Wherever the border ran, there could be no Protestant state in Ireland that did not include too large a minority of Catholics, no British state that did not include too many people whose emotional patriotism was Irish. Geographical distribution defeated the logic of partition.

Oddly enough the early years of devolved government in the North saw a sharp controversy between the Unionist government and the Protestant Churches. The government wanted to build up a unified system of education, but denominational forces eventually frustrated this.[19]

In this struggle the Protestant Churches were encouraged, and to a large extent co-ordinated, by the Orange Order. This body, officially named the Loyal Orange Institution of Ireland, and organized in Loyal Orange Lodges, responsible to the Grand Lodge of Ireland, dates from 1795. Originally composed mainly of Anglicans, it became during the Home Rule controversies a focus of Protestant resistance appealing to members of all the Protestant denominations. In the early days the lodges, as such, took part in violent attacks on and reprisals against subversive Catholic organizations. Songs sung in lodges and tunes played at marches celebrated some of these encounters. In modern times the threat or use of physical force passed first to the Ulster Volunteer Force (UVF) of 1912, and in the current troubles to the Ulster Defence Association (UDA) and to some smaller but perhaps more sinister groups, one of which has revived the title UVF. The Orange Order on the other hand became an organization for the maintenance of Protestant ascendancy by legal and 'respectable' means. It has, for example, the right to nominate members, distinct from the constituency representatives, to the Ulster Unionist Council. It counted, prior to the seventies, among its membership virtually all Unionist members of Parliament, whether at Stormont or Westminster, and in consequence all members of the Stormont government. Membership was, in fact, an indispensable condition of political advancement. It protected the employment of Protestants by its influence over employers, which is a polite way of saying that it contrived systematic discrimination against Catholics. Local authorities, except in the few districts with a Catholic majority, were dominated by members of the local lodges. Very many clergy were members, usually as chaplains to lodges, some of which had ties with local churches. Clergy saw in the Order an instrument of social responsibility among working men: there were, for instance, 'temperance' lodges. During the marching season, July and August, the lodges parade ostentatiously in the streets, demonstrating Protestant supremacy, but for the most part avoiding Catholic areas. The Royal Black Preceptory, the Apprentice Boys of Derry (whose organization commemorates the action of apprentices in closing the gates of Derry against James II's army when the Governor was preparing to surrender), and the Independent Orange Order are smaller bodies with similar practices.

It is easy to condemn this whole movement as unjust and sinister. In fairness it must be pointed out that from the first proposals for Home Rule the Protestants saw not merely their ascendancy but the survival of their way of life endangered. The principle 'civil and religious liberty' was proclaimed by the Order in defiance of a Church that was seen in such countries as Italy and Spain to tolerate no opinions but its own and which, it was feared, would exercise a similar intolerance in Ireland if, by a dissolution of the Union, power fell to the Catholic majority. Once partition had given Protestants their territorial share of power in Ireland, the maintenance of partition became the prime object; and that was best assured by discouraging the growth of the Catholic population in Northern Ireland. The only way to do that was to render conditions such that many Catholics emigrated. The order was seen by large numbers of sincere and well-meaning Protestants as a defence of their civil and religious liberty against a continuing threat. The irony was that that defence could only take the form of a restriction on the civil and religious liberty of Catholics.

Again it is necessary to guard against misrepresentation. Nothing in the laws of the Northern State discriminated against Catholics as such. The electoral law gave universal suffrage at Parliamentary elections, both for Stormont and Westminster; in elections for town and county councils it gave the vote to ratepayers only, and more Catholics than Protestants failed to qualify. The educational law provided for controlled and voluntary schools, the latter being less than wholly funded from public money. If the Catholics insisted that all their children should attend voluntary schools, they must pay the price; anybody else wanting to run a voluntary school must do the same. It was the manner in which action was taken within the law that constituted discrimination; and the Orange Order was seen, by both sides, as an effective instrument to achieve this. For long it was virtually the only forum for common action by Protestants of different denominations; but as time went on a more charitable and constructive relationship began to be built up between the Churches at an official inter-church level.[20]

This slow thaw in ecclesiastical relationships coincided with the succession in March 1963 to the premiership of Northern Ireland of Captain Terence O'Neill, whose aim was to engage in 'bridge-building' between the unionist and nationalist communities. If the latter could be persuaded to play a more constructive part in parliamentary and local affairs, if any demonstrable discrimination against them could be identified and removed, if friendly relations with the Republic could be established and maintained, then the basic status quo of Northern Ireland as a part of the United Kingdom, necessarily governed by the majority of those resident in it, might be secured. So, for the first time, a Northern Ireland Prime Minister visited nationalist towns and Roman Catholic schools; nationalist MPs at Stormont were persuaded to act formally as HM Opposition; and in 1965 Mr Sean Lemass, Taoiseach, or Prime Minister, of the Republic, accepted an invitation to visit Captain O'Neill at Stormont. At the same time a vigorous attempt was made to improve economic prospects, the Prime Minister appearing at a number of 'Ulster Weeks' in the principal British cities, while the Minister of Commerce, Mr Brian Faulkner, was successful in persuading a considerable number of British, European, and American firms to set up factories in the province.

Lord Brookeborough had been Prime Minister for twenty years. Had Captain O'Neill been granted half his predecessor's time to work out his policies quietly at his own pace, Northern Ireland might have been by 1980 comparatively prosperous and contented. But it was not to be. He was not moving fast enough for those who looked mainly to the grievances of the Roman Catholic population, such as an electoral system that kept their influence to a minimum in the local government of certain towns and gave them a consequent disadvantage in the allocation of council houses; an economic policy that favoured the eastern part of the province, accentuating unemployment in such predominantly Roman Catholic towns as Londonderry and Strabane; the practice in mixed areas of discrimination against Roman Catholics in the private sector of employment. Underneath all these factors lurked the issue of national identity: if all practical injustice were eliminated, would this large minority ever acquiesce in their constitutional separation from the rest of Ireland? Lord Brookeborough's view had been that they would not, from which he drew the conclusion that they must be kept in their place, as politically impotent as possible. 'These people are our enemies,' he said.[21] Captain O'Neill's view was that if they were treated justly within the state and made materially more content they would accept the continuance of partition. 'Give them jobs and houses and they will live like Protestants'[22] was his later insensitive way of putting it. By 1968 the nationalist leader, Mr Eddie McAteer, was saying 'There has been talk of change but nothing has been done to take up the talk.' That was very nearly true, and soon the pent-up frustration would erupt. On the other hand, Captain O'Neill was moving much too fast for many of his own supporters. The Cabinet was divided: some ministers were upset because he made them conform to new standards of fair play, some were ambitious and always ready to play to the unionist gallery against him. As soon as events became critical, support in the all-powerful Ulster Unionist Council dwindled. Time would show that whenever a Unionist leader went too far in accommodation of the other community, he would be overthrown. And eventually the Unionist Party itself would lose ground to movements on its right such as Vanguard and the

Democratic Unionist Party.

This last was the creation of the Revd. Ian Paisley, who first emerged from obscurity in the 1950s and 1960s as the opponent of ecclesiastical rapprochement and then took on an increasingly political role as the 'troubles' ensued. Son of a Baptist minister and ordained by his father and two other ministers, Mr (later Dr)[23] Paisley founded the Free Presbyterian Church in 1951. He had never been a member of the Presbyterian Church in Ireland. From his headquarters in a small mission hall in east Belfast he conducted evangelistic campaigns with a pronounced anti-popish emphasis, and gradually spread the denomination, of which he was permanent Moderator, over Northern Ireland and into fringe areas of the Republic. When the Irish delegation to the World Council of Churches returned from New Delhi in 1961 and held a public meeting in Belfast, Free Presbyterians picketed the hall with such tasteful placards as 'Fulton, whoremonger', a reference to the humane and scholarly Moderator of the Presbyterian Church in his contacts with supposedly unevangelical Christians. When a Roman Catholic preached in Westminster Abbey, Mr Paisley and his friends were at the door. When Archbishop Michael Ramsey went to see the Pope, Mr Paisley went to Rome also—to be refused entry by the Italian authorities, as one likely to cause a breach of the peace. By threat of disturbance he helped to prevent the appearance at Belfast Cathedral of the Bishop of Ripon, Dr Moorman, a prominent advocate of Anglican–Roman Catholic dialogue.[24] In 1966 he protested as usual against the so-called 'Romeward trend' of the Presbyterian Church. On the opening evening of the General Assembly he marched with his followers from east Belfast, through a predominantly Catholic area, where a riot was averted with difficulty by the police, and took up his position outside the Assembly Hall. When the guests, who included the Governor, Lord Erskine, himself a Scottish Presbyterian, and Lady Erskine, emerged to cross the street for supper in the Presbyterian Hostel, they were greeted with jeers and scuffles. The effect of this on Lady Erskine, whose health was poor, was such that she could no longer live happily in Northern Ireland, and consequently Lord Erskine resigned without completing his term of office.

Even before this Mr Paisley's activities had begun to extend to the political sphere. At the United Kingdom election of 1964 an Irish tricolour flag had been displayed at the headquarters of a republican candidate in West Belfast. This was strictly illegal, but the authorities had not made a practice of acting in such matters against those who were, in the circumstances of an election, their political rivals. Mr Paisley said that if the police did not remove the flag, he would. Knowing what that would mean, the Minister of Home Affairs, Mr Brian McConnell, reluctantly ordered the removal of the flag. There ensued four days of rioting, the worst since 1935, and fifty people were injured.

Meanwhile Mr Paisley's Sunday congregation outgrew his small hall and he took to hiring the Ulster Hall for his services. At these an evangelistic message was combined with constant attacks on the Roman Catholic Church and disparagement of those clergy and politicians who were prepared to seek better relations with it. Believing all this to be a poisonous influence, the late Jack Sayers, editor of the *Belfast Telegraph*, refused to accept advertisements from the Free Presbyterian Church. Paisley's riposte was to name his own weekly journal, founded in April 1966, the *Protestant Telegraph*, with the implication that that was the Telegraph true Protestants would read. This paper became the vehicle for what seemed to many to be scurrility and scandal-mongering against all who sought any degree of reconciliation between the communities: a Protestant minister had only to allow himself to be seen shaking hands with a 'popish' priest and he would find himself described as a traitor, an apostate, or one a-whoring after strange gods. At first it was possible to laugh at these attacks, but later, as violence increased, it was no longer a joke to be named in a periodical which, whatever the intentions of its publishers, was widely read by Protestant paramilitaries and assassination gangs.

Further riots occurred in 1966 when Mr Paisley and two of his ministers were charged with unlawful assembly following the scene outside the General Assembly. Refusing to pay their fines, they were imprisoned, and 2,000 of their supporters protested riotously outside the prison. They were released on completion of their sentences just in time to snowball the car of Mr Jack Lynch, the new Taoiseach of the Republic, when he arrived at Stormont to visit Captain O'Neill.

The rise of Paisley represented the most complete form of religio-political symbiosis that Ireland had experienced. This was not simply a matter of most members of a given denomination supporting a particular party. Before long there would be a political party, the Democratic Unionist Party, whose leader was identical with the Moderator of the Free Presbyterian Church. With many of the qualities essential to a popular leader, and, indeed, with the potential of a populist dictator, Mr Paisley knew exactly how to enlist religious fervour in support of a political programme, so that the latter, appealing speciously to the supposed material interests of his followers, was given the sanctity of a religious crusade; and both were essentially negative. The religious cause was 'No Popery' and the political cause was 'No Surrender': the total effect was no change, no progress, no reconciliation, no hope.

With this focus of intransigence growing on their right it was not likely that the traditional unionists would hold fast to Terence O'Neill when his bridge-building policy encountered rough weather. With the growth in 1968 of the Northern Ireland Civil Rights Association, designed to provide a focus on the other side for the grievances of the minority, the storm was about to break.

2 Ecumenism in Ireland 1945–1968

In Ulster, 'the Twelfth' means one thing only. Colour, excitement, the shrill piercing sound of flutes, the drone of bagpipes, banners billowing in the breeze with their pictorial reminders of the Siege of Derry, the Battle of the Boyne, William III landing at Carrickfergus, and many another bit of the folklore that goes to make much of Ulster's Protestantism what it was and is. For the Twelfth is not all high-jinks or fun and games. 'July the Twelfth' is a national holiday in Northern Ireland, holiday and holy day for the marching Protestants of the Orange Order, but a different kind of day for the Catholics, who do not greatly relish it. It is a day whose significance is more than hinted at in memorable lines from the pen of Louis McNeice, poet and Belfast-born:

> Over which country of cowled and haunted faces
> The sun goes down with a banging of Orange drums.[1]

The Orangemen were on parade as usual on 12 July 1980. Though the pattern of the day's events was very much as usual, they claimed that record numbers of new members were on the march that year.

They paraded to a large number of venues throughout the Province and to one in Donegal. At each a formal meeting accompanied by an act of worship was held and at all a series of identical resolutions was put to the assembled brethren and duly passed. Those resolutions contained the following:

As Orangemen we take seriously our commitment of a Christianity which is Christ centred, Bible based, and true to the beliefs of the Primitive Church.

As Protestants we are determined to continue to declare that faith in and by our Churches as Christians together in the unity of truth and brotherhood.

We are resolved to stand firm for the Protestant faith against those who would destroy it by accommodation to error or false doctrine, by manipulation or mis-use.

Welcoming the recent withdrawal of the Presbyterian Church in Ireland from the World Council of Churches, we shall continue to strive to stiffen the resolve of church leadership, so that they will stand for truth against error and superstition, and will not sell their heritage for an appearance of unity.[2]

Those resolutions were the kind of thing the Order had been saying for years. The only differences were the new content caused by the action of the Presbyterian General Assembly, to be treated later, and an emphasis on the rising tide of unemployment. This was embodied in a manner not hitherto noticeable in July resolutions. 'We deplore the economic state of the United Kingdom and the gross unemployment which persists here. We appeal to the Government to continue to consider Ulster's lack of natural resources and its peculiar trading difficulties. Our concern for the unemployed is not less than that of others who are also aware of the soul-destroying effects of idleness and its peculiar dangers for young people. We want British rights for British citizens everywhere.' In the context of this chapter, we may leave on one side comment on the recognition of social ills arising from unemployment and on the terms in which the demand for British rights was couched. For the present purpose the references to Protestantism and Orange determination 'to stiffen the resolve of church leadership' are more important.

On the same day, the Revd. Ian Paisley was addressing a rally of members of the Independent Orange Order. (It should be noted that he is not, though he once was, a member of the mainstream Order.) The *Coleraine Chronicle* of 19 July 1980 gave him a six-column banner headline. It read in three-quarter-inch capitals 'Keep an Eye on Cardinal Hume—Dr Paisley.' The report quoted him as saying that evil advisers of the Queen were seeking by every Jesuitical trick to subvert and overthrow the Protestant throne and that sinister forces were abroad seeking to undermine the Protestant constitution of the land which was brought about by the 'Williamite Revolution Settlement'. He went on to refer to the planned visit of HM the Queen to Rome, and was stated to have asked, 'Why should the Queen of the United Kingdom and the Dominions across the Sea have to veil herself in black in a subservient manner to the Roman Catholic Pontiff?' He was further reported as saying that the sinister figure on the horizon in England was Cardinal Hume, 'the Benedictine Archbishop of Westminster—someone on which [*sic*] every Protestant should keep his eye'. 'There is no doubt about it', he said, 'the Jesuits in England are flying a kite testing the temperature of the water and all Protestants must be alerted to what is taking place.' He alleged that the Bible was under attack 'from the scourge of ecumenism, the authoritarianism of Romanism and the rationalism, common among those who would perpetuate the falsehood of evolution'. He was quoted: 'Protestants should be aware that even although they adhere to those who reject Romanism, ecumenism, modernism and communism that their children are a prey to the pernicious teaching of evolution. Teach mankind that they are no better than the beast and they will act no better than the beast.'[3]

With such resolutions and speeches like these part of Ulster's July oratory and way of life, the fact that ecumenical activity of any kind exists in the province is far more remarkable than any failure to develop it fully. No wonder that the same Louis McNeice, son of a Church of Ireland rector who was later to be an outstanding bishop, felt that he did not belong to the Ireland he wanted to call his own. Even as a boy, during the First World War, he considered that he was 'banned for ever from the candles of the Irish poor'.[4] The belligerent phrase 'Romanism, ecumenism, modernism and communism' is not so much a variation on a theme as a frequently repeated articulation of the theme in words that hardly vary.

'Romanism' is a word to fan many a smouldering ember of Ulster Protestant suspicion into the strongly burning flame of 'No Surrender' and no truck with the Roman Catholic Church. If you ask an Ulster Protestant to explain his anti-Catholicism, as like as not he will refer you to what 'has happened to Protestants in the South'.

Given the population figures in the Republic, it would be difficult for the Catholics of any diocese to think naturally and spontaneously in ecumenical terms. If you are a Catholic, when you stand on any one of a thousand hill-tops and see nothing but Catholic farms and homesteads, your first thought is hardly likely to be about the sinful divisions of Christendom. Quite obviously, then, ecumenical attitudes and outreach in the Republic between the wars and after 1945 were not easy. There were, however, friendly enough relationships among Anglicans, Presbyterians, and Methodists. But with the Church of Rome it was a different matter. Rightly or wrongly, the Protestant Churches, and in particular the Church of Ireland, were and are still convinced that Catholic teaching and practice with regard to mixed marriages have played a large part in their numerical decline. The need to halt or reverse that decline explains, in part, the long and difficult road along which Catholic and Protestant have to travel, if you are to make any ecumenical progress.

With the exceptions of Belfast and Londonderry, Northern Ireland is still very much a rural area, where memories are long. The country churches, the meeting-houses, and rural grave-yards tell the story of natives and planters. Many Protestant lowland farmers boast with pride that their land has been 'in the family' for three hundred years and more. The other side of the coin recognize the possibility of envious eyes looking down on them from smaller holdings and workers' houses on the hills and mountains. The sense of kith and kin, and especially Scottish kith and kin, of strong Reformation stock, is not a natural breeding ground for reaching out across the divide. Belfast and Derry, the largest cities, with generations of cyclical violence in one and immortal memories of the siege in the other, and both with huge unemployment problems, too often, though naturally, think in sectarian terms.

Two other factors have had their effect. The first is the relative self-sufficiency until recent times of the Irish Churches. Roman Catholic church attendance is still very high, though how high it is hard to say. Until comparatively recently Protestant attendances, judged by Western standards, were the same. Congregations in provincial towns and more populous country areas are large. When economic and demographic factors are not at work, theological insights about ecumenical encounter and a sense of urgency are hard to come by.

The second factor is Dr Ian Paisley. No study of Irish ecumenism would be complete without further and fuller reference to him. In his own way, he is as significant in that study as Vatican II. Large and strong physically, he bestrides the religio-political scene like a Colossus. Possessed of a brand of Ulster humour that gets through to large numbers of his followers, he can, when he wishes, exude a *bonhomie* in stark contrast to the impression created by many of his television appearances. His energy and considerable ability to sway crowds with his oratory make him a force to be reckoned with. Yet he was laughed at and dismissed by church leaders and politicians in his early days as an incongruous and irrelevant figure. With an uncanny eye for publicity and an ability to use the colourful and damaging descriptive phrase, he has over the years avidly seized every opportunity to attack what he calls 'ecumenical clergymen' and the 'ecumenical churches'. The pages of his *Protestant Telegraph* bear frequent witness to his hostility to the Roman Catholic Church, the World Council of Churches, and everything to do with ecumenical activity. The

World Council, or its associates, may be from time to time 'pro-Rome', 'pro-communist', 'pro-fascist', or 'pro-terrorist'.[5] The implications are obvious. If a Council spokesman shows the slightest sign of deviance from the strictest of strict fundamentalist orthodoxy or biblical infallibility, or if he is known to have conferred with a priest, or to have said something in favour of co-operation with Rome, he is almost certain to be denounced as a 'modernist' or 'Pope-head'. The loud reiterations of his many charges have had their effect on a Protestantism that constantly feels itself under threat.

Over the years, Ian Paisley has fed the fears and suspicions of evangelical Protestantism with his rumbustious attacks. Away back in the 1950s he was already well known for his attacks on the WCC and its Irish member-churches. In the autumn of 1962 a loyalist organization had invited him to preach at a parade service in a Methodist Church in Lurgan, Co. Armagh. Its minister, the Revd. James Wisheart, whose evangelical credentials were impeccable, and his officials, whose necessary permission had not been obtained, did not sustain the invitation. They came in for a bitter attack, and in the December 1962 issue of the *Revivalist* Mr Paisley wrote: 'The methodist, presbyterian and episcopal churches are all members of the World Council of Churches. At the time of the ban they were officially represented at the Pope's Vatican Council. This Council aims at re-uniting so-called protestantism with the Roman Catholic church. With this aim the methodist, presbyterian and episcopal churches of Lurgan are in agreement. We are outspoken critics of the World Council of Churches and the Harlot Church of Rome.' Although none of the denominations had representatives, or observers, at the Vatican Council, the laying of the charge was not without effect. In January 1964 his target was the late Cardinal Bea's declaration that 'about co-operation by the Secretariat with the World Council of Churches there is no difficulty in principle'. He wrote 'Rome officially states that the World Council of Churches does not stand for any doctrine irreconcilable with Catholic dogma. In other words, the World Council of Churches is in agreement with Rome's doctrines. The World Council is here seen in its true light. Its massive dictatorial international organization is directed towards unity with Rome'.[6] After Archbishop Fisher's historic visit to the Pope, the tone of the criticism was predictable, but the language, though familiar to his Ulster hearers, was markedly different from that to be produced in later years for the pages of Hansard. 'Lord Fisher of Lambeth, the first professing Protestant Archbishop of Canterbury to visit the Pope since the Reformation, and the fore-runner of a whole line of Protestant leaders who have gone "to slabber on the Pope's slippers", has stated publicly that the term "protestant" should be dropped. That is but another step in conditioning the people for the Roman take-over.'[7] And when political capital could be made, so much the better. In the spring of 1966, he wrote at length about Archbishop Ramsey's visit to the Pope and about the protest mounted by himself and others. He had strong words about Dr Ramsey himself: 'The Archbishop is a traitor—a traitor to the Constitution—and I charge him and indict him of high-treason against this realm.'[8] Later in the same article he wrote: 'The Pope said to Dr Ramsey that he was glad that the bridge which had been broken down between Rome and England, he (the Archbishop) had repaired. By the grace of God we will place the dynamite of Protestant Truth under this re-constructed bridge and blow it to smithereens. The Archbishop is like Terence O'Neill—he is a modern bridge-builder: A bridge and a traitor are alike in one thing—they both take you to the other side. In this day of crisis both O'Neill and Ramsey would like to take us to the other side.'[9] He summed it all up in an early pamphlet on the World Council of Churches: 'Our opposition to this ecumenism is because of its opposition to the Gospel.' No self-respecting Ulsterman enjoys being described as an enemy of the Gospel. For a church or cleric to be thought 'weak' on one or more of the crunch issues or doctrines is enough to breed suspicion in many of Northern Ireland's Protestant faithful. It unsettles them, and demonstrably over the years has caused increasing friction inside the main-stream churches. To say the least, it lowers the ecumenical temperature. That temperature had been a long time rising.

As early as 1905 the Presbyterian and Methodist Churches established a joint committee 'to confer from time to time on matters of common interest'. In 1910, that seminal year for the ecumenical movement, the Presbyterian Assembly made an approach to the Synod of the Church of Ireland which resulted in the establishment of a similar Presbyterian–Anglican joint committee. The aim was 'to encourage the cultivation of friendly relations between the two churches and to co-operate in philanthropic, social and religious work, so far as such co-operation may be found possible'. The minutes of this body, which held its first meeting in Dublin on 18 October 1911, reveal how narrowly the field of co-operation was defined. The Home Rule crisis of 1912–14 passes without a reference. The Great War is noted only in the sentence: 'The subject of temperance and the war was discussed.' In 1916 we read: 'The deputation on temperance, which the Lord Lieutenant had promised to receive on the 28 April last could not be carried out owing to the Sinn Fein rebellion which took place that week', and that is the only reference to the Anglo-Irish struggle that continued until 1922. On 10 March 1922 the committee recorded that 'The subject of possible joint action on the matter of education, especially in view of the altered political conditions in Northern and Southern Ireland, was discussed', and that is the only allusion to partition. A comparison with the minutes of the Irish Council of Churches for the past decade reveals the immense distance travelled in half a century towards joint action in relation to public affairs.

This committee continued in existence until 1945, but it seems to have been little more than a formality after the founding in 1923 of the United Council of Christian Churches and Religious Communions in Ireland. During the inter-war period serious attempts were made to bring the Protestant Churches in Ireland along the road towards unity. These sprang, as did the United Council itself, from the influence of the Lambeth Appeal of 1920. Talks in 1921–3 came to nothing, but were revived in 1932. A joint committee of the Presbyterian and Anglican Churches proposed mutual participation in future ordinations, and put forward a method of achieving mutual recognition of ministries. The Primate, Charles D'Arcy, favoured progress along these lines, but J. A. F. Gregg, then Archbishop of Dublin and later to succeed D'Arcy in the primacy, opposed any form of mutuality that was not accompanied by a scheme for full organic union. In 1935 the Dean of Belfast, later Bishop W. Shaw Kerr, moved in Synod that the Church of Ireland 'fully and freely recognises . . . the validity, efficacy and spiritual reality of both ordination and sacraments as administered by the Presbyterian Church'. Gregg moved an amendment which had the effect of terminating the negotiations. They were not resumed until the late 1960s, on the very eve of the outbreak of civil unrest.

If progress towards union was halted, the work of the United Council was not. In the early years after the Second World War, it was concerning itself with evangelism, the Christian reconstruction of Europe, the organization of 'Home and Family weeks', the tax on Bibles imported into Eire; participating in the British Council of Churches scheme to assist Austrian Protestants, helping refugees from Hungary and the Near East; and supporting Inter-Church Aid. Other forms of inter-church co-operation began to develop apart from the Council. A few earlier experiments in co-operation between Methodists and Presbyterians paved the way for 'federation schemes' in the far west, and joint work in the new housing areas of Belfast. These, in their turn, encouraged Methodists and Presbyterians, and Methodists and Anglicans in the sixties and seventies actually to share buildings. Meanwhile the joint education work continued, though in many ways it had little impact on ecumenical thinking as such.

It goes without saying that the Roman Catholic Church played no part in all of this. There was, however, one breakthrough. The United Council formed a committee on unemployment, and this committee decided to involve some Catholics in its work. Such was the genesis of the Churches' Industrial Council, which was in the fifties and sixties the only inter-church body with Roman Catholic participation. As such, it was under constant pressure to deal with matters not strictly within its brief. It fostered personal relationships between clergy. It showed the possibility of common action. In later years, these achievements were to stand Northern Ireland in good stead.

Before Vatican Two had run its course, both sides of the Irish ecclesiastical scene, in spite of all the obstacles, were changing. In Protestant circles, the name of the Revd. Michael Hurley SJ, was becoming increasingly familiar. Operating from the Milltown Seminary in Dublin, he had initiated correspondence with a number of Protestant ministers and clergy on both sides of the border. He was making exploratory visits to Belfast and acquiring a first-hand knowledge of Protestant thinking and attitudes. He delivered a much-publicized lecture in Milltown on the Ecumenical Movement; he wrote on Irish Anglicanism, and published a commentary on John Wesley's famous letter written in 1749 from Dublin to a Roman Catholic.[10] The signs were already evident that his restless interest and indefatigable determination would not be content until he participated in some new ecumenical venture, however impossible or unlikely it appeared to others. In 1963 he published his *Praying for Unity*.[11] It was a series of prayers, meditations, and informatory chapters dealing with the larger Irish churches. In retrospect, perhaps, the most significant thing about the book was his being able to persuade no less a member of the Northern Hierarchy than Dr William J. Philbin, Bishop of Down and Connor, to contribute a foreword. Three short sentences from that foreword were for their day prophetic. They still make significant reading: 'The world would be able with something like a good conscience to hold aloof from Christians as long as Christians hold aloof from one another.' 'In the Gospels we find no justification for a self-satisfied faith or for any cold-shouldering of those who are not fully of our community.' 'We must not forget our Lord's refusal to repudiate those in marginal positions, while at the same time we must not fail to give full value to His will for complete unity.'

Michael Hurley was not the only Catholic theologian or thinker giving his attention to the ecumenical imperatives. By 1970 three prestigious journals, the *Irish Theological Quarterly*, *The Furrow*, and *Christus Rex* had printed a number of well-documented articles on issues raised by Vatican II, and especially on different facets of ecumenism. Contributors included the Revd. Principal Haire of the Presbyterian College. From our point of view, perhaps the most interesting of all the articles was one by Brian McNamee, OMI, in the January 1969 issue of the *Irish Theological Quarterly*. It printed *in extenso* a remarkable statement made by Bishop Doyle of Kildare and Leighlin over 160 years ago. 'The reunion of the Churches alone would affect a total change in the disposition of men and would bring all classes to co-operate zealously with one another. . . Protestant and Catholic theologians should meet to ascertain the points of agreement and difference between the Churches.'

Organized but unofficial contact between Catholic and Protestant clergy began with what are known as the Glenstal and Greenhills conferences. Both of these are held on Catholic property and they have been very influential. 'Glenstal' goes back to the spring of 1964, when the Abbot at St. Columba's Abbey, Glenstal, Co. Limerick, the Revd. Father Joseph Dundass OSB, made contact with the Anglican Dean of St. Patrick's Cathedral, Dublin, then the Very Revd. John Armstrong, later and in succession Bishop of Cashel and Ossory and now Archbishop of Armagh and Primate of All-Ireland.

Through him, he also reached the Very Revd. Dr T. A. B. Smyth (Presbyterian) and the Revd. Robert A. Nelson (Methodist). His purpose was to set up a conference for theological discussion. The first, of what was to become an annual residential event, was held on 23 and 24 July 1964. Over the years, many theological issues have been discussed, always with major contributions from each side. Although press statements are issued at the conclusion of each conference, no findings are drawn up. This has ensured a freedom of discussion not likely otherwise. Glenstal was immediately recognized as a success by those attending. Their numbers, however, were relatively restricted, because of geography, the residential nature of the conference, and the fact that it was held in midsummer. The decision in 1966 to launch 'Greenhills' was a natural consequence. It also has become an annual event. Its location at the Presentation Convent, Greenhills, Drogheda, on the banks of the River Boyne, makes it easy of access from both North and South. The yearly attendance is drawn from Roman Catholic, Presbyterian, Methodist, Church of Ireland, Society of Friends, Orthodox, Salvation Army, Reformed Presbyterian, Lutheran, and Moravian communities of both sexes, and both clerical and lay. As at Glenstal, time is given to united worship as well as to discussion. Since 1966, even though on occasion January weather has been inclement, careful choice of subjects and speakers has attracted large numbers and has made possible a significant contribution to the growth of a deeper ecumenical spirit. The Revd. Principal John M. Barkley, of Union Theological College, Belfast (Presbyterian), who is a regular participant at both conferences, has commented: 'On the Roman Catholic side, the conferences are well attended by representatives of the religious Orders and the laity, but attract few parish priests. On the Protestant side, theological professors and a good number of clergy attend, but the representation of the laity is weak. This means that what is said and done does not seep down to the parish level. . . On the other hand, the friendship and understanding created are deep, sincere, and lasting, and, had it not been for Glenstal in particular and to a lesser extent Greenhills, it is doubtful if the Ballymascanlon meetings would have come into being with so little opposition.'[12] Principal Barkley's reference to the Orders underlines the contribution made by the Servite Monastery in Benburb, County Tyrone. Its publications and its occasional meetings and conferences, with attendances at one time frequently checked and car numbers noted by suspicious Protestant anti-ecumenists, were also, and still are, important nurseries of new attitudes.

On the Protestant side, ecumenical interest in the immediate post-war years stemmed, for the most part, from clerics and lay-folk, who in pre-war days had come under the influence of the Student Christian Movement. There were enough of these in the United Council of Christian Churches and Religious Communions in Ireland (whose grandiloquent title has long since been superseded by the shorter and more workaday Irish Council of Churches) to make new ventures possible. They were able with some difficulty to persuade their pre-war veteran colleagues to consent to the holding of post-Amsterdam and post-Evanston World Council of Churches conferences.[13] These were held in Belfast and Dublin respectively. They brought a new dimension to ecumenical thinking which, in its turn, was to encourage the development of inter-church co-operation. It is incidentally a tribute to the magnanimity of the Church of Ireland House of Bishops that an abrasive speech by Dr Richard Hanson at the Dublin conference did not prevent them from electing him years later to the vacant see of Clogher.

In the 1960s the Council was to become a better-known and more active body. In 1956 it had been able, with the good will but far from generous support of its member-churches, to appoint its first paid official, a part-time organizing secretary, the Revd. Carlisle Patterson. Two conferences held in the wake of the Dublin conference on possible forms of inter-church co-operation were also formative.

Perhaps the most significant development of the 1950s had been the initiation of the Murlough House Conferences. In 1958, the late Bishop Frederick Mitchell of Down and Dromore had attended his first Lambeth Conference. Some time before it, the Revd. Carlisle Patterson had attempted to enlist the Bishop's support for his work with the ICC. He had met with no great success. But shortly after the conference, the Bishop sought to renew the contact. Mr Patterson recalls the Bishop's words: 'Mr Patterson I owe you an apology.' Dr Mitchell explained that the recent meetings at Lambeth had made an indelible impression on him. The presence and influence of bishops from the younger churches had shattered his concept of a self-contained and self-sufficient Irish Anglicanism. What could he do to help the work of the Irish Council and what it stood for?[14] The short series of Murlough House Conferences was the result. The Marquis of Downshire had recently made his large residence and grounds at Murlough near Dundrum, Co. Down, available to the Church of Ireland for the winter months. The first of the conferences was perhaps the most exciting and stimulating of them all. The opening keynote address by the late Principal J. Ernest Davey of the Presbyterian College, Belfast, was delivered against the noise and frenzy of a winter gale. Fearlessly, and with the integrity for which he was so noted, he met the problems and difficulties of free church–episcopal relationships head-on. What he said was calculated to make or mar the conference. It made it. Murlough brought a new depth to Irish Protestant dialogue.

The years 1962 and 1963 were turning-points. Dr Charles Ranson, a minister of the Irish Methodist Church serving as Director of the Theological Education Fund with its headquarters in New York, and a former General Secretary of the International Missionary Council, was on special leave in Ireland for the carrying-out of his duties as President of the Methodist Church in 1961–2. He gave impetus to ecumenical thinking. Presbyterians, Anglicans, and Methodists had started a joint church for the somewhat cosmopolitan population resident at Shannon Airport. New possibilities were in the air. In 1961 the Church of Ireland bishops had initiated a study of the implications of various church union schemes. The following year the Methodist Conference indicated its willingness to enter into conversations with other member-churches of the World Council of Churches regarding the implications of the New Delhi statement of the Council for Church relations.[15] In 1963 the Inter-Church Relations Committee Report to the Presbyterian General Assembly stated: 'Never in the history of the Church has there been such general interest in the subject of Church unity.' Had previous and subsequent Assembly reports and discussions been similar, the Irish ecumenical story might well have been different. But the writing was already on the wall, not only for the Presbyterians but for all who had eyes to see. Opposition to the ecumenical trends of the time was already becoming vocal and organized; in due course the issues of church union and the World Council of Churches would come near to tearing apart the Churches whose leadership had 'stepped out of line'. In 1961 it had taken all the skill of a respected former Moderator, Dr Austin Fulton, to pilot a resolution through the Assembly, that was to become, as it were, in succeeding years the criterion by which ecumenical affairs were to be judged. The resolution affirmed the Lord Jesus Christ as sole King and Head of the Church and the only Mediator and only Redeemer of Men. It recognized the Word of God, as set forth in the Scriptures of the Old and New Testaments, as the only infallible rule of faith and practice, the Supreme Standard of the Church. There was a recognition of the historic creeds and the acceptance of Holy Baptism and the Lord's Supper as the only Sacraments of the Church. It emphasized the status of the Presbyterian Church as a historic part of the Church of Christ and it stressed the obligation of Churches, as living Churches obedient to a living God, to consider and reform their doctrine and practice in accordance with the Word of God as set forth in the Scriptures.

The next year, the Assembly warned any potential church union negotiators to be specially careful that 'no impression is left that the Assembly is prepared to consider departure from its unanimous affirmation of 9 June 1961 regarding the status etc. of the Presbyterian Church as part of the Church of Christ'. Before the warning was finally sounded, it had been necessary to secure the withdrawal of an amendment designed to ensure that there should be 'no impression that the Assembly is prepared to consider any form of union which would require her ministers to accept ordination by a bishop in apostolic succession (so-called) or anything equivalent thereto'.

The time had come for more than talking about the nature of the Church and ideas of a united Church. The Presbyterians were the first to take soundings. They clearly had no thought of Anglican participation. They made contact with the Congregationalists, Reformed Presbyterians, and Methodists. By 1963 Congregationalist–Methodist–Presbyterian negotiations were under way. After a year, the Congregationalists withdrew. The report on the initial year's work had split them evenly 'down the middle'. Meanwhile the Church of Ireland was on the move. They too took their soundings and in 1964 three elaborate and cumbersome sets of negotiations started: Church of Ireland–Methodist; Church of Ireland–Presbyterian: and Methodist–Presbyterian. These were too much for even the most argumentative of negotiators; they were consequently merged in 1968 into what are now known as the 'tripartite discussions'. Their long and thorny history is traced in Chapter 9, on 'Ecumenism 1969–1980'.

In 1968 the Presbyterian Moderator and the Methodist President[16] received and accepted invitations to attend and greet the General Synod of the Church of Ireland. But before they could enter the Synod hall, let alone speak, they were required to wait in an ante-room while protocol requirements were set. They were then formally permitted to appear and address the House. Having spoken, it was indicated that it would be considered fitting if they withdrew. Ten years later each Church annually receives as a normal fact of life teams of observers from the other two Churches. What is more, Roman Catholic observers now attend the General Synod.

Relationships with the Roman Catholic Church were, however, another matter. So far, with the exception of Glenstal and Greenhills, there had been almost no meeting of minds between Irish Roman Catholics and Protestants. In the 1950s, the Presbyterians and Methodists had little, if anything, to say good or bad about the Church of Rome. It was left to the Primate of the Church of Ireland, the late Dr J. A. F. Gregg, who was congratulated at the General Synod of 1956 on forty years of service as a bishop, to make the running. Again and again his strong convictions and scholarship were evident in his presidential addresses to the General Synod. In 1951 he was concerned about Mariolatry and the Roman claim to the mono-poly use of the word 'Catholic'. In 1954 he went out of his way to pay tribute to the stand of Eastern Orthodoxy against the Church of Rome.

The 1960s brought a different mood. Irish Catholicism was already being influenced by John XXIII, the 'caretaker' Pope, and Vatican II. While as yet there had apparently been no major changes on the ecumenical front, other developments had been taking place. Mass in the vernacular and the new emphasis on Scripture had been noted by Protestants, as well as being experienced by Catholics. Even if, at this stage, there was no ecumenical *démarche* forthcoming from the Irish Hierarchy, many Protestants were beginning to realize that, sooner or later, far-reaching developments were inevitable, and that con-sequential decisions would be demanded from them.

By 1964 the Presbyterians, in response to a query from the United Presbyterian Church in the USA, could see 'evidence of change' as far as Rome was concerned. But it was a guarded admission and, above all, it was 'not clear that there is any change in doctrine'. Even if dialogue should be agreed, it must be under 'the guidance of the Holy Spirit and must not be undertaken with any vain illusions or in a spirit of irresponsible enthusiasm'. For Protestants there were two main problems:

Catholic power, and papal infallibility. Because of these 'many Presbyterians for political and doctrinal reasons were uneasy about dialogue with the Church of Rome'. The Inter-Church Relations Board completed its report with the warning, 'The history of Ireland is such that progress must be slow and the building up of a spirit of co-operation and trust after centuries of mistrust and suspicion will take time.' Ominously, at the General Assembly of that year, thirty-two members of the Assembly had, at their request, their names recorded as dissenting from the Assembly's decision to endorse its member-ship of the WCC, even with 'awareness of the dangers and difficulties and opportunities involved'.

In 1965 the Church of Ireland General Synod was equally guarded about the Vatican Decree on Ecumenism. Pending any sign of public reaction to a statement by the Irish Hierarchy, it was content to say 'the practical results will be watched with interest'. In the same year, the Methodists realized that guidance was needed for ministers and lay persons who might receive invitations to attend Roman Catholic services, or who contemplated issuing invitations for Roman Catholics to attend, or speak at, Methodist meetings or services. In 1966 the Church of Ireland Primate, Dr James McCann, told his Synod that a new day had dawned, and that sectarianism was outmoded. The same year the Methodists issued a courageous and significant document, *The present situation in Ireland*. It deliberately based on Holy Scripture a reasoned case to encourage social justice and the elimination of sectarianism.

It was clear that attitudes were changing. At official level new initiatives were being tried. But in the after-light, it is equally clear that the rearward defences were left unmanned. Early in 1964 a south Belfast Presbyterian minister, Dr John H. Withers, a well-known and respected preacher on radio and television and Moderator of the General Assembly in 1968, and a neighbouring Methodist colleague, the Revd. Robert Nelson, a lifelong ecumenist and later to be President of his Church, had, unknown to each other, arranged for Roman Catholic priests to address groups connected with their congregations on the same Sunday evening.[17] Ian Paisley had, with typical opportunism, mounted a vociferous barrage of opposition. It was a chance to stir up Protestant opposition to another sign of the alleged 'Romeward trend'.

The clamour over the two invitations was no more than a whisper compared with the frenzy evoked in early 1967 by the announcement that Dr John Moorman, the Bishop of Ripon and Chairman of the Joint Anglican–Roman Catholic Commission, was to speak in St. Anne's Cathedral (Church of Ireland) Belfast. The unfortunate Dean Cuthbert Peacocke, later Bishop of Derry and Raphoe, was subjected to abuse, pressure, and threats of damage to his cathedral. Massive separate demonstrations were planned by the Orange Order and by Ian Paisley and others. Evangelical Protestantism was enraged. With no support apparently forthcoming from any level, ecclesiastical or secular, the Dean was in an impossible position. He withdrew permission for the Bishop's visit.

The courts of that year endeavoured to recapture lost ground. At the General Assembly, the Presbyterians took note of the ecumenical crises through which the Churches were passing. They were particularly conscious of the growth of 'Paisleyism' (*sic*) and of the effects of the 'Bishop of Ripon affair'. They asked the question 'Why not leave ecumenism alone?', to which their reply was 'We can no more opt out of our ecumenical situation than out of the social and industrial environment in which we are placed.' Meanwhile the Standing Committee of the Church of Ireland, at its February meeting, had expressed 'its grave concern at the threats, which forced the cancellation of the [Bishop's] visit' and declared 'that the right to freedom of speech must be preserved, whether one agrees with the views of the speaker or not'. It called upon every member of the Church of Ireland 'to resist to the utmost any attempt to dictate to the lawful authorities of the Church what action they should or should not take either generally or in any particular set of circumstances'.

All brave words, but the damage had been done. The Churches had not been ready for an onslaught that was to have dire effects on the 'sickly growth . . . of ecclesiastical expediency'—Ian Paisley's description of ecumenism.[18]

As so often happens, however, non-theological factors had been drawing the Churches to actions they might never have taken otherwise. Paisleyite threats, police action, and subsequent crowd behaviour in the Divis Street area of Belfast produced, as has already been seen, street rioting of the kind that was to become all too familiar before the decade was out. It also produced a joint call for the restoration of peace from Church of Ireland, Methodist, Presbyterian, and Roman Catholic leaders in Belfast. This statement and a meeting between representatives of the recently formed Churches'

Industrial Council and community leaders from the lower Falls (including some thought to be 'activists') held in Methodist premises were judged to have been helpful in quelling the violence.

The next significant development, by a strange irony, had to do with the setting-up of the New University at Coleraine.[19] A meeting of the representatives of the joint Boards of Education (Church of Ireland, Methodist, Presbyterian) decided to take action to ensure that there would be nothing in the Charter of the University to disadvantage pastoral care by the Churches of students and staff, or to preclude the setting-up, if so desired, of a faculty of theology. Those present realized the advantage of involving the Roman Catholic Church in any approach to the government. Cardinal Conway received a deputation[20] in his home, Ara Coeli in Armagh, and promised to give further thought to the case they had made. They finally decided to write to the Prime Minister, Captain O'Neill, requesting that he should receive a deputation to be headed by Cardinal, Moderator, President, and Primate. The result was electric. The Secretary of the Cabinet, the late Sir Harold Black, almost immediately on receipt of the letter was sent to see the signatory[21] who had been responsible for its dispatch. Stormont had considered such a joint approach inconceivable. In the event, the terms of the Charter were considered accept-able. Equally, and if not more significant, the approach to the Cardinal had opened new doors.

New Year's Day 1968 was another important milestone. Pope Paul VI had called on Catholics throughout the world to regard 1968 as a Peace Year. Responding to an initiative, in late December 1967, from the Methodist President,[22] Cardinal Conway had tentatively inquired about the possibility of a joint request to the Irish people to pray for peace and work for it. The Moderator, President, and Primate[23] replied affirmatively and accepted, with a minimum of alteration, the draft he had been asked to supply. The result was massive front-page publicity in all the Irish dailies on 1 January. Some printed photostat copies of the call with its appended signatures. More than one editor asked where the signatories had met. The truth was not dis-closed that they had not dared to meet together. Corre-spondence,[24] telephone, and a personal emissary, a brother of the Cardinal, who little knew what he was carrying, ensured the authenticity of the document and its publication. It was a major break through as far as official contact with the Roman Catholic

Church was concerned.

The first meeting of all four leaders took place almost unnoticed a few months later at the official opening of the new Armagh Planetarium. By a judicious seating-arrangement, Cardinal Conway and Prime Minister Terence O'Neill were placed side by side. The press took notice of the latter encounter, but missed the first.

When the crunch came it caught the Irish Churches at a time of transition. The ecumenical trends had gone far enough to raise the Paisley opposition and to produce apprehension among the more conservative members of the main denominations; they had not gone far enough to ensure that the Churches would be able to function together immediately as a reconciling force. If the political crisis had arisen a decade earlier the Churches would have taken sides, as they did in the Home Rule crisis at the beginning of the century; a decade later, the Churches might have achieved a relationship that would have enabled them to rally their forces quickly in a united movement for reconciliation through reform. As it was, each denomination was divided between those who looked forward in ecumenical terms, and those who looked back to the doctrinal and political certitudes of an earlier time. Most of the leading figures belonged to the former group, but a majority of the rank and file, ministerial and lay, were still counted with the latter. When the heat was on, the waverers tended to go that way. Hence the phenomenon that we shall see endlessly repeated in the pages that follow: Christian leaders making constant appeals for moderation and reconciliation, but forced always to look over their shoulders to see how far they were isolating themselves from their own flocks. For generations their predecessors had been content to sow the wind of denominational rivalry and mutual disparagement; now, when supremely the need arose to speak Christ's reconciling word, they would reap the whirlwind. The secular world outside the province has been more aware of that whirlwind than of the men and women standing firm among its buffetings for the vision of unity and peace.

3 Civil Rights or Nationalist Insurrection?

The civil rights march in Londonderry on 5 October 1968 is generally thought to mark the outbreak of the current troubles. This was a new kind of activity on the part of those discontented with the state of affairs in Northern Ireland. It was not an assertion of Irish nationalism but a protest against 'second-class citizenship'. There is no doubt that the Northern Ireland Civil Rights Association (NICRA) took its cue from Martin Luther King's movement among the Negroes of the United States and that the Washington march was the pattern for the march in Derry. Active student support in this early phase of the agitation reflected the general student unrest of the later sixties, of which the most violent manifestation, the uprising of students in Paris, had occurred that summer. Spurred on by these examples, NICRA, which had both Catholic and Protestant members, planned its protest to draw attention to a number of standing grievances felt mainly by the Catholic population.

The most fundamental of these concerned elections for local authorities. There was universal suffrage for parliamentary elections, but only ratepayers had a vote in local council elections; furthermore, in some places, particularly in the city of Londonderry, ward boundaries were arranged to give an advantage to Unionists. Thus arose the cry of 'one man, one vote' and for an end to 'gerrymandering'. Once elected, councillors controlled the allocation of publicly provided housing, and gave preference to their own supporters. During the previous summer a particularly blatant example of this had aroused vigorous protest, when Dungannon Rural Council allocated a house at Caledon to a nineteen-year-old single Protestant girl, passing over homeless Catholic families.[1] So a system of points to ensure fair priorities in housing was another demand. The allegations about discrimination in this and other municipal matters led to the demand for an ombudsman. The item in NICRA's programme that came nearest to the traditional nationalist viewpoint was a call for the repeal of the Special Powers Act, which existed to enable the Unionist government to control subversive activity. This in practice meant activity to bring partition to an end.

Public opinion outside Northern Ireland strongly supported these demands, and within the province many who upheld the existing constitutional arrangement saw there was justice in them. Hence we find the Churches, Protestant as well as Catholic, talking in terms of reform, even of repentance, prepared to advocate to the government measures of conciliation that they certainly would not have supported if the agitation had been of the traditional kind, directly seeking Irish reunification. The authorities, on the other hand, could see no difference: this was the old wolf, even if it appeared to be wearing sheep's clothing.

The violence of 5 October, so widely displayed on the television screens of the world, arose directly from this difference of view. NICRA, claiming rights that should belong to all, planned a march through the whole city, disregarding the convention that each side only marches 'in its own territory'. It claimed not to be exclusively representative of 'one side'. The Protestant organizations, like the authorities, were quite sure that it was. If a breach of the peace was to be avoided, they argued, the march must be kept out of the Protestant Waterside district. The result was a confrontation between the Royal Ulster Constabulary (RUC) and the demonstrators. Heads were broken, including those of some opposition Stormont MPs, and the Unionist government, whose Minister for Home Affairs, Mr William Craig, had ordered both the re-routeing and the police action, was depicted to the world as oppressing a population seeking no more than fair treatment.[2]

The confrontation was followed by a weekend of rioting in Derry and Belfast in which students, later calling themselves the People's Democracy, played an active part. Further civil rights marches were arranged in a number of towns and their potential dangers increased by counter-demonstrations organized by the Revd. Ian Paisley and Major Ronald Bunting, a lecturer in mathematics whose wartime commission gave a military aura to the crowds he 'commanded' on the streets.

The reaction of the Protestant Churches to these events was divided: official church committees and officers for the most part supported the Prime Minister's policy of 'bridge-building', and recognized some justification for the civil rights protests.

On 14 October the Primate, the Moderator, and the President[3] issued a joint appeal 'for a period of calm to consider the implications of recent events and for prayers for the preservation of peace and goodwill'. The Moderator (Dr J. H. Withers), preaching on 13 October, said that 'the first task was for leaders of Church and State to call for calm, then fearlessly to analyse the causes of unrest and where justice was being denied to any section and driving it to despair. A Methodist, Dr. Hedley Plunkett, was saying 'We have been satisfied with mere tolerance and the old sores have been allowed to fester'. The Revd. Carlisle Patterson, another leading Presbyterian minister, summed up the feelings of many when he said: 'We cannot evade the truth that for years we have known of various forms of social injustice and political discrimination within our community and that we have found it mentally more comfortable, politically more acceptable and socially more convenient to acquiesce in these things.'[4] At the same time many individual clergy of the Protestant churches, particularly those associated with the Orange and Black Institutions and the Apprentice Boys of Derry, took a different view, and called for the maintenance of law and order: 'People responsible for defying the law, whether MPs or others, were morally responsible for any suffering that resulted', said the Revd. Henry Holloway, a Methodist minister preaching in Belfast Cathedral.[5] But some saw the 'law' that had been broken in Derry as the arbitrary decision of one man, a very partisan minister of the Crown.

On the same Sunday the Roman Catholic Primate, Cardinal Conway, welcomed 'the call by leaders of the Protestant Churches for an examination of conscience by everyone into the significance of recent events' and associated himself with 'their desire for lasting peace and harmony in the community'. 'I know', he said, 'the people who are suffering from these injustices well enough to realize that they will respond to any credible sign that their position is going to be remedied soon.'[6] When the Government Committee of the Presbyterian Church called for a meeting with leaders of other Churches and of political parties, the Roman Catholic Bishop in Belfast (Dr William Philbin) said he would consider the message 'with great interest and sympathy'.[7] The Executive of the Irish Council of Churches (ICC), meeting on 21 October, prepared a resolution for the Council which called for 'consultation with representatives of the Roman Catholic Church with a view to discovering how the Churches together can make an effective contribution towards improving community relations in Ireland'. When the full Council met on 7 November this was changed to 'consult with responsible church leaders on what practical steps might now be taken to advance the work of reconciliation'. The resolution also called on the government and local authorities 'urgently to consider the need for reform' and expressed the hope that 'our Roman Catholic and other fellow-countrymen will seriously examine in what ways they can alleviate the effects of those of their policies which tend to divide the community'.[8] Here is a subtle shift from what the Churches might do together to what the other Church ought to do; and the shift occurs when the issue is taken to a wider forum. A few days later 'The Voice of Ulster's Christian Ladies' was loud in condemnation of all support for Captain O'Neill's policy of 'appeasement'.[9]

Another march was planned for Derry on 15 November, and the previous night both cathedrals in the city were open for a night-long vigil of prayer. NICRA planned to march within the city walls (an enclave sacred to Protestants since the defence of the city in 1689 against James II's Catholic Army). Major Bunting promised 5,000 men to keep them out. The Londonderry Churches' Industrial Council appealed to the Prime Minister to allow the march as planned. Dr Paisley said: 'The Protestant clergy of Londonderry's so-called Churches Industrial Council have been unmasked as supporters of the law-breaking communist-inspired seditious amalgam of the so-called civil rights movement.' In the event the 15,000-strong demonstration halted at the police barriers; large numbers then entered the walled city as individuals and reassembled in the Diamond where a sit-down protest took place. No violence occurred.[10]

A fortnight later it was Armagh's turn. The Roman Catholic and Anglican Primates, both with their Sees in that city, issued a joint appeal for restraint. This was the first example of joint action at that level. When it was all over and little violence had occurred, they acted separately. Dr McCann praised the RUC and Cardinal Conway the NICRA stewards. Meanwhile, under pressure from the British government, which was at last alerted to the potential dangers of the situation in Northern Ireland, Captain O'Neill was preparing to meet many NICRA demands. Finding the intransigence of Mr Craig an obstacle to his policy, he dismissed him from the government and made a broadcast appeal for support. The response to this was gratifying, but, as events would show, insufficient.

The year closed with Christmas appeals for peace: 'The only sure and lasting foundation for peace is justice,' said Cardinal Conway. Already, however, students of the People's Democracy had announced a four-day march from Belfast to Derry. In the early days of January this took place, harassed at intervals by loyalist crowds and eventually subjected to brutal assault at Burntollet, where the road passes through a cutting favourable to ambush with stones and other missiles. The arrival of the mauled procession at Derry led to disturbances, following which the RUC entered the Roman Catholic Bogside area and behaved in a fashion that led to bitter accusations and to an official inquiry. This was carried out by a Scotland Yard officer[11] who complained of a 'wall of silence' put up by the policemen whom he questioned; in September it was announced that sixteen members of the RUC would be disciplined. Sixteen leading Protestant clergy, convened to initiate the consultations with the Hierarchy for which the ICC had asked, scathingly condemned the actions of Protestant elements at Burntollet and also wrote to the Prime Minister asking for a commission of inquiry into the causes of strife. O'Neill acknowledged that this letter had greatly helped him in persuading the Cabinet to agree to the setting-up of what became known as the Cameron Commission.

One of the main grievances at Londonderry was, as we have seen,[12] that ward boundaries were so arranged that the Protestant minority elected a majority of the councillors. O'Neill had earlier told a deputation of clergy that he would very much like to rectify this but that the Unionists would not hear of it: Derry was 'a sacred cow'. However, on 30 January 1969, he did replace the corporation by a commission nominated by the government. Later in his memoirs he called this 'the greatest of the reforms I was able to achieve' and considered that if it had been done years before, the 'explosion' of August 1969 would never have happened.[13] In 1980 the Roman Catholic Bishop of Derry (Dr E. Daly) spoke warmly of the impartiality of this Commission which had, he said, prepared the way for more normal relations between parties on the district council which superseded it in 1973.[14]

The early months of 1969 were characterized by further civil rights demonstrations, leading to clashes whether because of counter-demonstrations or because of re-routeing by the police. When a march was proposed for Newry the local Protestants, numbering less than 20 per cent of the population, were very alarmed. Their clergy took action on two fronts: they appealed to Ian Paisley not to bring in thousands of Protestants from elsewhere to counter-demonstrate, and they asked the Roman Catholic Bishop of Dromore (Dr Eugene O'Doherty) to join in an appeal for restraint. Dr Paisley complied but Dr O'Doherty thought intervention unnecessary. In the event the marchers resisted re-routeing by the police and considerable violence occurred. The Protestant clergy then issued a statement distinguishing between the 'humanitarian aims' of the genuine NICRA leaders and the fact that the movement was 'becoming the tool of agitators and avowed enemies of the rights of any but themselves'; they went on to say that 'if there had been a more noticeable and more active desire to preserve peace . . . on the part of our fellow (Roman Catholic) clergy, the situation might have been different'.[15] Among the signatories of this statement was the Revd. William Arlow, then a rector in Newry and later to become an outstanding leader in the Christian pursuit of reconciliation.[16]

The Moderator, Dr Withers, announced in January that conversations were being sought with the Roman Catholic Church, 'seeking to understand their dogmatic positions and equally to interpret to them our own Protestant evangelical theology'.[17] In the same week a *Directory on Ecumenism*[18] was issued in Dublin permitting Catholics in certain circumstances to attend Protestant services and to engage in common prayer. On 31 January the leaders of the Protestant Churches met Cardinal Conway. Arrangements were made for a standing joint consultative committee which in the months to come advised the church leaders about joint action. Before this meeting the Cardinal and northern Roman Catholic bishops issued a statement about the current unrest. They complained that recognition had not been given to serious abuses about jobs, houses, and franchise until the people took to the streets. They castigated 'people allowed to impede lawful and peaceful demonstrators with the threat or use of force', and on the other hand 'small groups of subversive militants who have associated themselves with Civil Rights for their own ends'. The bishops went on to pay tribute to the service in the cause of social justice rendered in recent months by many Protestant members of the community including leading churchmen, and to welcome the government's setting-up of a commission of inquiry into the causes of unrest.[19]

This commission had been announced on 16 January. Lord Cameron, a Scottish judge, was assisted by Sir John Biggart, Dean of the Faculty of Medicine in Belfast, and by Mr J. J. Campbell, a leading Catholic educationalist. By the time the Commission reported,[20] confirming what everyone knew but not everyone would admit, that the main contentions of NICRA were justified by the facts, Captain O'Neill had long since resigned. Mr Craig he had dismissed; another minister resigned in protest at the reforms, and a third, Brian Faulkner, tried to upstage the Prime Minister by resigning in support of universal local government franchise, which was not yet included in the reform programme. This was a complete change of front on Mr Faulkner's part: Professor James R. Boyd revealed that at a private meeting between clergy and Cabinet ministers he had strongly made the case for ratepayer franchise in local elections. Faced with growing disaffection in his parliamentary party the Prime Minister tried to take advantage of the support expressed in response to his broadcast by holding a general election. But he had not thought out clearly how he could use this instrument to defeat dissident elements within his own party. The result, announced on 25 February, was confused and did him little good. The most important outcome of the election was to bring some of the civil rights leaders, notably John Hume, into Parliament in place of the older nationalists. After a few months these joined forces with other Catholic members to form the Social Democratic and Labour Party (SDLP), henceforth the main political voice of the minority.

When the election was called, the Moderator said he could not commit his Church to the support of any one party or personality, but the Primate, with more than a hundred of his clergy, signed a statement of support and confidence for the Prime Minister.[21] Dr Paisley announced that he would have a candidate oppose 'every O'Neillite', and an organization called the New Ulster Movement[22] was founded, its chief object being to ensure that there was an O'Neillite candidate wherever the official Unionist candidate was against the Prime Minister's policy. This movement, largely led by Christian laymen of various denominations, while ineffective in its immediate electoral object, developed into a significant political factor in the years that followed. From its ranks was formed, about a year later, the Alliance Party, designed to attract voters from both communities, which it has done ever since with varying, but not decisive, success. During the election campaign efforts were made, particularly through editorials in the Belfast *News Letter*[23] and the *Church of Ireland Gazette*, to persuade Cardinal Conway and the northern bishops to 'recognize' the Constitution by paying formal calls on the Governor or the Prime Minister. It was suggested that if this were done the question of rights within the state could receive proper attention, for that issue would no longer be confused with the question of the state's legitimacy. Cardinal Conway's position remained unaltered: he accepted the existence of the state *de facto* and worked with its agents in practical matters, but would not go out of his way to show any positive cordiality towards it. He had already paid a visit to Government House: but at the Governor's request this had not been made public.[24] It must be remembered that Cardinal Conway, although himself a native of Belfast and resident, as Archbishop of Armagh, in Northern Ireland, was head of a Church four-fifths of whose members were citizens of the Republic. Political parties in the Republic had consistently questioned the legitimacy of the northern state, although so far that issue had not been raised by NICRA within Northern Ireland.

During March and April O'Neill steadily lost ground in both his parliamentary party and in the Unionist Party as a whole. In April water and electricity supplies were endangered by explosions. These were commonly supposed to have been perpetrated by the IRA, but were suspected at the time and are now known to have been the work of 'Loyalist' groups anxious to render the Prime Minister's position impossible. Confrontations in the streets continued, and a major clash between police and community took place in the Bogside district of Derry. On 25 April, in a bid to reduce tension there, the two local bishops, accompanied by a Presbyterian and a Methodist minister, rode in the same car to visit old people in the affected areas, an action immediately described by the Ulster Protestant Volunteers as a 'publicity seeking jaunt'. The Anglican bishop and his Protestant companions were blamed for 'acquiescing in what was obviously a carefully planned move by the Roman Catholic Church to curry sympathy in the outside world for its alleged persecuted minority in Northern Ireland'.[25] In fact the proposal had come from the Methodist minister (the Revd. George Morrison). When the simplest gestures of solidarity and compassion are represented as giving in to a sinister conspiracy it becomes very difficult to display Christian charity in a way that effectively improves matters.

Sunday 27 April 1969 was a day of prayer. Cardinal Conway pleaded in a sermon with parents to exercise more control over their children, easily carried away by the excitement of conflict. The Protestant clergy of Derry held a meeting in the cathedral and passed a resolution advising restraint, supporting the RUC, and pledging to work for harmony. Roman Catholics could join them in visiting the poor, but not yet in commenting on the situation. Prayer did not avail for Captain O'Neill, who resigned the next day because he lacked support in his own party. Leaders of the Churches heard the news of his fall as they sat together in the Cardinal's study considering the possibility of a joint appeal.

O'Neill had gone, destroyed by his friends rather than by his enemies. Major James Chichester-Clark, elected leader of the party by one vote over Brian Faulkner, inaugurated his premiership with an amnesty, which had the effect of releasing Ian Paisley from prison, whither he had gone after the election rather than pay a fine for obstructing the police in Armagh on 30 November. There was a momentary relaxation of tension with conciliatory utterances from all sides; even at an Apprentice Boys' service it was said that the Orange Order existed to uphold Protestantism but not to eradicate or abolish Roman Catholicism.[26] On 1 May the Irish Council of Churches welcomed the new Prime Minister's intention to pursue the programme of reform, called upon the Churches and sections of the community to consider ways in which they could contribute to the cause of social reconciliation, and instructed its executive to consider how to set up a full study of the role the Churches could and should play.[27] The summer was, however to see an outbreak of violence of a different order from any that had gone before, ending not only Chichester-Clark's 'honeymoon' but also, by placing the main responsibility for security on the British army, his effective control over policy.

Before that happened the Protestant Churches held their annual gatherings, the first opportunities for these representative bodies to review the situation. Primate McCann, opening his last General Synod, said 'We must stand firmly for the equal rights of every man' and 'be seen firmly opposed to all forces of fanaticism, religious and political.' Next came the Presbyterian General Assembly, held this year exceptionally in Dublin. This entailed a visit from President De Valera and so gave Ian Paisley the opportunity of denouncing the Moderator (Dr J. T. Carson) for 'grasping the hand of a murderer'. The retiring Moderator, Dr Withers, reviewed 'the many statements of Christian principle' issued by the Church during the year and emphasized Presbyterian support of just reforms and their willingness to acknowledge a share in the 'sins of apathy and discrimination'. He felt sorrow and disappointment that 'the Roman Catholic Hierarchy, while condemning violence, had not felt able, in spite of repeated requests, to acknowledge that their people too . . . had contributed to the malaise of Ulster'.[28] Similar complaints were made about the same time by Anglican and Methodist clerics. In private the Cardinal revealed the hurt that these statements had caused him and was irritated by the fact that this had not been made an issue when the Church leaders met. At the Methodist Conference, the normal rotation of which brought it also to Dublin this year, the report from Londonderry, so far the scene of the most serious confrontation, claimed that 'Methodist lay people and ministers have sought to demonstrate the message of reconciliation to a wounded and embittered society.' At about the same time the Society of Friends issued a pamphlet by Denis Barritt of which the message may be summed up thus: 'Look at the effects of television reporting—clarify the terms Protestant and Catholic—look again at shared education—support the Northern Ireland government's reforms.'[29] A joint inquiry by the Churches into these matters was suggested.

There was increased rioting after the Twelfth of July when Orangemen annually celebrate the Battle of the Boyne. On 21 July the first men landed on the moon and Ulster's lunacy erupted. By the first Sunday in August sermons against violence were being ineffectually preached in most of the churches. A call to ban all marches, including the traditional ones, was supported by church leaders on both sides. Eventually a ban for one month was imposed, but only after 15,000 Apprentice Boys had marched through Londonderry on 12 August. Cardinal Conway felt bound to say that he 'could not understand why a parade—lasting five or six hours and accompanied by dancing women singing party songs and firing off miniature cannon— was allowed to take place in a city which was tinder dry for an explosion. In the name of God who loves all men, Catholic and Protestant, Jew and Gentile, let no more wood be piled on this destructive fire.'[30] But to call off their traditional celebrations of past victories seemed to the Protestant organizations tantamount to present surrender.

This demonstration in fact sparked off riots in which the police had to use CS gas. By 14 August the British army was called in to assist the police in Derry. Belfast Catholics took to the streets in large numbers to draw off pressure from those in Derry. They found themselves faced, however, not by police reinforcements drawn from the other city, but by Protestant crowds armed with cudgels and petrol bombs who followed the police into Catholic areas and burned down large numbers of houses occupied by Roman Catholics. At this point a revealing episode occurred: the Revd. A. J. Beattie, assistant minister of a nearby Presbyterian Church, was asked to go to Cupar Street and act as Protestant spokesman in contact with Roman Catholic priests of the Clonard monastery. He met the Superior, Father McLaughlin, and each undertook to hold a meeting of local men, of their respective persuasions, and to appoint thirty stewards to keep the peace by mounting guard at a critical intersection. As Mr Beattie was duly holding his meeting John McQuade, a Unionist MP at Stormont, turned up. Let Mr McQuade speak for himself in words he used before the Scarman Tribunal:[31] 'Mr Beattie informed me that he with a Roman Catholic priest and a Republican had a peace pact. I informed the people that there was no need for any peace pact; if people would obey the law of the land and recognize the constitution there was no other need. I then warned the women and children to go to their homes and keep off the streets. I told the men they would have to be prepared to defend them.' The Tribunal commented: 'We have no doubt that owing to Mr McQuade's intervention the meeting failed of its purposes.'[32] That night saw the burning of many Catholic houses in Bombay Street, one of the ugliest incidents of the riot period. Interviewed by the authors in 1980, Bishop Philbin told a parallel story on the other side. He and a parish priest had just concluded a mass meeting, at which Roman Catholic men had agreed to proposals that would keep the peace, when a Roman Catholic politician, Paddy Devlin, (later to be a valuable Minister in the power-sharing executive), arrived, and by spreading rumours about what was happening destroyed the positive atmosphere which the clergy had painstakingly established. It is much easier to sabotage reconciliation than to achieve it.

On 15 August troops began to be deployed in the Falls district of Belfast, and on the next day, at the urgent request of Bishop Philbin, they also took up positions in the Ardoyne. Evictions of people living in mixed areas were now in full swing, and the soldiers could do little to prevent them. A number of people lost their lives by shooting; the Dublin government set up field hospitals near the border, and called for a United Nations peace-keeping force.

The general reaction of the Churches to this August crisis was practical: halls were opened to receive the homeless, and volunteers tended to their needs. In east Belfast a peace committee was established which became a model for similar efforts elsewhere. Its leader was David Bleakley, who, as a former Labour MP at Stormont, could engage the trade unions, and as a leading Anglican layman could ensure the support of the Churches.[33] Members of these committees, including Protestant and Catholic clergy, patrolled the streets at night, calming fears, scotching rumours, and, on occasion, physically occupying ground between opposing mobs. Bishops of both persuasions were visitors to the east Belfast Committee's Centre in a Presbyterian hall. Less dramatically, many Christian people went out of their way to call on friends and acquaintances of the other persuasion to assure them of continued goodwill. At the shipyard the shop stewards called a mass meeting to ensure that the Protestant majority in the work-force did not intimidate or expel the Catholic minority. Led by Sandy Scott, assisted by Eric Gallagher, who spoke to the men in the name of Christian charity and at their request prayed with them, this venture was successful and set a pattern that was followed by industry generally. At this period it was possible to find men working at the same bench in the daytime who had been throwing stones—or worse—at each other at night.

The intervention on a large scale of British troops involved the Westminster government more closely; indeed many would hold that this was the moment at which Stormont should have been suspended and the government which provided the force taken responsibility for policy. If the initiatives towards inter-party government eventually taken by Mr William Whitelaw had began early in 1970, before the situation had been embittered by two further years of bloodshed and the introduction of internment, things might have been very different. As it was the British government sent over the Home Secretary, Mr James Callaghan, whose department was responsible for relations beteen the British government and the authorities at Stormont.

4   The Destruction of a Regime

The deployment of British troops in the streets and the visit of the Home Secretary marked the beginning of much closer involvement by the British government in the affairs of Northern Ireland. This was to lead, in less than two years, to the suspension and eventual abolition of the provincial parliament and government that had been set up in 1921.

Mr Callaghan made a brave attempt to restore the situation, working through the existing machinery of Stormont to insist on reform.[1] At this period it was thought that if the Unionist government could be persuaded to remedy the specific grievances of the Catholics, it would be possible to preserve unscathed the constitutional arrangements made in 1921. Mr Callaghan's visit afforded another opportunity for the Churches, along with political parties and other bodies, to set out in statements to him their respective assessments of the position.

Without waiting for the Home Secretary's arrival, Cardinal Conway and the northern bishops of his Church issued a statement on 23 August[2] strongly controverting the Unionist government's line. The facts, they said, of 14 and 15 August were that 'the Catholic districts of Falls and Ardoyne were invaded by mobs equipped with machine guns and other firearms. A community that was virtually defenceless was swept by gunfire and streets of Catholic houses were set on fire. We ask all to realize that among Roman Catholics belief in the impartiality of the Ulster Special Constabulary[3] is virtually non-existent.' The official view was that an armed insurrection had occurred and that Protestant crowds, though admittedly out of control, were trying to help the police restore order, a view sustained in a letter to the press by five Protestant clergy working in the districts concerned. The Catholic bishops said that 'a necessary precondition for any restoration of confidence . . . must be an open recognition of these facts',[4] that is, of their diagnosis. What they in fact got was the appointment of a tribunal of inqury under Lord Justice Scarman to establish the facts. This tribunal took two years over its work, and by the time it reported its conclusions had little practical bearing on the current situation.

In reply to these assertions of the Cardinal and bishops, the Moderator, Dr Carson, said that 'they will, in my view, be regarded by many as not likely to add to the spirit of mutual trust and confidence on which we must try to build'.[5] It is, however, only fair to add that the Roman Catholic bishops did call upon their people 'to remain calm and to avoid all words and actions which could in any way increase tension'.[6] The Anglican Primate, Dr George Simms, who had assumed office in the midst of the storm, stayed for three weeks in a Belfast rectory, and walked the riot-torn streets every evening with the rector, Canon Eric Elliott. He said, 'During my evening visits to certain Belfast city areas this week, I met a new kind of co-operation. This gives hope that all denominations can work together as neighbours, as responsible partners in community problems and in countless practical courtesies and joint ventures, without compromising their religious loyalties.'[7]

The *Protestant Telegraph* wrote robustly of the Cardinal's 'lies', but his diagnosis of the August violence was given credence by the relief and enthusiasm with which Catholic districts greeted the British troops, whom they saw as protectors, and James Callaghan, whom they regarded as an umpire there to see fair play by the Unionists. These were hardly the attitudes to be expected from insurrectionaries. Mr Callaghan walked the streets in a reassuring, avuncular manner, and met leading people of all persuasions. These included Dr Paisley, to whom he said, 'But all men are children of God.' 'No,' came the instant reply, 'they are the children of wrath.'[8] 'The Voice of Ulster's Christian Ladies' was heard again, claiming that 'the ecumenical drive' in all the Churches had led to the defection of hundreds to Paisley's Free Presbyterian Church. Most of the Callaghan conversations were private, but the Presbyterian Church published its submission to him, and this may be taken as a fair expression of the point of view of the Protestant Churches generally at this stage.

After pointing out that their Church functioned in both states, and that the causes of conflict were not mainly religious, the Presbyterian statement continued:

Religiously, however, there is a strong conservative body of opinion within our church who suspect the modern ecumenical trends and the more liberal policies of our church courts and church leaders as implying a weakening or betrayal of fundamental Reformation principles which all, indeed hold dear . . . There remains . . . a deep seated distrust of the Roman Catholic Church, not only in its doctrines but also in its power structures. Our Church seeks to serve and to speak fairly for the honest conservative as for the more liberal views of our membership.

The Church supported the general constitutional position of Northern Ireland, and regretted that this had never been 'accepted frankly by Eire or by the northern minority.' Their pressure to change it 'has in turn engrained deeply into the northern majority a strong sense of distrust, a "besieged" mentality and a resentment against those who would claim all the benefits of their social provisions while persistently denigrating their society'. Pointing directly to the problem facing all Church leaders in Ulster, they continued: 'As a Church we have perhaps suffered more than any other for the degree to which our leaders have been prepared to go in advance of their members', in giving 'a lead to their thinking in these matters'. Much, they claimed, had been done on a personal and practical level 'to mitigate the events of this year'. 'There is a widespread feeling that much less effort has been made, both by the news media and by the authorities, to understand the Protestant as well as the Roman Catholic in Ulster . . . Perhaps most of all' a new climate 'depends on the readiness of the Roman Catholic community to make changes in some of their traditional attitudes and policies, at a time and on a scale to be compared with the changes to be required of the majority.'[9]

In spite of the defensive nature of this formal statement, the Moderator (Dr Carson) acknowledged at a meeting between Mr Callaghan and the Protestant church leaders that the Protestant Churches shared a common sense of shame for what had happened. Eric Gallagher spoke of an unofficial liaison committee already existing with the Roman Catholic Church, and Mr Callaghan was astonished that it was thought necessary to keep this constructive move confidential because of likely reactions in some circles.

Mr Callaghan went home promising protection by the army, reforms by Stormont, and another visit in six weeks' time to monitor progress. As he went the four church leaders appeared on television together for the first time, and were interviewed by Kenneth Harris.[10] It was remarked that they said little to each other and replied individually to questions, but it was a beginning. Cardinal Conway said that 98 per cent of his people would oppose a united Ireland brought about by violence. Archbishop Simms said we all had to educate our people in the application of Christianity not just to personal life but to public problems. Dr Carson wished the northern minority would identify with the state as the southern minority had done. That led the Cardinal to ask if the Protestants in the south were 'satisfied', to which Dr Simms said in effect 'Yes', but drew attention to the different dimensions of the problems and to the impact of mixed marriages. All expressed the hope that people would keep calm for six weeks during which the reforms called for by the Home Secretary could be introduced.

At this point the Prime Minister (Major Chichester-Clark) summoned a peace conference consisting of church leaders, representatives of the trade unions and industry, and other prominent citizens. He and Brian Faulkner were the only politicians present. The Cardinal and the Primate, or their representatives, attended the successive sessions. To some degree this conference helped to reduce tension, but it had no lasting results. That September many areas in Belfast were cut off by barricades, and the clash of rival mobs was frequent. Clergy joined with the police in trying to keep people apart, and Dr Paisley on more than one occasion, at the request of the authorities, prevailed upon Protestant crowds to go home quietly. The army constructed a permanent barrier, ironically named the Peace Line, between and Falls and Shankill roads in Belfast. The Prime Minister demanded in a broadcast the dismantling of unofficial barricades, and on 15 September, following up a suggestion made by a Protestant clergyman at the peace conference, an urgent visit was paid to the authorities in London by Father Padraig Murphy and Mr Tom Conaty. Thereafter Bishop Philbin and Father Murphy helped to negotiate voluntary removal of the barricades on the Catholic side. This averted a clash with the army, which still enjoyed good relations with the Catholic population.

Shortly afterwards the Cameron report[11] on the initial causes of unrest appeared. It showed that the grievances of the civil rights movement were by no means imaginary. Cardinal Conway found it very fair and a remarkable achievement; Archbishop Simms asked that it should not be used for recrimination but positively; Dr Carson, the current Moderator, said it merited careful study and showed that there were 'legitimate causes of dissatisfaction'. It must be remembered that these statements were made against a background of bitter protest by William Craig and others, who had said all along that this inquiry, because it could not compel evidence on oath, would be used as a propaganda instrument by 'the enemies of Ulster'.

There followed a winter during which almost every weekend saw rioting on the streets; neither the early closing of public houses nor the warnings of politicians and churchmen availed to prevent threatening mobs of both factions from assembling and acting in a manner that forced the army to use CS gas and other methods of control, devastating in their effect upon relations with the local population. A quotation from the *Protestant Telegraph* illustrates the atmosphere prevailing in some quarters:

There is every reason to believe that Jesuit infiltrators have wormed their way into positions of prominence in the ecumenical movement, especially in the Church of England, and have been largely instrumental in the sell-out of Protestantism. One of these Jesuits is the present Archbishop of Canterbury, Dr Michael Ramsey. Dr Ramsey has demonstrated to the world that he is an idolator, a liar who had repudiated his ordination vows, and the wearer of a cardinal's ring, a gift from the Pope, to be valued at £250,000. Some time ago the Pope appointed some new cardinals, but did not give the names of the men appointed. There is little doubt that Dr Ramsey has been appointed a cardinal. . .[12]

Against this background the government, in response to strong pressure from Downing Street, persevered with its programme of reform, pushing bill after bill through a reluctant Parliament and bringing the head of the City of London police, Sir Arthur Young, to reorganize the RUC and to provide it with a proper reserve, on lines recommended by a commission under Lord Hunt. The B Specials[13] were disbanded, and the Ulster Defence Regiment, a local force under British Army command, was formed. It is impossible to detail the incidents of this period but it is important not to underestimate the effect on public opinion of the constant turmoil, for which each side held the other responsible, and which authority seemed powerless to control. To take an impartial stance, indeed to see any merit in the other side's case, took considerable independence of mind at such a time; to express it was a matter of moral and indeed physical courage. The moves made by church leaders during this winter must be viewed in that light.

In November Dr Arthur Butler, who was to prove a man of great wisdom and grace during the years of ordeal, was installed in Belfast as Anglican Bishop of Connor. 'Faith, hope, and love', he said 'must be brought out of the pages of the Bible, out from between the walls of churches, into the streets and into the hearts of all our people.'[14] Dr Farran, the Roman Catholic Bishop of Derry, praised the people of that city for their restraint, and thanked the army. The Revd. Donald Gillies, Presbyterian minister in the Shankill district of Belfast, protested against a smear campaign on the local residents following their demonstrations in the streets: they did not believe that the RUC was returning to Catholic areas as a police force but 'by compact with the lawless'.[15] The *Presbyterian Herald* announced that all were sinners and 'it is not possible to justify the claim that either side is taking a Christian way'.[16] True enough, but if the Christian way meant taking neither side, those who tried to follow it found themselves without a base of support in the community. The Protestant leaders called a day of prayer for 2 November—perhaps an ill-chosen date, as it enabled First Antrim Presbyterian Church to keep the observance by holding a thanksgiving for the defeat of the Gunpowder Plot![17] That is a prize example of the Ulster capacity to justify from the past a partisan stand in the present. When Father Denis Faul alleged partiality on the part of law-courts in Ulster he was publicly rebuked by Cardinal Conway. In December the Cardinal and the Anglican Primate attended together a demonstration at the Armagh Planetarium on 'The Star of Bethlehem'; each spoke of 'an enormous increase in friendly relations between members of the churches'. Yet 'Catholic' and 'Protestant' remained for the news media the most favoured terms to identify the warring factions.[18]

On 2 March the statue in Belfast of the Revd. Hugh Hanna, a Protestant champion of earlier days, was blown up. Dr Paisley immediately demanded (unsuccessfully) its reinstatement, and a Belfast paper took the opportunity to reprint from *Punch* of 1857 a pointed ditty:

> Behind the harbour office wall,
> Roaring Hanna,
> Girt by your Lisburn lads so tall,
> Roaring Hanna,
> What's faction's flame or hatred's gall,
> What's riot, bloodshed, row or bawl,
> Roaring Hanna,
> To one who boasts the inward call,
> Roaring Hanna?[19]

Against fanaticism reason's ironical question was as ineffective then as it is now. And in the same month the New English Bible, inaugurated in England at Westminster Abbey and in Scotland at St. Giles', was almost surreptitiously introduced to Ireland at a service, by invitation only, held in the small Chapel of Unity at Methodist College, Belfast, lest the protests of Roaring Hanna's modern champion should lead to a breach of the peace.

But the church leaders continued to struggle against the results of their own traditions. When Cuthbert Peacocke was enthroned Bishop of Derry, he announced his resignation from the Orange Order. The first tentative steps towards formal dialogue between the Protestant Churches and the Roman Hierarchy were taking place this winter. Following a deadlock in the electoral college, the bishops of the Church of Ireland elected to the rural bishopric of Clogher Richard Hanson from Nottingham, an Anglo-Irish theological professor of strong liberal views, born in Dublin and educated at Trinity College. This was to prove one of those cases of going too far too fast, the memory of which is so inhibiting to those who work for Irish reconciliation. Dr Hanson's forthright exposition of modern views on the Bible and his well-publicized comments on clerical membership of the Orange Order put too great a strain on the canonical obedience of some of his clergy, and after three unhappy years he returned to the academic life in England.

Easter 1970 saw a singularly violent commemoration of the 1916 Rising,[20] which went on for several days and led to the partial evacuation of the Protestant population from New Barnsley, an enclave in west Belfast's predominantly Catholic area. Dr Paisley, ostensibly engaged in succouring Protestant refugees, is thought by many to have stimulated the fears and encouraged the evacuation for purposes of anti-Catholic propaganda. Protestant church leaders made a joint statement of their deep concern 'that so many of our families have been in so much fear as to be compelled to leave their homes'.[21] They appealed for 'the rejection of any attempt at reprisals or retaliation'. Cardinal Conway said that the Roman Catholic community in Northern Ireland had 'suffered too much for too long from real grievances for it now to have to suffer from the activities of [its own] hooligans', while Dr Philbin said, 'I little thought that a day would come when Protestants could allege that fear of trouble involving their Catholic neighbours caused them to leave their homes and when Catholics would attempt to occupy houses so vacated.' Meanwhile Bishop Butler considered the New Barnsley situation so serious that he cancelled other engagements in order to worship with the congregation there; but the Revd. Donald Gillies in a letter to the *Daily Telegraph*[22] said the events of Easter week necessitated 'the mounting of a massive Protestant counter-attack'. Evictions and intimidation went on, and by July the Protestant withdrawal from New Barnsley was complete. Before long it was being stated that forced removals in Belfast represented the biggest displacement of population in Europe since the immediate aftermath of the Second World War. Such was the end of well-meaning attempts during the previous decades to 'integrate' housing.

On 20 April Dr Paisley held his own 'day of prayer' and stated that without divine intervention he would 'not have been able to defeat the Unionist Party machine'.[23] In the same week the Belfast Methodist Synod called for 'full justice for all sections of the community, a determined effort to understand the hopes and fears of every section, and full support for the forces of law and order in establishing conditions wherein political questions were settled only on peaceful and democratic lines.' At the end of May campaigning began for the United Kingdom general election of 1970. As the contest began the northern Roman Catholic bishops issued a statement in which they said:

The overwhelming majority of our people do not want violence . . . It would be a stab in the back for any individual or group deliberately to provoke violent incidents . . . but there is some evidence that it may have happened in recent days. If this is so then in the name of God and the whole Catholic community we condemn it . . . Most of our neighbours here are our fellow Christians, united with us in love and worship of the same God and the same Lord and Saviour, Jesus Christ.[24]

This is the first reference, albeit veiled, to the activities of the by now revived IRA, which were to replace the communal rioting by an organized terrorist campaign. Nine days later came the first joint statement by the Cardinal and the leaders of the three main Protestant Churches. It was mainly concerned to deny that the conflict was a religious war. Divisions 'arise from deep and complex causes—historical, political and social—but the religious differences between professing Christians are not a primary cause'.[25]

That year at their summer meetings the governing bodies of the Churches took a significant step. They authorized the setting-up of a joint group on social questions, duly appointed by the Roman Catholic Hierarchy on the one side and the member Churches of the Irish Council on the other.[26] Meanwhile the governing bodies severally took stock of the worsening situation. The statement of the Methodist Conference may be taken as typical, since there is not space for full consideration of them all. The Conference began by reaffirming the obligation to demonstrate Christian love to opponents as well as to friends, its conviction that any form of injustice is contrary to God's will, the duty of the civil power to maintain order, and the requirement binding all citizens to obey the duly constituted authorities. It proceeded to welcome and support the continuing programme of reform. It then urged the organizers of traditional parades and marches to consider whether they should 'continue to exercise their rights in this connection', and in any case to avoid provocative behaviour if they did. Referring to the current UK election, the Conference went on to remind parliamentary candidates of their obligation to speak and act with a full sense of responsibility to the whole community, avoiding appeals to religious prejudice, and it called on the public to use their votes with a full awareness of their responsibility. It warned of the illicit importation of arms, condemned all resort to force, and reaffirmed its belief in the sanctity of life, calling the taking of life for political ends unequivocally 'murder'. It then commended the efforts being made to improve community relations, and listed seven lines of action which ordinary church members could take to that end.

The Presbyterian Assembly and the Anglican Synod expressed similar views, and the Roman Catholic Hierarchy at the same season issued a statement roundly condemning violence as 'a betrayal of the Catholic community, a stab in the back'. 'It is no justification', they said, 'for such conduct to say that there was provocation or to say, even with justice, that much worse deeds have been done by others and have gone unpunished.' They pointed to the progress made in reform and hinted that further instalments would be hindered, not encouraged, by unreasonable conduct on the Catholic side. 'Next to love of God the greatest commandment is love of our neighbour. Our neighbour, as the catechism teaches us, is "mankind of every description, even those who injure us or differ from us in religion".'[27]

Any effect that these appeals might have had was nullified by a particularly harsh military operation that took place in July 1970, a thirty-six-hour curfew and house-to-house search on the

Lower Falls Road in Belfast. Whatever may have been the operational reason for this, it completed the alienation of the Catholic community from the British army, which a year earlier had been regarded as protectors, and led Cardinal Conway to state that 'Measures taken to establish law and order should be taken impartially.' August saw a fresh outburst of violent conduct on both sides, followed by the now familiar appeals to reason and charity from bishops and other church leaders. Bishop Quin, of Down and Dromore, praised restraint shown in east Belfast, but warned of wild and subversive talk among Protestants directed against the government.[28] He had clearly been hearing of attitudes that later took shape in the Ulster Defence Association and other Protestant paramilitary bodies. We may note that on both sides, within a few weeks, bishops had given warning of sinister organizations of which the public was still largely unaware.

And so into the third winter of strife, a time when nothing seemed to change: endless incidents, repeated assertions of all-too-familiar viewpoints, a growing sense of frustration, and a job to do caring for the victims of eviction. On 15 February Cardinal Conway was interviewed on UTV and claimed to have condemned violence twenty-three times. He spoke of the limitations to the bishops' authority over lawless elements, and, movingly, of the social deprivation of areas from which Catholic violence sprang. The Catholic Church held that it would be wrong to try to unite Ireland by force. In the course of the interview the Cardinal revealed that he had never had the opportunity of discussing matters with the Prime Minister, and he would be glad to do so. Within a fortnight such a meeting was arranged. It is characteristic of the frozen practices of Northern Ireland that such an encounter did not occur until within a month of the end of Major Chichester-Clark's two years as Premier. A quotation from the *Protestant Telegraph*[29] may help the reader understand the slowness of public men to make unaccustomed contacts: 'Within a week of Cardinal Conway's appeal to meet Chi-Chi, the tête-à-tête took place in secret. So far the public has been left in ignorance as to what actually was said, or what bargains were made, or what concessions agreed.' Chichester-Clark was not looking for bargains with the Cardinal, but for stronger initiatives against lawlessness from Westminster. In March, saying that these were not forthcoming he resigned, to be succeeded by Brian Faulkner. Again, as on the occasion of Captain O'Neill's resignation, the church leaders were in session together when news of the impending resignation came through.

The new Prime Minister exhibited a dynamic approach that had been lacking in his predecessor. He went outside the Unionist Party to invite David Bleakley, whose peace-committee work has been mentioned before,[30] to be Minister of Community Relations. He made no attempt, however, to find a seat in Parliament for Mr Bleakley, and thus limited his tenure of office to six months. When that time expired Mr Faulkner made another innovation and brought Dr G. B. Newe into the government, with cabinet rank as minister of state. He was the first Roman Catholic to hold office in a Northern Ireland government—but before Dr Newe's six months of non-parliamentary ministerial life expired the Stormont government had ceased to exist.

Chichester-Clark's first August had brought the army on to the streets, and Faulkner's August was to bring internment. But initially there was new hope. Incredibly the province began celebrating its fifty years of statehood with a Jubilee Festival and an exhibition of its achievements. By this time the only matter raised by the civil rights campaigners in 1968 that had not been granted was the abolition of the Special Powers Act. On 22 June Faulkner introduced into Parliament his plan for parliamentary committees which would give the Opposition influence over administration and legislation. This proposal was cautiously received by the SDLP, but inter-party talks were actually in progress when the killing by soldiers of two rioters in Derry on 9 July caused the abrupt withdrawal of the SDLP, not only from the talks but from Parliament itself.

At the General Synod the Anglican Primate praised the new Minister of Community Relations and spoke of encouraging developments in relations between the two communities. A united service with Roman Catholics present took place in Portadown—perhaps, in view of the outspoken Protestantism of many people there, the most unlikely place in Ireland for such a gesture. The Methodist Conference developed further the ideas of its statement of the previous year, but felt it necessary in so doing to reaffirm its loyalty to the principles of the Reformation, and at the Presbyterian Assembly ecumenical hesitations led to an unsuccessful attempt to withdraw that Church from the World Council of Churches. Meanwhile between March and August Cardinal Conway five times in sermons proclaimed the sinfulness of murder, whether of civilians or soldiers.

The increase in explosions and shootings, as compared with rioting, convinced the government that the general unrest was now being fomented by the IRA, and indeed on 19 May there took place in Belfast the first IRA funeral with 'full military honours', when over 1,000 uniformed members paraded openly on the Falls Road. Believing that the defeat of this organization was the key to a return to normality, Faulkner resorted on 9 August (without consulting his Cabinet[31] but with the reluctant consent of the British government),[32] to the traditional weapon of detention without trial. The result was counter-productive. Intelligence was not up to date, and many leading figures were not seized. Others, who had long since abandoned subversive methods, were. Within a month many of those arrested had been released—a tacit admission that the wrong ones had been taken. In that month more people had died violently than in the preceding three years, and an effective propaganda advantage had been conceded to the enemies of the state.

The introduction of internment confronted the Churches with a dilemma. It was a manifest interference with human rights, but it was directed against people whose actions denied the rights of others. It was no novelty in Ireland, north or south. If it had not been bungled, it might have been effective in restoring order for a period during which remaining grievances could have been tackled. On the day of internment Cardinal Conway appealed to the Catholic population 'not to allow their feelings at the present time to lead them into situations where they could suffer serious injury or death'. A few days later he was saying that 'abhorrence of internment was as deep and wide-spread among Catholics' as their dislike of violence. The position of the Protestant Churches was of necessity more equivocal. The government, through the Ministry of Community Relations, was anxious for church support for a ban on loyalist marches which it had imposed as a kind of counter-weight to internment. In the absence on holiday of the leaders, their appointed and authorized substitutes, justly aware like the government of the need for 'something for everybody', called for loyalist restraint and obedience but also, with certain provisos, gave guarded support to the measure of internment. A few days later, interviewed on RTE, Archbishop Simms without disclosing that he had not been personally present, said that those who drew up the statement had agonized for hours and reached their decision 'with the sound of gunfire in their ears'. They did not know at the time that only Roman Catholics had been interned in this first swoop. Later a considerable number of loyalists were to join them in prison, and in 1975, with the benefit of hindsight, a joint working party of the Churches[33] agreed in disapproval of detention without trial. This was some months before the system was finally brought to an end by the third British Secretary of State, Mr Merlyn Rees.

In the immediate aftermath of internment a Roman Catholic priest, Father Hugh Mullen, was shot dead while giving the last rites to a wounded man. Bishop Arthur Butler attended the requiem mass for this first clerical casualty, and was roundly condemned by a select vestry in his own diocese for conduct 'incompatible with the teaching of the Church'.[34] By September the papers were recording the hundredth death since the troubles began. Soon rumours began to circulate of brutal treatment of internees in the quest for information. Reports to this effect were made by Father Denis Faul and Father Patrick Walsh to the joint *ad hoc* committee of Protestant and Roman Catholic clergy that had been meeting spasmo- dically ever since the Burntollet outrage in 1969. The committee informally passed on the allegations to Mr Faulkner, suggesting that an inquiry was needed. This was set up under Sir Edmund Compton, and in November its report, attempting a subtle distinction between 'torture' and 'ill treatment', but recommending the prohibition of certain practices, was quickly accepted by the government. These findings occasioned little church comment on the Protestant side, but the northern Catholic bishops issued a sharp protest against the practices now revealed as having occurred.

Despite the bitter reaction among Catholics following internment—which included the withdrawal of many Catholics from public life and the mounting of a civil disobedience campaign—the Roman Catholic bishops of Northern Ireland, led by the Cardinal, issued a statement in September, of which the main thrust was that 'there is a small group of people who are trying to secure a united Ireland by force' and 'one has only to state this fact in its stark simplicity to see the absurdity of the idea'. This statement had been preceded by a personal one on similar lines by the Cardinal, and was followed by one from the whole Irish Episcopal Conference (30 September)[35] which attributed much of the current violence to reaction against internment but declared it, all the same, to be 'grievously wrong'. At the same time criticism from within their own Churches of the Protestant leaders for being too accommodating to the other side became more vocal. Sermons of an increasingly belligerent character were reported in the newspapers.

But if some felt that the Protestant leaders had gone too far in the pursuit of reconciliation, others were impatient. 'In Ulster', wrote the Revd. John Stewart,[36] Methodist minister in Woodvale, Belfast, 'everyone claims to be a Christian. Yet it is here that soldiers say they lose any religion they ever had . . . What are the churches doing to make their witness? We blame the media but we ought to be making the news for the media to take up.' The Churches were poverty-stricken in the area of public relations, yet 'the basic Christian principles of the people were shining like gold amid the bombs and rubble of human suffering'. It was not political restraint that had held them back from 'losing their cool' but basic reverence for life. Later the same minister pointed out the way in which church leaders were tied to the institutions of which they were part: 'the very democracy of the church systems mirrors the weaknesses of the society in which they witness'. Yet many, he granted, were speaking out as never before.

As these conflicting views were being aired, first came the atrocity at McGurk's bar in Belfast on 4 December 1971, in which fifteen Catholics lost their lives, and then the shock of 'Bloody Sunday'. On 30 January 1972 paratroopers in Derry, in a riotous confrontation, shot thirteen people dead. The wave of revulsion in the nationalist community led to the burning of the British Embassy in Dublin. Immediate reactions in Northern Ireland were of shock and a demand for more exact information. Only Dr Paisley gave unqualified justification to the army. Cardinal Conway at the funeral spoke of 'this national day of mourning'. Within a week the four church leaders had found it possible to issue a joint statement,[37] sharing the grief and pain, recognizing the depth of feeling, and underlining the extreme danger of the resulting situation. 'In face of everything we once more ask our people to make a greater effort to understand each other's point of view and to accept one another in our differences?' Yet another inquiry was set up, under Lord Widgery, the Lord Chief Justice of England, the outcome of which failed to satisfy the aggrieved. Indeed it gave a fillip to those who wished to denigrate British justice.

At this point the two Anglican bishops in Belfast issued a joint warning to the effect that, 'amid serious and mounting pressures aimed at altering the status, institutions and structures of Northern Ireland we feel obliged to state that . . . the majority of members of the Church in our dioceses will not be coerced into the society and community of the Republic of Ireland as it is at present constituted'.[38] That particular development was not in fact to occur; but an alteration of the status, institutions, and structures was indeed at hand. Faced with a steady deterioration of the security position, tragically illustrated by an explosion at the Abercorn restaurant in Belfast[39] on a Saturday afternoon which killed two women, gravely maimed several more, and injured altogether 130 people, and also with a fatal explosion at Aldershot barracks in England, Mr Edward Heath's government proposed to take direct control of security policy in Northern Ireland. This was not acceptable to Mr Faulkner's Cabinet. The British Parliament immediately passed legislation to prorogue—in the first instance for one year—the subordinate Parliament at Stormont and to replace the government responsible to that Parliament by a British department of state. Thus the system of devolved government instituted in 1921 was brought to an end. It was Good Friday,[40] set apart by the Churches as a day of prayer for Northern Ireland.

The particular grievances adduced by the civil rights movement in 1968 had masked a more fundamental grievance: the failure of a long-standing monopoly of power by one party, representing a community of identity, to find ways of associating with it in government representatives of the minority community. Yet in fairness it must be said that for many years that minority community had held aloof from participation and indeed from recognition of the state, mainly because they sought the unification of the country. Now neither group would have any political power, until the devising of a new system enabled the Parliament of the United Kingdom to restore devolved government. The Churches had failed to prevent this débâcle; but it is fair to say that in their attempts at mutual understanding and reconciliation they had at least made more progress than the political parties. In every joint act or word, however limited and ineffectual these often seem, they were affirming the common Christian conscience of communities whose patriotic aspirations were incompatible.

5 Private Armies and Political Progress

Mr William Whitelaw, who was appointed Secretary of State for Northern Ireland after the suspension of its Parliament, was soon to find himself confronted by paramilitary forces on both sides. His day-to-day problem of averting open civil war was for many months acute. 1972 was, statistically, the worst year of violence. On the other hand, progress towards a political solution of the fundamental problem seemed to be greater during his term of office than at any other time. This was because no one of the local political parties was now clothed with the responsibility and authority of government: Unionist and Nationalist alike were out of office, deprived of a parliamentary forum, and seeking to negotiate with the United Kingdom government in the person of Mr Whitelaw conditions under which local autonomy could justly be restored. In the event a new form of government, providing for participation by politicians of both communities and for a new pattern of relationships with both Westminster and Dublin, was devised and put into effect, only to be brought down by the direct action of those 'loyalist' forces which had been gaining in strength and organization during Mr Whitelaw's period of office.

The split between those Unionists who were to co-operate in the new departure and those who were to wreck it was already foreshadowed at the transition to direct rule, and there is no doubt that within the Protestant Churches a similar division of opinion was developing. William Craig had said as early as March 1971 that an attempt by the British government to rule Northern Ireland would be met by massive resistance and by a provisional government. In February 1972 he had announced the formation of Ulster Vanguard, 'an umbrella' for traditional Unionist groupings. Open, an umbrella can be a symbol of comprehensiveness; closed, it can be used as an offensive weapon. Vanguard was to become the spearhead of attack on the new regime. Six days before the suspension of Stormont there had been a Vanguard rally of 50,000 in Ormeau Park, Belfast, reminiscent in its style of Hitler's mass rallies in the thirties, and when direct rule was announced Mr Craig called a two-day general strike and a rally at Parliament Buildings; he declared that he would demonstrate that he could make the province ungovernable. There was indeed a near-universal stoppage of work, not all of it voluntary, on 28–9 March, while the legislation to effect direct rule was going through Westminster. The demonstration at Stormont was, however, somewhat deflected from its original purpose when Mr Faulkner and his Cabinet, still in office, were the first to appear on the balcony of Parliament Buildings and took the cheers that Mr Craig intended for himself. A handshake between the two leaders in the presence of the crowd meant nothing in terms of subsequent events.

Faulkner had already agreed to facilitate the transfer of power by remaining in office while the legislation was passed, and on the next day he announced that he would co-operate with Mr Whitelaw. It had been announced that an advisory commission of local people would be appointed to help the Secretary of State, and this in fact acted as a kind of lightning-conductor: in condemning the 'coconut commission' and refusing absolutely to work with it, the Unionist Party let off the necessary steam without specifically refusing to work with the Westminster Ministers themselves. The Civil Service rallied to the new team as the legal government of the country, and enabled it immediately to assume control of the administration.

Meanwhile Ian Paisley, who saw direct rule as a step towards the formal integration of the province with Great Britain, a course which he at that time favoured, said in characteristic terms that 'the voice of Mr Craig and the advice of Mr Craig are the voice and advice of folly'.[1] Thus the three leading political figures on the Protestant side were at loggerheads, and before long many ordinary Protestants came to feel more confidence in Mr Whitelaw than in their squabbling local leaders; if he could have remained in office throughout 1974 things might have turned out very differently.

That is not to say that direct rule, especially at the beginning, was supported by all who declined to support Vanguard. Many felt that not only had they been deprived of the self-government they had enjoyed for fifty years, but that their local Parliament had been the only bulwark against the reunification of Ireland. A mere fortnight before its suspension the Provisional wing of the IRA had called for a three-day truce to give the British government a chance to accede to their 'terms', one of which was the abolition of Stormont. It was not difficult to represent the government as having conceded to this demand and having begun a process that would end in an all-Ireland solution. These feelings were reflected in a statement issued by the Government Committee of the Presbyterian Church:

We deplore the decision of the United Kingdom Government to prorogue the Northern Ireland Parliament and the consequent denial to democratically elected representatives of the people a voice in the government of their country; and we further deplore that this action taken now is above all at the expense of a peaceful majority who have sought to maintain their cause in an orderly and lawful way. We speak for a people in Northern Ireland who, without consent, are now suffering a massive deprivation of their constitutional and civil rights and a substantial disfranchisement, exceeding any previous curtailment of local voting rights, such as have caused widespread protests in the past. This is being done after they have suffered, patiently and resolutely, prolonged and violent attacks upon them both by hand and tongue. The pain and loss of confidence thus engendered towards those responsible for all this, both in Ireland and beyond, should not be underestimated or disregarded.

These strong words were nevertheless accompanied by a call to 'keep as our first aim the peace and welfare of our land and the reconciliation of our divided community'. The Irish Council of Churches appealed to all political parties to co-operate in the provisions of the Westminster legislation and, in a reference to the suspension of the local Parliament in the first place for one year, 'to use the next twelve months as an opportunity to act constructively'.[2] The Methodist President (the Revd. C. H. Bain) said: 'Our people are always prepared to accept legitimate authority', and Archbishop Simms hoped that the British Prime Minister's statement 'will be carefully studied in a spirit of calmness'.[3] While some prominent lay members of the Churches were leaders in Vanguard, the Protestant Churches corporately settled for acquiescence in the new regime.

But what of the Roman Catholics? In theory the direct rule of Great Britain over part of Ireland was even more obnoxious to the nationally minded than the system of local autonomy; but in practice the British were likely to be more fair in their treatment of the minority than the Unionists had been. Cardinal Conway said in a broadcast interview in Dublin that he now looked for an end of the IRA campaign and hoped that progress could eventually be made towards reunification in a new state by peaceful mutual agreement. This was scarcely calculated to allay Protestant fears, and a few days later in Rome he was content to advocate 'a new political structure in Northern Ireland in which all parties would participate in government' and to say that 'a united Ireland could safely be left to history'.[4]

For a moment it looked as if the Cardinal's hopes of an end to the violence might be fulfilled. Women in Roman Catholic areas organized themselves to appeal for peace and to act as intermediaries between the IRA and the authorities, moves which received formal encouragement from Cardinal Conway and then from the four church leaders acting together. On 29 May the Official wing of the IRA called a cease-fire which has lasted ever since, though it has not prevented sporadic hostilities against other Republican movements. Early in June Sean MacStiofain, chief of staff of the Provisional wing, announced that they had had contacts during the previous winter with Protestant clergy with a view to a truce. One of the authors was involved in one of those contacts, and Eric Gallagher accordingly writes in the first person from notes made afterwards.

During the early autumn of 1971 my wife and I had discussed several times whether or not I should try to make a personal approach to the IRA with the idea of (a) speaking as a Christian and an Irishman about my concern at what they were doing, (b) pointing out that violence was counter-productive and that a Protestant backlash was inevitable, and (c) asking for political rather than military action. This thought remained with me for some time, and then one day Father Desmond Wilson[5] came to see me. He had a contact, very concerned about violence, who said there was a desire to meet us both, and, if possible, some right-wing politicians. In the event I went by myself to meet the contact at Father Wilson's house. 'Jim' arrived and proved to be sensitive to all that the campaign was doing—in suffering, in killing, in destruction, and in corruption. He was anxious to see it ended, and others shared his concern. I pointed out that I had no authority from anyone and could not be a negotiator, but that I would convey a message to anyone who might be helpful.

For a couple of weeks I heard nothing, but then Desmond Wilson came to see me. A message had come through asking whether we would be ready to talk to some people of influence the next week. So on the following Monday we set of with 'Jim' in Desmond's car. Near the border we came upon a military road-block. Amazingly we were thumbed through without having to stop. We came to Dundalk and to the venue which was, ironically enough, the Imperial Hotel. After a few minutes Sean MacStiofain[6] appeared in the customary white Aran sweater and khaki-green slacks. We were taken to a private room, and 'Jim' was summarily dismissed. Later Rory O'Brady and Joe Cahill[7] arrived. Only Christian names were used, but there was no doubt about identities.

Then followed a conversation that I will remember vividly all my life. I told them of my own background, of my father's attitude to life and his willingness to pay the price of his convictions, of my Christian faith and its implications for me, of my love of my country, and my wish to see it happy and its people contented, of my fears for the future, of the implications for the Protestants of all the violence that their campaign was causing, and finally of my wish to see that campaign ended. MacStiofain spoke first, followed by O'Brady. The two men were an interesting contrast: MacStiofain obviously self-disciplined and a disciplinarian, a man who had been through imprisonment, who did not want to destroy, but was ready to carry out that destruction and require others to share in it in order to impose his will. O'Brady on the other hand was the self-assured, articulate proponent of the emerging *Eire Nua*[8] philosophy. It was no trouble to him to talk, and I must confess it was no trouble for me to listen. All the time Joe Cahill sat silent. On the hour and the half-hour he produced an ear-piece from his pocket and listened for a few moments to a small receiver, after which he would announce 'All quiet so far.'

Eventually Sean MacStiofain showed his hand. They were after a two-week truce during which the British forces would be withdrawn to barracks and some declaration of intent made by Britain. Could I get a message to Harold Wilson? I then asked 'What about Mr Heath? He is after all the Prime Minister.' I can still remember what MacStiofain said: 'Eric, if you can do that we will be very grateful. But you must not do anything to put yourself at risk.' The message was duly delivered, but nothing transpired until June 1972, to the events of which month we now return.

On 19 June, under pressure from hunger-strikes and faced with serious problems of prison accommodation, Mr Whitelaw conceded 'Special category status' to convicted prisoners whose crimes had political motivation, making their conditions of imprisonment similar to those of the internees who lived in compounds largely organized by their own officers. This was a decision that led to much trouble later on, but at the time it no doubt made it easier for the Provisionals to announce on 22 June that all offensive operations would cease at midnight on 26 June. They killed at least seven people in a last round of carnage before the time of cease-fire arrived. 'The peace is a fragile thing', said Cardinal Conway, calling on parents to see that youngsters did not break it and on public figures to avoid inflammatory statements. It was indeed fragile: it lasted fourteen days, during which eleven people were killed. That was precisely the period suggested in MacStiofain's message to Mr Heath. Holding that the cessation of hostilities removed any impropriety in his negotiating with the Provisional leaders, Mr Whitelaw received them in London. No doubt they asked him for the declaration of intent to leave Ireland about which they had talked to Eric Gallagher. They did not get it, and on the very next day the cease-fire broke down, ostensibly because the army refused to permit the housing of some Catholic families in Horn Drive on the western outskirts of Belfast. But who can doubt that the real reason was that it had failed of its purpose? The British were not receptive of the 'terms' which the Provisionals had sought an opportunity to put. During the 'truce' a Roman Catholic chapel in the Ardoyne had been blown up, and elsewhere hundreds of Protestant neighbours had attended the funeral of two Catholic brothers shot in the streets. Such are the anomalies of 'peace' and 'war'.

Meanwhile, as ordinary people entertained a fleeting moment of hope that the 'Catholic' paramilitaries would give up, their 'Protestant' counterparts grew daily more active. Within a few days of Mr Whitelaw's arrival he and the public were made aware of the existence of the Ulster Defence Association. This body, which had grown out of the miscellaneous vigilante groups formed in the days of continuous rioting to protect particular Protestant streets from incursion, now numbered many thousands. Indeed a deputation from the Irish Council of Churches had warned Mr Faulkner in the autumn of 1971 that in certain areas every street had been called upon to organize a patrol and every household to designate a male member to participate;[9] this was the organization of a co-ordinated force. The Prime Minister had brushed the matter aside. Now, on 6 July, Captain Lawrence Orr said in the Commons that it was not surprising, seeing that the IRA had not laid down their arms, that other armed forces outside the control of the Crown should have appeared. At this Mr Whitelaw expressed shock, as he had been led to believe that the UDA was not armed; but there was no doubt that a great many were, and some had already appeared in the courts on arms charges. The existence of Catholic 'no-go' areas, particularly in the large Bogside–Creggan enclave at Derry, where for many months the government's writ did not run, was a bitter grievance to the Protestants, and the UDA tried to force Mr Whitelaw's hand by setting up barricaded Protestant areas, at first for brief stated periods and then with a threat of permanency. Efforts by the army to prevent this led to confrontations, the most serious being at Ainsworth Avenue in west Belfast during the Provisionals' truce, when 8,000 masked men faced the army, and it was reported that a further 20,000 were on call. On that occasion an uneasy compromise was achieved by which for a brief period unarmed UDA men and soldiers patrolled the area together.[10] Meanwhile in east Belfast the ravages of 'tartan gangs', groups of young Protestant vandals, made the streets unsafe for any to whom they took objection.

In this confused and threatening situation, which lasted through most of 1972, the action of the Churches consisted for the most part of day-to-day remedial measures and *ad hoc* comments rather than any consistent plans for peace. In some quarters low morale was reflected in wild utterances: 'We who see God in all men see none in these subhumans,' said one minister, normally known for his liberal views, of the bombers and gunmen. 'They deserve pity for their sick minds must lead each one of them to purgatory, hell fire and lunatic asylum.'[11] Others put the blame elsewhere: speaking to the Irish Association of Priests in Dublin Mr Brian Walker, chairman of the New Ulster Movement, asked:

Where but in Christian Ireland could murder and bloodshed be perpetrated day by day while church leaders, clerical and lay, wring their hands in pious horror but at the same time appear to offer excuses and explanations for the excesses of their adherents?. . . Double-talk and double-think have been used to persuade the Irish people that death and violence, hatred and bigotry are the purest and noblest methods for pursuing political objectives.'[12]

It must be said, however, that the impression of double-talk sometimes arose from the sense that clergy had of the need to say something against the other side in order to gain a hearing for the restraining advice they sought to give to their own people. A report to the General Synod of the Church of Ireland in that year also referred to a 'double standard . . . which justifies actions on the part of one section of the community while condemning similar actions on the part of another. There must be a total condemnation of *all* killing and wounding, the infliction of mental and moral anguish, and particularly the suffering and involvement of children'. Clergy were not lacking who in ugly situations had the courage to take their own side to task. Father Hugh O'Neill in St. Eugene's Cathedral at Derry said: 'Up to now the IRA has been asked to stop. Now they are being told to. Let them heed before they are made to . . .' People were prepared 'to protect those who were guilty of behaviour that was wrong in principle'. And he made the telling point: 'if there had been a truce at the introduction of direct rule all the internees would be home now'.[13] A few days later the Revd. Brian Hanna, an Anglican rector in Derry, supported Father O'Neill and applied his words to gunmen on the Protestant side. In 'Free Derry' women encouraged by his words approached the Provisionals with a demand for peace, and such was the public revulsion against violence that Father O'Neill rashly said: 'The IRA is finished.' Shortly afterwards forty priests in Derry called on all Roman Catholics to support peace initiatives in the city.

With its eye on tartan gangs and the UDA the Presbyterian General Assembly of 1972 reaffirmed 'opposition to those who counsel or condone violence as a solution to the problems of Ireland and detestation of the behaviour of those who practise or permit intimidation or hooliganism; and . . . the conviction that the principles of law and order must be accepted as applying to members of our church as much as to others'. To this Assembly were reported not only the bitter words of its Government Committee about direct rule quoted above, but another statement which read: 'Though the majority of our people in Northern Ireland may give political support to the Unionist Party and a lesser number be members of the Orange Order, yet as an organized Church of some 400,000 souls we are not committed to these or to any other institutions or parties.'

When the by-now customary resolution of admiration and thanks to the security forces and public services came before the Assembly, the Revd. Terence McCaughey of Dublin moved to delete the army from the list of those thanked, because of alleged brutality in interrogation, house searches, and control of riots; 'Bloody Sunday' had occurred since the last Assembly.

Mr McCaughey was hissed and booed, and his amendment overwhelmingly defeated.

In the week following the Assembly a letter appeared in the press signed by fifteen Presbyterian ministers supporting the ministers of the Shankill Road in their criticism of the UDA. It was impossible to call on the IRA to stop, and yet to ignore this body: Counter-violence was no solution. The ministers expressed their solidarity with the Roman Catholic priests who were working for reconciliation and similarly criticizing the paramilitary element in their own community.[14] A few weeks later Bishop Cahal Daly, a northerner holding a see in the Republic, of whom we shall hear more, warned, in the same spirit, of 'Al Caponism'. The only people who thought a military solution possible, he said, were the extreme republicans and the extreme loyalists; in both these groups a gangster element was by now apparent.[15] In late August Father Thomas Cunningham of St. Agnes's protested in his sermon at evictions carried out by the IRA, and was noisily interrupted.[16] Two Sundays later a statement by Father Padraig Murphy condemning some specific murders was read in all the churches of his large west Belfast parish.

The resumption of hostilities by the Provisionals was quickly followed by 'Bloody Friday', 21 July 1972, when twenty-two bombs exploded in Belfast and nine people were killed, most of them at Oxford Street bus station. In his book, *Memoirs of a Statesman*, Faulkner regards this as the turning-point of Mr Whitelaw's rule, the moment at which he grasped that the IRA had to be defeated and not appeased. Certainly action followed: on 24 July the army entered the 'no-go' areas and removed the barricades. There was now no part of the state in which the government was not at least trying to exercise its proper authority.

At the end of September Mr Whitelaw convened at Darlington a conference of Northern Ireland political parties to consider the future government of the province. The SDLP declined to attend because the government had not made a firm statement of intention to end internment. The DUP declined because the Secretary of State had refused to hold a public inquiry into the shooting of two civilians on the Shankill Road. Hence only the Unionist, Alliance, and Labour parties were present, this last represented by the late Vivian Simpson, a former lay missionary in Africa, whose work as MP for Oldpark, a mixed Roman Catholic and Protestant constituency, had earned the respect of all but the bigoted on both sides. Ideas discussed at this conference led, through subsequent Green and White Papers, to the Constitution Act of 1973, under which the ill-fated Assembly and Executive were set up.

Meanwhile the Revd. Joseph Parker, whose fourteen-year-old son had been killed on 'Bloody Friday', held a seventy-two-hour hunger-strike in protest at the refusal of some of the parties to go to the conference. The Governor of Northern Ireland was present at the launching of a League of Prayer and Reconciliation; and the church leaders called for ecumenical services of prayer on Sunday 1 October. On that day Londonderry's first ever joint service of Roman Catholics and Protestants took place. At Armagh the two primates worshipped together, but the Presbyterians held aloof. In Belfast 3,000 people gathered at the City cemetery; because of its location many Protestants had for a long period feared to visit the graves of relatives, but now, on the invitation of Catholics who vouched for their safety, they did so. There was an attempt to disrupt a service in Portadown on this day of reconciliation, and a bomb threat at the service in Armagh. Bishop Hanson of Clogher in characteristic vein, described the Orange Order as 'somewhere between the old-fashioned Sunday School and a not very efficient mafia that hibernated during the winter'. But to some who had criticized the Order in the past it now seemed a source of stability and restraint compared with the Protestant paramilitary bodies that had grown up. A few weeks later, on the eve of his departure to a chair of theology at Manchester, Bishop Hanson summed up his view of the situation by saying that church leaders had been making the running in a very spectacular way but the clergy had not found it possible to follow their lead. They were torn between what the leaders were calling for and what they knew their people wanted or didn't want. This was to state the difficulty, but perhaps to underestimate the courage of many clergy in meeting it.

By now the government's discussion paper, offering alternative solutions to the problem of associating the minority community with government in the province if local autonomy were restored, had appeared. At its autumn meeting in 1972, the Irish Council of Churches responded to this document by commending it to church members, to the general public, and to the political parties for careful and objective consideration; by urging all parties to act responsibly to make the greatest possible use of the opportunity to seek a peaceful, just, and speedy solution to Northern Ireland's continuing problems, and to press on with the necessary programme of development, reconstruction, and reconciliation; and by urging citizens, organizations, and leaders of all sections of the community 'to recognize and acknowledge that any system of government for Northern Ireland, however democratically determined, will work effectively, justly and peacefully only if all are prepared to give heart and will to make it work'.[17]

Of all the years in a decade of strife 1973 was the one in which the most progress seemed to be made towards a just resolution of Northern Ireland's problems. It was the only time that constructive political measures reached the point of implementation, and it was also a year of notable advances in the relations between the Churches. During the year there came to power in the Republic a government formed from those parties perhaps less doctrinaire in their traditional approach to the issue of partition than the Fianna Fail Party which had been in office since 1957. In the last month of 1972 a referendum in the Republic had ended the special status accorded by the Constitution to the Roman Catholic Church—a move that meant little in practice but seemed at least a gesture to Protestant opinion, north and south.

Violence was the constant background to these hopeful signs, and its prevalence was no doubt largely the reason why so much of the progress was ultimately stultified. Bombing of property on a large scale was an almost daily occurrence, and assassinations of individuals in the streets and in their homes were frequent. Cardinal Conway was outspoken in his condemnation of what he called 'a second campaign', and pointed out that, whatever the IRA might be doing, more Catholic civilians than Protestants were losing their lives—to which an army spokesman replied that Catholics had killed 197 soldiers and that Protestants had killed two. Nevertheless, the same spokesman was able to reveal that between April 1972 and November 1973 the weekly level of bombings had fallen from forty to fifteen, and of shootings from 600 to 100.[18] Stanley Worrall remembers the year as the one of hoax bomb-alerts. Day after day the telephone would ring and a gruff voice would announce that there was a bomb in his school. To evacuate 2,000 children every time would have reduced school life to chaos. He was virtually certain that the calls were false, and usually restricted action to an unobtrusive search by janitors while the school went on working; but supposing that on just one occasion he had been wrong . . . People in responsible positions, even if they never suffered injury or damage to their property, were constantly subject to that kind of strain. This must not be forgotten in judging the suspicions and timorous attitudes towards radical change which eventually prevailed.

Parish clergy had their own problems, not least of which concerned funerals. When, on either side, but more frequently in the case of the IRA, 'volunteers' were 'killed in action', the funeral would be carried out with 'full military honours': marching men in masks or wearing dark glasses, flags on the coffin, volleys of shots at the graveside. The authorities were reluctant to use force at funerals to prevent such celebrations; clergy were reluctant to deny Christian burial, but deeply disturbed at their own participation as representatives of a Church that consistently condemned violence. As Bishop Cahal Daly put it: 'The paramilitary bit is done by the IRA once the remains are taken from the church. The priest knows that an ugly situation will develop if he tries to intervene to prevent it. He hesitates to bring further anguish to the stricken family'.[19] And on the other side the UDA or UVF likewise would appear, without the prior knowledge of relatives or clergy, to surround and escort a coffin as it was borne along the streets.

The depth of feeling aroused by such displays is illustrated by a statement made in January by Methodist members of Vanguard, demanding to know why church leaders had been silent when the Roman Catholic Church extended its privileges and ritual to known IRA murderers.[20] In February St. Anthony's Roman Catholic Church in east Belfast was vandalized, and similar incidents occurred elsewhere in the course of the year. Bishop Philbin was not the only one who thought these attacks resulted from a supposed connection between the Roman Catholic Church and the IRA, which he, of course, firmly repudiated. Protestants in their turn repudiated those who attacked churches; many helped their Roman Catholic neighbours in 'tidying up', and later in the year the papers in Belfast carried pictures of the Anglican Bishop Quin handing over £600 towards the repair of St. Anthony's.

Nevertheless, against this unpropitious background encouraging steps were being taken. On the ecclesiatical front two major development occurred in 1973: the issue of a report entitled *Towards a United Church*[21] and the holding of the first official conference between the Roman Catholic Church and the others. This was held at the Ballymascanlon[22] Hotel near

Dundalk on 26 September 1973, and the name 'Ballymascanlon' became a kind of code-word for the movement which originated in the meeting. In 1973 the first such meeting was seen as 'historic', and was greeted with enthusiasm by all those concerned for reconciliation in Ireland. The press tended to regard it as a 'peace conference', and expressed impatience when proposals for the solution of the political problem did not emerge. It became necessary to emphasize that this was a dialogue about the standing issues that divided the Churches, and that any political outcome would be the indirect result of improved relationships and the removal of misunderstandings.

The participation of the Protestant Churches in the Ballymascanlon dialogue was not allowed to pass without criticism. Dr Paisley threatened to disrupt the conference, but when the day came he contented himself with a picket of about 100 people. These gathered at the hotel gates and sought entry. When the police explained that the hotel management objected to a demonstration inside the grounds, Dr Paisley carried a letter of protest up the quarter-mile-long drive and returned to his group outside. Within minutes the conference organizers made a public statement that the protest was based on a misunderstanding: the talks were not secret, the press being invited to attend; and they were not aimed at church union. A few weeks later the Revd. Robert Bradford, a Methodist minister who had been associated with Dr Paisley's protest, launched a campaign against Methodist participation: 'Methodists awake—to the dangers of dialogue with Roman apostates.' Five months later this hitherto unknown young man was to capture from the Official Unionists the prestigious Westminster seat of South Belfast. He held it, later as an Official Unionist, until he was assassinated by the IRA on 14 November 1981. In the summer of 1974 Mr Bradford journeyed to Cork for the Methodist Conference and proposed a number of 'hard-line' resolutions and amendments; on none of them did the number of his supporters reach double figures, and a few weeks later he announced his resignation from the Irish Methodist ministry.

The successive stages of Mr Whitelaw's policy received general support from the Churches. In March he held a referendum on whether Northern Ireland should remain in the United Kingdom or join the Republic. The aim of this was to settle the issue of nationality independently of elections, which could then, it was hoped, be fought on other issues. Well over half the total electorate turned out to vote for the British connection; only a handful voted against.[23] An IRA boycott, backed by intimidation, prevented the true strength of the anti-partitionist vote being recorded. Shortly afterwards the government published a White Paper[24] setting out its definite proposals: these were for an assembly of seventy-eight members elected by proportional representation, from which would be chosen an executive to run the Northern Ireland departments. If the executive contained an adequate representation of the minority community, the government would devolve some of the powers previously exercised by the Northern Ireland Parliament. A Council of Ireland would be set up to co-ordinate the work of the two governments in Ireland.

It is an indication of the dangerous state of public opinion that before the paper was issued the leaders of nine Churches made a joint call for restraint after its publication, stressing the need for careful study, and pointing out that snap judgements would influence people who would never read the paper itself. At its spring meeting of 1973 the Irish Council of Churches commended this action of the leaders and expressed gratification that the Churches through their appropriate committees had been able to give the paper careful and detailed study. The Council called for continued study and for increased political involvement on the part of all citizens, expressing the hope that through a constructive approach to the proposals a satisfactory way forward might be found.[25] We must now turn to those denominational reactions, with which the Council had expressed general satisfaction. A few days after the publication of the paper Archbishop Simms had said: 'We welcome the White Paper as a fair and workable basis from which to move forwards. It has long been apparent that peace and progress could only be achieved through co-operation in various ways by all sections of the comunity.'[26] The Presbyterians had been more guarded: the General Board had issued a long statement which began by asking people to think things out, to respect the views of others, and to seek to live and work together. 'Nothing in the White Paper violates Christian conscience or justifies any action holding the community to ransom or resorting to violence.' However, the Committee felt that the paper in supporting rights did not emphasize enough the corresponding obligations and the need for protection against those who would deny them: 'We are concerned', it went on, 'lest the proper emphasis on the obligation to co-operate with minorities here may be an unfair erosion of the traditional rights of majorities.' As for the Council of Ireland.

As a Church in Ireland, north and south, we should welcome proposals for sincere co-operation between those areas. This, however, must be based on mutual respect and self-determination, not on unilateral claims and inter-ventions. Further we fear that the greater the disparity in standing between those taking part in the Council of Ireland, drawn from a sovereign Parliament and from a regional Assembly, the less real the partnership that it offers.

The Committee in fact feared 'a self-destroying policy of appeasement, not reconciliation'.

In uttering these warnings the Presbyterian authorities were reflecting the fears of many of their members, and events were to show how strong those feelings were. Some will ask whether a more positive reaction might not have so influenced the climate of opinion that the proposals would have had more chance of success; but by this time the mood of repentance that appeared in so many of the church utterances in 1968–9 had given way to a feeling that all the concessions had been expected of the Protestant side and none had been forthcoming from the Catholics. If the local Catholics had suffered certain injustices in the past, the Catholics of the Republic had maintained unabated their insistent propaganda against partition, and their constitutional claim to the whole island. If that were granted, the injustice to the Protestant majority in the north would, it was believed, outweigh any previous injustice the other way. Accordingly the time had come to warn the British government of deep-seated Protestant feeling, while dissociating the Church from the threats of violent action being uttered by Vanguard's leaders. It is noteworthy that in its report to the General Assembly a few months later the Government Committee said: 'There is always the danger of people arguing as if their own concerns and ideas, whether liberal or conservative, moderate or militant, were of obvious Christian inspiration, whereas those with whom they disagree were moved simply by political calculation and personal prejudice.' There was a resolution before the Assembly to 'endorse the observations of the General Board on the British Government's proposals'. Ministers of 'the right' moved to add the words: 'stressing the responsibility of the Government to maintain law and order and to take firm steps to end violence without which no political settlement can work, the Church's ministry of reconciliation is impeded and the Christian concern that men of any faith or none should live together in peace is vain.' This amendment was carried, but immediately ecumenically-minded ministers moved a further amendment to omit all the words following 'can work', and to substitute 'and they further stress the responsibility of all, including ourselves, to work with sacrificial love so that men of any faith or none can live together in peace'. This was also carried, and the whole debate is instructive in showing the constant tension between the demand for peace by enforcement of the law and the call for peace by reconciliation.

The Methodist Conference welcomed 'the present opportunities given to the people of Northern Ireland to express their wishes for the future government of the province', and called upon 'all citizens to use their votes at the Assembly elections in a responsible manner', being 'convinced that to secure a stable democratic society the ballot box must replace violence and civil disturbance'. With the report *Towards a United Church* and the Ballymascanlon conference in mind, the President (the Revd. H. Sloan) said: 'Only when the sectarian barriers are broken down in the Churches themselves will we have the right to preach reconciliation to all the people'.[27] On the day he spoke a car-bomb killed six people in the hitherto peaceful town of Coleraine.

By then the date of the Assembly election had been set for 28 June. The results showed an unprecedented range of eight parties represented. Forty-nine members were prepared to explore the possibility of government on Mr Whitelaw's lines, and twenty-nine were not. Members of the Unionist Party were on both sides of this divide, just as earlier they had been for and against the hapless Terence O'Neill; this was thanks to the complete autonomy of local associations in the selection of candidates. July being the close season for church meetings, little formal church reaction to the results was recorded; but the Orange Order, in preparation for its annual demonstrations on 12 July, asked for the Assembly to be made unworkable and rejected all the White Paper's proposals. On the last day of July the Assembly met to elect a chairman, who would appoint a committee to draw up during the summer recess standing orders for its business. The 'loyalist' groups created a scene of chaos that boded ill for the future, but nevertheless the essential business of the day was transacted.

The Constitution Act, under which these arrangments were made, had formally abolished the Northern Ireland Parliament and the office of governor, and in August Lord Brookeborough, who had for so long been Prime Minister in that Parliament, died. A memorial service was held in Belfast Cathedral, attended not only by the Unionist 'establishment', but by the British Prime Minister and the Secretary of State.[28] In his address the Bishop of Connor, Dr Butler, praised the courage, conviction, and charm of the late Prime Minister, but under the heading of 'conviction' quoted *The Times* obituary as saying 'he was convinced that Roman Catholics should be excluded from responsibility and participation'. Dr Butler added: 'It could be argued that had he thought differently and acted differently Northern Ireland would not be in its present unhappy state'—a mild enough observation, in all conscience, when twenty years of Brookeborough's administration had left the minority community in the state of mind that revealed itself in 1968. There was an immediate storm of protest at the Bishop's comment, the gist of which can best be summed up in the words of Mr Ernest Baird, at that time a Vanguard member of the Assembly. He spoke of Bishop Butler 'doing a proper burying job on a man's reputation when he is dead'. The scales, he said, 'are fast falling from the eyes of the laity of that Church as they see the infiltration of the higher clergy by citizens of the Republic devoted to the ideal of a Republican Ireland . . . Increasingly the laity refuse to follow their shepherds on the stony road to Dublin.'[29] This is an interesting example of the way in which the slightest deviation from uncritical adulation of the Unionist leadership can be interpreted as wholesale treachery and unqualified advocacy of a united Ireland. Yet by now the Unionist politicians themselves had a long record of mutual recrimination and abuse.

Mr Faulkner said that he regretted the controversy, but he did not say that he regretted the sermon. For by now he was set on a course Lord Brookeborough would never have endorsed. He was negotiating with the leaders of the other parties, under Mr Whitelaw's guidance, the composition of an Executive which he would lead and which would satisfy the requirement of the Constitution Act that representatives of the Catholic community should be included. Eventually, after long discussion, against the background of stormy scenes in the Assembly, an agreement was reached by which Mr Faulkner would lead an Executive of eleven Ministers, six Unionist, four

SDLP, and one Alliance, with four other ministers outside the Executive.

There followed the next stage of Mr Whitelaw's plan to establish relations with the Republic. A tripartite conference was called at Sunningdale in England between the governments in London and Dublin and the Executive-designate in Belfast. At this conference, over which Mr Heath presided, some said dictatorially, agreement was reached for a Council of Ireland to consist of seven Dublin ministers and seven from the Northern Ireland Executive.[30] The government of the Republic accepted that there could be no change in the status of Northern Ireland until the majority there accepted it. The British government solemnly renewed the pledge to support the wishes of the majority to remain in the United Kingdom.

The Church of Ireland bishops immediately supported the Sunningdale agreement and said that it could 'provide the basis for building a fair and peaceful society in Northern Ireland'.[31] The Presbyterian General Board said that it provided 'a positive, constructive step towards a framework of better understanding and co-operation between all the people who share life on this island'. The Board was, however, 'keenly aware of differing reactions in church and community'. But people should remember,

that we live under the rule of the God of justice and love, and that our human relationships one to another and the exercise of government are to be judged accordingly. There can be no perfect government for sinful men . . . yet Christianity obliges us to respect those in authority, to live peaceably and to share our rights and advantages with others, even to the point of sacrifice.

The Board hoped that the Council of Ireland would not be used 'as a means of forwarding the interests or political aspirations of one section over another' (i.e. of promoting a united Ireland), and it called upon 'all public representatives to disown unruly and violent behaviour which can only bring their calling into disrepute' (a rebuke to 'loyalist' members of the Assembly).

Dr Paisley set up an action committee 'to reinstate their civil, religious and democratic rights', and a few days later published an advertisement in the Ulster papers which roundly condemned the Sunningdale agreement. His assertions, dubious as they were, were widely believed, and assuredly influenced voters in larger numbers when a general election ensued in February.

For already events outside Northern Ireland were leading to

the eventual collapse of all that had been accomplished. The worsening condition of industrial relations in England led Mr Heath to withdraw Mr Whitelaw from Northern Ireland affairs even before the Sunningdale conference, in order that his gifts for conciliation might be used on a wider front in Britain. An inexperienced Secretary of State, Francis Pym, never had a chance before Mr Heath's deepening crisis led him to call a United Kingdom election in February, which gave the voters of Northern Ireland an immediate opportunity to repudiate the Sunningdale settlement.

But that is to anticipate: meanwhile the settlement had majority support in the Assembly, and on 1 January 1974 powers, excluding law and order, were devolved by the Secretary of State upon the 'power-sharing' Executive.

6 Ulster Says 'No'

On the first Sunday of 1974 many sermons expressed good wishes to the Executive as it assumed the powers now delegated to it. Hopes were entertained for 'a return to normality' in the conditions of everday life, but, of course, this was no return to the political conditions prior to direct rule. It could be seen, according to one's point of view, as a considerable advance towards 'just' government in Northern Ireland and more friendly relations in the island as a whole, or alternatively as a gross betrayal of the interests of the Protestant community in the North. For they were being asked to accept an electoral system, proportional representation, which the main political parties in Britain had consistently declared unacceptable to themselves, and a pluralist state of a type not acceptable to the Catholics in their part of Ireland; further they were to concede control over certain aspects of their affairs to a Council of Ireland in which the larger state seemed likely in the long run to have a preponderant influence. In retrospect it seems probable that partnership government—'power-sharing' as it was called—might have succeeded if it had not been linked with all-Ireland institutions.[1] In the event Ulster said 'No' to both in 1974, first by electoral verdict and then by direct action; and it said 'No' again in a more considered way in 1975, when it elected to a Constitutional Convention a majority committed to opposing this form of solution.

It was between these events that the Churches and churchmen made their most dramatic moves to promote reconciliation; but the political tide had already set very strongly against the kind of structures which reconciliation might entail. Consequently the action of the Churches, while contributing to a mitigation of hostile feelings, had little practical effect on the search for acceptable political institutions. If the Churches could have acted in 1972 as vigorously as we shall see them acting at Christmas 1974; if they had conducted their Peace Campaign before the decisive loyalist

victory in May 1974 rather than after it, they might have
prepared a state of mind in their members that would have given
Mr Whitelaw's programme a chance of success. But their own
inter-church relationships, gradually established in the face of
the troubles, had probably not reached in 1972 the level of
mutual confidence necessary for such action.

The opponents of 'power-sharing' had not been invited to
Sunningdale—and adroitly declined when the government
under pressure issued a last-minute and very ungracious
invitation. This gave them a grievance which they exploited
fully. On 4 January, only four days after Mr Faulkner took
office, his policy was repudiated by the Ulster Unionist Council
by 427 votes to 374. A few days later he resigned the leadership
of the party, to be succeeded by Mr Harry West, who, because
of SDLP participation, was bitterly opposed to the participation of Unionists in the Executive. Mr Faulkner's supporters
in the Assembly formed a new party, later known as the
Unionist Party of Northern Ireland (UPNI), and began to
organize in the country; but already it was apparent that the
'Unionist' element in the coalition no longer represented the
Unionist Party outside the Assembly. Bishop Butler's plea in a
sermon on the Feast of the Epiphany that the people of
Northern Ireland, like the Magi, 'return to their own country
by another way', i.e. regain devolved government by accepting
new institutions, fell on deaf ears.[2] A background of renewed
violence did little to help considered judgement. The arrival of
Mr Liam Cosgrave and other Dublin ministers at Hillsborough
Castle on 1 February to discuss details of the Council of Ireland
was represented as provocation— and yet, as an illustration of
the confused state of Unionist opinion, it may be noted that
some days later the Ulster Unionist Women's Council voted to
support Mr Faulkner.

Then out of the blue came the United Kingdom general
election. Confronted by a challenge from the trade unions Mr
Heath felt he had no alternative but to go to the country. It is
said that both Mr Whitelaw and Mr Pym saw the danger for
Northern Ireland's fragile new beginning in an election at this
moment; but their efforts failed to persuade Mr Heath, who had
to think of the interests of the United Kingdom as a whole. And
so, before the Executive had had time to show that it could rule
fairly, and while those opposed to it were still smarting from the
'betrayal' of Sunningdale, the Ulster electorate had a chance to
express itself and did so in no uncertain terms. The Official

Unionist Party (now committed against Faulkner), the Democratic Unionist Party, led by Ian Paisley, and the Vanguard Unionist Party, led by William Craig, formed an umbrella organization called the United Ulster Unionist Council (UUUC), and won eleven of the province's twelve seats at Westminster, defeating in seven constituencies pro-Faulkner Unionists, most of whom were the retiring members. The twelfth seat, West Belfast, was held by Mr Gerard Fitt for SDLP. All the anti-Sunningdale candidates were supported by 422,000, while 296,000 voted for those—of all parties—who supported the Executive.

The Labour Party came to power, but with so small a majority that the eleven Ulster Unionists could have kept Mr Heath in office if they had not been alienated by the recent events. The new Secretary of State, Mr Merlyn Rees, was confronted with a situation in which the electorate had clearly disowned the Assembly that it had elected seven months earlier. He was faced with noisy demands for a new Assembly election to correct this anomaly, and with quieter advice to try to play down the Council of Ireland in an attempt to save the power-sharing Executive. He declined both.

The Churches had avoided direct pronouncement during the election campaign, in accordance with the general principle that they do not advise their members how to vote. The General Board of the Presbyterian Church, meeting seven days before polling-day, had merely urged all 'to exercise their democratic responsibility'. Some indication of the mood of the Church is given by the decision of the same meeting to approve a delegation to the All-party Committee on Irish Relations, recently set up by Dail Eireann. It was reported subsequently that:

the delegation dealt with the reactions produced by directly linking the search for reconciliation and other proposals for a settlement with the goal of a united Ireland. The reactions produced by the territorial claims in the Eire Constitution were underlined and the importance of a change in contributing to mutual confidence. If co-operation and association were to mean more than mere toleration and assimilation steps should be taken towards building up a genuinely plural society in Eire as well as in Northern Ireland.

The election was followed by an uneasy period during which Mr Faulkner made repeated attempts to prove that the Council of Ireland had no teeth—and he would not propose its ratification unless that were made perfectly clear. Meanwhile Mr Cosgrave made similar efforts to prove to his supporters that he had not betrayed the principle of a united Ireland by giving *de facto* recognition to the northern State. In March Captain Austin Ardill, a Vanguard leader, said that if the plans for a Council of Ireland were changed there could be a fresh political deal that would not exclude power-sharing.[3]

At the spring meeting of the Irish Council of Churches there was a motion on the agenda in the name of two southern members 'that the Council would welcome the early ratification and implementation of the Sunningdale Agreement'. This was opposed by Dr Weir, Clerk of the Presbyterian Assembly, on the grounds that a large section of opinion had been unrepresented at Sunningdale. He said, prophetically as it turned out, that if the election result was discounted they could hardly be surprised if people resorted to violence.[4] After considerable debate the Council passed *nem con* the following:

That the Council welcomes the principle of power-sharing as offering an opportunity for all sections of the community in Northern Ireland to make a positive contribution to the public good. That it endorses the principle incorporated in the Sunningdale Agreement of mutual respect for divergent aspirations in Northern Ireland and between Northern Ireland and the Republic of Ireland.[5]

This very pointedly declined to support the Council of Ireland, and drew the clear distinction between the internal and external aspects of the settlement, a distinction which Mr Rees, probably because he feared SDLP withdrawal from the Executive, was refusing to entertain.

Meanwhile violence continued, and, if the reports that survive are typical, Easter sermons were much more concerned with the security situation that with the political one. Bishop Philbin looked back to Irish history, with its 'illusions of patriotic grandeur and inflated self-righteousness . . . Right back to early times there had been failure to agree, internal conflict, the use of murder as a political weapon and addiction to extremes.'[6] A new voice was heard: just two years after he had been seen, then a curate, on television screens waving a white but blood-stained handkerchief to British troops as he sought to minister to the dead and wounded on 'Bloody Sunday', Edward Daly had been appointed Bishop of Derry. He now warned young people against the danger of getting caught up in a violent organization and being unable to leave it. He called the bombers cowardly and immoral: 'How can anyone who professes to be a

Christian continue to do this sort of thing?'[7] In April he proposed a phased release of internees in return for a cease-fire by the Provisionals; and he asked the army to desist from 'detaining, questioning and releasing' innocent people, which 'served only as means of recruiting for military organizations'.[8]

Bishop Philbin aroused controversy at this time by declining to confirm some Roman Catholic children who had not attended a Catholic school.[9] The dispute did little to help rational discussion of the issue of separate education, on which Mr Basil McIvor, Minister of Education in the Executive, now sought to take an initiative by putting forward a proposal for Christian 'shared schools', in the management of which representatives of more than one denomination would participate.[10] Initially this was opposed by the Catholic authorities, and the fall of the Executive prevented the discussions that might have led to an experiment by mutual consent. Early in May Mrs Monica Patterson, a Catholic, issued a pamphlet with a foreword by Father Desmond Wilson entitled *The Hungry Sheep of Ulster*, in which she studied the decisions of the Second Vatican Council and suggested that the Bishops were setting limits to their implementation in Ireland. In the same week the second Ballymascanlon Conference was held.[11]

On 21 April the Archbishop of Canterbury, Dr Michael Ramsey, preached in St. Anne's Cathedral, Belfast. At a given point in the sermon the leader of a Free Presbyterian group called out 'All true Christians leave.' A number of people rose and walked out, but the Archbishop went on to speak of thousands longing and praying for reconciliation. 'The future lies with those who have such thoughts in their hearts.'[12]

On 20 February the press had mentioned for the first time a body calling itself the Ulster Workers' Council. The official trade-union movement had always been non-sectarian. While some unions in Northern Ireland are affiliated to unions in Britain, the movement as a whole finds expression in the northern committee of the Irish Congress of Trade Unions (ICTU). These facts had done much to prevent the conflicts of 1969 and 1970 from spreading to places of work. As time went on, however, loyalist workers grew dissatisfied with this ambiguity and formed, first, the Loyalist Association of Workers (LAW) and later the UWC. LAW had helped Vanguard to secure the protest strike on the introduction of direct rule. UWC was now preparing for a much more decisive trial of strength. On 21 April it threatened a general strike unless fresh Assembly elections were held. On 10 May it made its threat more precise: a vote was to be taken in the Assembly on 14 May confirming the Sunningdale agreement; if the Assembly so voted, said the leaders of UWC, a general strike would follow immediately. And it did.

The strike started at 6 p.m. on 15 May and ended at 11 a.m. on 29 May.[13] It was a fortnight of political and moral confusion, of material hardship in varying degrees, and of deep and wearing anxiety. When it ended with the fall of the Executive, there were those older people who remembered the emotions of September 1938, when the Munich agreement brought intense immediate relief mingled with shame and dismay; but the majority rejoiced simplistically at the foiling of a supposedly malicious plot against Ulster. To them it was the Sunningdale agreement, and not the insurrectionary strike, that was immoral.

It was far from clear at the start whether loyalist politicians were involved in the preparations for the strike. Certainly it was called by the UWC, and for a day or two the UUUC kept in the background. Mr William Craig was the first to make clear his support. As its success became more likely the politicians allowed their association with it to become more open, and when it was over the papers published a photograph of Mr Harry West walking triumphantly with two of the principal leaders of the UWC. On the first day of the strike Mr Stanley Orme, Minister of State, met the leaders in company with political representatives. Thereafter the Secretary of State declined to talk, or let his ministers talk, with the strike leaders. As the tension mounted, moderate opinion, including that of church leaders, sought to persuade him to modify this position; and it is difficult to see how he could have avoided doing so if there had not been the expendable Executive. Eventually the Unionist members of the latter joined in the clamour for talks, and resigned when the Secretary of State continued to refuse them; but that resignation largely removed the *casus belli* and the strike ended without the government being involved in any negotiations. It was this that enabled direct rule to be resumed in relative calm.

How far was the support for the strike attained by intimidation?[14] That there was intimidation is unquestioned; and behind the UWC, giving the orders, stood the 'Ulster Army Council' enforcing them, in some cases with proven acts of violence. Road-blocks were effectively used to prevent people going to work. It would, however, be foolish to suggest that the strike lacked widespread willing support. The voting figures of February showed that a large majority of Protestants shared its aims, whatever they might think of its methods. A feeling of communal solidarity was at least as powerful as fear of the consequences in persuading the Protestant working class overwhelmingly to comply with the instructions of the UWC. The failure of the trade unions to secure a return to work, even when leaders like Len Murray were present to lead a collective march back to the shipyard, revealed the general popular backing for the UWC.

The organizers played their hand with considerable skill. Declaring that essential services would be maintained, they ensured supplies of bread and milk, and allowed food shops to open for certain hours each day. They maintained electrical power at a level that kept the system going and enabled householders to have a few hours of supply each day, provided that industry took none. They issued passes to those whom they would permit to pass the road-blocks, and doctors, nurses, and other 'essential' personnel queued at the offices of the self-appointed junta to get their cards. There was a constant threat to animal foodstuffs, but enough was allowed through to keep the support of the Protestant farmers, who demonstrated in favour of the strike by blocking roads with their tractors at the weekends, but otherwise got on with their summer work. When at long last the government intervened to secure the supply of petrol the position had further deteriorated as a result of the Prime Minister's ill-considered broadcast, in which Mr Wilson accused the Ulster people of sponging on the British tax-payer, a remark that evoked bitter resentment on the part of opponents as well as supporters of the UWC. The strike leaders responded to the government's initiative by placing on the government the responsibility for taking over all the essential services they had so far maintained. Gas was cut off, total closure of the power stations announced for Tuesday midnight, water and sewage workers withdrawn. The army would have to do everything from now on; in spite of an earlier impression given by the government that it could cope, it had not the resources in manpower or technology to do so. Hence the final crisis in which the Executive crumbled and in doing so saved the face of Mr Rees.

The Churches played little official part in affairs during the strike. When it started the clergy and senior laity of the Church of Ireland were away at Dublin for the General Synod, and as late as 19 May the Bishop of Connor was saying there that most people wanted power-sharing to succeed; members of the Executive were working well together, in a trusting and generous spirit.[15] It is doubtful whether he or his clergy realized what was happening until they got back from Dublin at the end of the week. For the most part the clergy seem to have spent their time succouring individuals in their parishes, and to have had little to say about the rights and wrongs of the strike while it was in progress. Some clergy affirmed that they would accept no passes from the UWC and, where their flocks were scattered, appointed congregational wardens in different areas to mitigate their own loss of mobility. Some, as we have seen, tried towards the end to set up negotiations between the strike leaders and the government.

When it was all over and direct rule had been resumed, the Presbyterian and Methodist Churches met in Assembly and Conference. The Methodists were in Cork that year, and whether because it was too near in time or too far in distance they passed no resolution directly referring to the strike. The Conference did, however, 'draw the attention of all citizens to the dangers involved in supporting movements and organizations which are not subject to the normal checks of public support and criticism, which are in defiance of the law, or use intimidation as a means to impose their will. It commends support for those politicians seeking a solution of the present troubles in positive and constitutional ways.' The Conference further drew attention to the 'danger of unelected groups of all shades of opinion gaining strength through the failure of governments and politicians to communicate adequately with the common people and to be sensitive to their anxieties and fears'. It also reaffirmed 'the right of all elected groups to participate in the processes and responsibilities of government or opposition'. This resolution had a ring of 'power-sharing' about it, but avoided commitment on the essential issue by including the words 'or opposition'—which is acceptable where parties based on political opinion have a chance of alternating between government and opposition, but begs the question where a structured minority is condemned to permanent opposition.

The Presbyterians, as always, gave a lot of time to public questions, and engaged in a long and complicated debate. The main resolution consisted of a preamble followed by seven sections. Dr G. B. McConnell and the Revd. R. J. G. Gray moved to add to the preamble the words 'It is essential that there should be a sharing of responsibility and power between different sections of the community and that intimidation of every kind be utterly condemned.' The strike, proceeding at least in part by intimidation, had resulted in the denial of the principle of power-sharing. The grave division of opinion in the Church was reflected in the vote: the amendment was lost by 191 to 209. An alternative amendment was then accepted without a count: 'It is essential there be co-operation between and acceptance of responsibility by different sections of the community *who are prepared to act for the community's good* and that intimidation of every kind be entirely condemned'. The words that we have italicized could be taken as excluding those who sought a united Ireland; taken in that sense, they would endorse the current Unionist view that power-sharing with some Catholics was possible, but not with the SDLP. But the words were vague enough for supporters of the erstwhile Executive to vote positively.

The long resolution continued with the statement that 'more regard must be paid outside the province to the hopes and fears of the majority as well as the minority here . . .' Then came a paragraph which declared that 'the different sections of the Northern Ireland community should refrain from invoking their associations with the people either of Great Britain or the Irish Republic as being in any way a substitute for seeking first to live in partnership with one another'. This was to go to the root of the matter, because fundamentally the conflict was less one of religion or culture than of allegiance. In seeking to subordinate the rival allegiances to the good of Northern Ireland itself, the resolution was embodying one of the arguments later to be used by the proponents of independence for Northern Ireland. The clause was carried by 141 to 121. The next paragraph supported the aim 'of positively involving the different religious, political and social sections of the community in practical responsibility', and commended 'the efforts of the former Executive members to make one form of power-sharing work'. It blamed the collapse on 'so much official discounting of popular misgivings and objections'. The Unionist politician Mr John Taylor moved an amendment adding the words 'for government in accordance with democratic practice' to the phrase 'practical responsibility'.

This was for him a polite way of saying 'majority rule', which in practice is equivalent to 'Protestant ascendancy'. His amendment was carried without a count.

Later paragraphs of the resolution suggested that accusations of bigotry had been used to discredit 'the real situation and the character of a host of men and women'. The events of the past five years had been the source of great evil to ordinary people and the threat of still greater evil. There followed a statement that 'democratic government cannot be exercised nor human rights defended by coercion for any length of time . . .' to which an amendment by the Revd. Ray Davey and the Revd. John Morrow (then and now, respectively, leaders of the Corrymeela Community) added: 'While recognizing the widespread support for the recent strike, we must condemn the fascist manifestations which it took on a number of occasions.' This was carried, and the Assembly moved into the calmer waters of the final paragraph which asserted:

Christians are called to seek a better way of truth and mercy, honesty and patience, justice and compassion, of looking after not only their own interests but also those of others, in public and in private life. More Christians need to hear this call and offer themselves in public service and political endeavour at this time of such great stress and need in the community.

We have recorded this debate at some length because it reveals the deep differences of opinion sincerely held within the Presbyterian Church throughout the decade, but at this point brought sharply to focus by the crisis of the strike; and because it reveals also the strenuous efforts of the leaders in the Assembly to avoid open disruption and strife within the Church. Skilful wording of resolutions can avoid schism; but it does not solve the problems or seriously influence the political and electoral activities of those who have been brought within the Assembly to a measure of verbal consensus.

On 12 July it was the turn of the Orange Order to express its view of the situation in the resolutions to be passed at the annual demonstrations. These deplored:

the decisions of successive governments: the disbandment of the Ulster Special Constabulary in 1969, the prorogation of the Northern Ireland Parliament in 1972, the abolishing of the office of Governor and the passing of the Constitution Act in 1973, which have done nothing to confirm that there is a will to defeat Ulster's enemies and bring the country to peace . . . By ballot box, Covenant and Petition the Ulster people have clearly stated their position.[16]

There was no mention of the strike, which had so effectively stated the position: that had been under other auspices.

The strike had in fact left Northern Ireland in a tense and dangerous situation. It was not simply that a promising political initiative in co-operation had been thwarted. There was now a sense of triumph among Protestant paramilitaries which could easily lead them to direct action against the other community, and in fact the number of Catholics murdered in their homes and in bars showed a significant increase. The failure of the security forces to prevent widespread illegalities during the strike suggested that they would be powerless to restrain civil war if paramilitaries on both sides took to the streets. It was difficult to see what political measures were available to resolve the situation. Mr Merlyn Rees quickly announced that there would be an elected convention to try and find a better solution than the one which had just been rejected. This proposal at least gave the politicians something to work for, although the Convention was not elected until the following summer.

A notable series of efforts to divert support from the IRA was made by Bishop Edward Daly in Derry. On 21 June he recalled Bishop Philbin's words that they are 'of the devil', and said that they should get no support in the community until a full and permanent cease-fire was declared.[17] On 4 August, preaching to the prisoners at Magilligan prison, he said: 'The quest of military victory by any side is futile and immoral at this stage . . . Derry has had enough of deaths, enough suffering, enough destruction.' It is understandable that, talking to these men, many of whom he had known since their childhood, he should have added: 'Internment without trial is equally wrong and immoral . . . British troops have contributed to the violence'.[18] Again on 1 October he called for an end to detention without trial, pointing out that resentment about it prevented acceptance of normal measures of law and order;[19] but in the same month he criticized demonstrations on the subject which had twice disrupted business and normal life in Derry city. At his diocesan Synod on 30 October the Anglican Bishop of Derry, Cuthbert Peacocke, warmly praised the utterances of his new Roman Catholic counterpart 'who had fearlessly condemned violence'.[20]

Meanwhile others were doing what they could to forestall the threatened resort to arms. Behind the scenes such figures as the lawyer Desmond Boal, outspoken champion of the loyalist viewpoint, and Sean McBride, veteran IRA campaigner of the twenties, and now recognized as an international statesman, seem to have made some contact, albeit fruitless. The SDLP made approaches to the UDA, but talks broke down when the former refused to abandon their ultimate aim of a united Ireland. In Belfast some officers of the Community Relations Commission succeeded in promoting direct contacts between paramilitaries on both sides. Stanley Worrall, together with a Roman Catholic solicitor and a member of the Society of Friends, was asked to be present at tripartite meetings of UDA, Official IRA, and Provisional IRA—the UVF declined to participate—and he soon found himself the chairman of a committee that was permitted to meet—a privilege indeed considering the risks involved—first in the Friends Meeting House in south Belfast, and later in a hostel run by Dominican sisters. This committee eventually organized a conference of some 150 members of their respective organizations and of an association of community groups. This conference met for a weekend in a seaside hotel in County Donegal and completely evaded the notice of the press. Men who openly boasted that they would shoot each other in the streets of Belfast shared tables in the hotel dining-room and danced with their respective wives and sweethearts for half the night. In a three-hour plenary session on the Sunday morning it emerged that everyone was appealing to the Provisional IRA to call off the violence, 'to get off the backs of the working class', so that talks on the basic problems could take place. The Provisional delegation was led by Jimmy and Maire Drumm, veteran republican campaigners, the latter Vice-President of Provisional Sinn Fein; Jimmy Drumm undertook to convey this expression of 'working class opinion' to the Provisional Army Council.

An independent line of contact with the Drumms had been established by the Revd. William Arlow, then associate secretary of the Irish Council of Churches. This was the indirect result of a gathering in Holland at which a wide variety of interests was represented. Through this contact, and no doubt assisted by the impact of the Donegal Conference, came eventually the news that the Provisional Army Council would be prepared to meet a group of Protestant clergy from the north, to discuss the situation and how it might be resolved. Stanley Worrall informed the government, through the British Ambassador in Dublin, that this invitation had been received and that it was intended to accept it. The authorities neither encouraged nor discouraged the move. It was not done behind their backs, but no message or suggestion emanating from the authorities was carried to the rendezvous.

So it came about that both the authors of this book found themselves in a car bound for the village of Feakle in County Clare—traditionally a republican stronghold—where would take place the meeting partly described in our opening pages. Just after dark on a December evening we arrived, and soon other cars brought our colleagues and some of the Provisionals. Small talk did not prove easy, and the offer to buy a round of drinks at the bar revealed more teetotallers among the Provos than among the clergy. Formal discussions were postponed until the morning, and some of the Provos arrived after we had gone to bed.

The atmosphere at the next morning's talks was courteous, and the discussion rational. It became clear that there were 'hawks' and 'doves' in the Army Council, at least six members of which were present. Our strategy was to try and strengthen the 'doves'. None of them questioned the justification of their violent campaign, which they held to be a legitimate military operation on behalf of an oppressed country. If civilians accidentally got in the way, what had happened when the RAF bombed Dresden? There were, however, clearly those who inclined to the view that it would at that juncture be right to call a cease-fire and 'go political'. We have already described the strong reinforcement which spokesmen for the clergy tried to give to this view, stressing the determination of Protestant opinion, as evidenced by the strike, and the continued fortitude of the people under attack. They would never give way to violence on the scale that the IRA could mount it. The only hope for a united Ireland was to win their hearts and minds; and every bomb postponed the day when such an outcome might become possible. In response to this the Provos accepted that the IRA could not win; but neither side could win. Therefore they were committed to continuing their campaign until the British got tired and made a declaration of intent to withdraw. This need not entail abrupt or early departure. A clear state-ment of future intention would suffice, but without that the campaign must continue.

Accordingly we attempted as we talked alone in the after-noon—when those liable to arrest had already departed because of the reported approach of the police–to articulate a formula which would satisfy the expressed minimum demands of the Provisionals without compromising the government's position.

Much play had been made with the word 'imperialism', which seemed to us totally out of date in the Anglo-Irish context. We thought therefore if the Provos wanted to get 'off the hook' of violence without loss of face, some repudiation of 'imperialism' by Britain might help. After all, the British were now in Ireland solely because a million Irishmen considered themselves British and were counting on British support. We therefore drew up a draft declaration that the British government might conceivably make and which would not, in our view, be a betrayal of reasonable people in Northern Ireland. We undertook to urge the government to make such a declaration if it would in fact enable the Provisionals to declare a cease-fire. The draft declaration was as follows:

1. HM Government solemnly re-affirms that it has no political or territorial interests in Northern Ireland beyond its obligations to the citizens of Northern Ireland.
2. The prime concern of HM Government is the achievement of peace and the promotion of such understanding between the various sections in Northern Ireland as will guarantee to all its people a full participation in the life of the community, whatever be the relationship of the Province to the EEC, the United Kingdom or the Republic of Ireland.
3. Contingent upon the maintenance of a declared cease-fire and upon effective policing, HM Government will relieve the Army as quickly as possible of its internal security duties.
4. Until agreements about the future government of Northern Ireland have been freely negotiated, accepted and guaranteed, HM Government intends to retain the presence of armed forces in Northern Ireland.
5. HM Government recognizes the obligation and right of all those who have political aims to pursue them through the democratic process.

The impending police raid described in the Prologue prevented any discussion of this draft with the full delegation, but in further talks after the raid O'Brady and his remaining colleagues reacted not unfavourably, and undertook to convey it to the Army Council. The next morning we all went home to await the IRA's response, and on the following morning 12 December, the news of our meeting was broadcast to the world, having been made public by the Irish police.

That was the very day that had been chosen for the launching of a concerted peace campaign by the leaders of the four main Churches. At the prompting and guided by the organizational skill of Dr Weir, Clerk of the General Assembly, the Cardinal, the Primate, the Moderator (the Revd. J G. Temple Lundie), and the President (the Revd. R. Desmond Morris), called on their people to 'let peace begin at Christmas time'. They appeared together on television, placed full-page advertisements in the press, issued countless car-stickers, and called rallies in Belfast and many other towns, at which thousands of people indicated their personal wish to 'Think, pray and talk peace'. The campaign was not intended to promote any particular 'solution' but rather to create an atmosphere in which public opinion would permit a solution to be found by the politicians. That the politicians should seize the opportunity was essential to the plan, and accordingly the four leaders paid visits together to the Secretary of State, the Prime Minister, and the Taoiseach. Some confusion was at first caused by the coincidence of this official campaign with the revelation of the encounter at Feakle. While Dr Weir participated in both efforts, the official leaders were not aware of the Feakle enterprise until it was made public, and at least one of them said it should not have happened. But after the initial shock the venture was seen by many as exemplifying the kind of initiative for peace that the leaders were calling individual Christians to make whenever the opportunity occurred.

As the Church Leaders' campaign gained momentum in the days before Christmas, the Feakle group was anxiously awaiting the response of the IRA to their draft. They had arranged to report to the Secretary of State in London, and the reply came on the very morning they were due to fly to Britain. It was said that the Army Council had spent eighteen hours debating their reply. The answer rejected the proposed formula and restated the tortuous self-justification that had been heard at Feakle, but it did announce a cease-fire for eleven days over Christmas and hinted at the possibility of this being extended if the British Army avoided offensive action. This message was conveyed to the Secretary of State and a full report of the talks made to him in the presence of his advisers. Mr Rees let it be known publicly that army activity would be related to the level of violence, which was a positive response to the cease-fire stopping short of a formal 'truce'. A direct appeal was made personally by one of the Feakle party to Andy Tyrie, the UDA leader, asking that Protestant asassinations should cease. He, of course, denied that men under his command committed them, but undertook to do what he could. During the eleven days no such killings of Catholics took place—if only that restraint had been maintained throughout the winter and spring! Between Christmas and New Year there was a considerable passing of messages through the

Feakle group to the government, seeking sufficient response to 'justify' an extension of the cease-fire.

The four church leaders were at Downing Street on 1 January as part of their peace campaign, and, no doubt, expressed concern that the cease-fire be maintained. On 3 January the Feakle group announced that they had no plans for further action. At the last minute the IRA extended their cease-fire until 16 January. Shortly afterwards the government announced that there would be no major change in internment policy unless the cease-fire were extended beyond that date, and also rejected all proposals for talks with the IRA through intermediaries or directly. As 16 January approached, Cardinal Conway urged an increase in releases, and Seamus Loughran, then spokesman for Sinn Fein, expressed disappointment at the government's lack of response. The deadline passed and the cease-fire lapsed. There was, however, no immediate resumption of violence, and the IRA turned Merlyn Rees's formula round, saying that their level of activity would depend on what the army did.

Meanwhile two of the top Provisionals present at Feakle had been arrested in the Republic. The four church leaders and the Feakle group expressed separately their bitter disappointment at the failure to maintain the cease-fire. On 15 January it became known that Mr Rees had authorized talks between two of his aides and representatives of Provisional Sinn Fein. No explanation of this apparent volte-face was ever forthcoming, and it seemed strange that talks which had been refused in the circumstances of cease-fire could take place while hostilities were nominally in progress. The Revd. William Arlow, though taking no part in these talks, ferried the Sinn Fein delegates in his car to Lane Side, a house beside Belfast Lough then used by the government for informal contacts. Two or three such meetings took place, while massive peace rallies organized by the church leaders took place in Dublin, Belfast, and Newry. On 31 January the report of Lord Gardiner's committee on measures to deal with terrorism was published: while greatly regretting internment and suggesting some changes in its administration, the committee recommended its continuance; it also called for the abolition of special category status for prisoners convicted of politically motivated offences. Neither of these findings was likely to mollify the IRA.

It is instructive to note two sermons preached on 26 January, during this period of anxious waiting for a renewal of the cease-fire. At Martyrs' Memorial Church Dr Paisley said:

We fight for our lives and our national identity. Mr Arlow has drunk the heady wine of ecumenism so deeply that his mind is in stupor and his eyes are blind to the plain unadulterated facts . . . The Lord will not deliver Ulster while her people do not realize that there are strange gods among us in the form of ecumenical clergy, those fickle, Feakle clergy who would lead the Protestants of Ulster astray.[21]

He went on to enumerate four duties: to be alert to the real nature of the attack, to acknowledge dependence upon God, to reaffirm to Roman Catholic fellow-countrymen what our principles are, to band together for the defence and resurrection of Ulster. Eric Gallagher on the same Sunday also had four points, principles rather than duties: ultimate loyalty is not to republicans or to loyalists but to God; everyone 'irrespective of creed, was of value and entitled to share in the common life; love was stronger than hatred; and a quest for forgiveness would do more for the country than continuing hostility and violence.[22]

On 9 February the IRA announced an indefinite cease-fire, presumably made possible by what had transpired at the talks with civil servants. This was, of course, the fulfilment of the immediate aims both of the church leaders and of the Feakle group, but neither was involved in the negotiations that led to it, nor can it be said what conditions were made or accepted by the government. 'Incident centres' were organized, for the reporting of events likely to jeopardize the cease-fire, and these were manned by Sinn Fein members who had direct telephone links with the security forces. It was feared that these gave Sinn Fein an acknowledged control over events in republican areas, and loyalists alleged that terrorists had been given limited powers of policing. Many felt that the IRA had been given a chance to renew itself when on the verge of defeat, and blamed the Feakle group for this. But the government had access to intelligence, and if the IRA had really been on the verge of defeat, the authorities would surely have rejected any cease-fire and destroyed them. Instead of that the government went far beyond any Feakle proposals to gain the renewal of the cease-fire. This suggests that they knew that hostilities on a disastrous scale were at that time possible; and this may have included a threat to the London Underground.

Opinions differ as to why this indefinite cease-fire broke down, although it was never formally revoked by either side. Some believe that it was never intended by the IRA to last, but simply to give them a respite for reorganization. Others think that the resumption of violence depended on a revival of support in Catholic districts and in the Republic, and that this revival occurred because of the actions of Protestants. Within a few days of the ending of the initial eleven-day cessation, the assassination of individual Catholics began again: on 7 and 9 January the Feakle party issued statements pleading for this to cease and warning of the consequences if it did not. The assassinations increased through February and the spring, although the IRA campaign of bombing was in abeyance. Then came the election for the Constitutional Convention, at which a substantial majority was returned pledged to oppose all forms of participation by the minority in shared government. The Convention did not need to meet; its outcome was obvious from the day of the count. Moderate Catholics were left with no hope of any attempt to resume the experiment in power-sharing that had collapsed with the strike. The climate was again favourable to direct action; the IRA 'hawks' were in the eyes of republicans proved right after all, and the movement acted accordingly. Ulster had again said 'No' to compromise, and had of necessity said 'Goodbye' to peace.

Nevertheless the great efforts that had been made for peace—mainly by the Churches and churchmen—during the winter of 1974–5 were not entirely fruitless. The cease-fire gave Mr Rees the chance to implement the policy of ending internment, which had been the aim of successive Secretaries of State since the British government inherited responsibiity for it from Brian Faulkner. Releases began early in 1975, and, in spite of set-backs to the cease-fire, continued until the last internee had been released at the end of the year. The power has never been used since, and in 1980 Parliament was asked not to renew it. The second consequence was more general: the public, especially in Belfast, started going out at night again. For years there had been almost a voluntary curfew; few went to places of entertainment and evening meetings were kept to a minimum. Now, relying on the cease-fire, all that was changed; and, as violence gradually resumed, the public refused to return to the habits of the early seventies. Week-night activities in churches, attendance at concerts and theatres, eating out, dances, and cabarets all took wing. While it is impossible to claim normality for central Belfast behind its security gates, elsewhere cars taking people out for the evening are as plentiful as in any other city. It was possible by 1978 to claim that the annual Festival of the Arts promoted by the Queen's University was the next biggest event of its kind after Edinburgh.

There was no solution; there was still an alarming incidence of violence, but there was also a more cheerful and positive enjoyment of life.

We must return to 1975 and trace the story of the ill-fated Convention. On 7 April the parties published their manifestos—a fatal step, for each side nailed its colours to the mast instead of announcing an intention sincerely to seek an accommodation. At the same time two well-known Roman Catholic priests, Father Faul and Father Murray, called for a boycott of the election because internment continued; but Cardinal Conway joined with the other church leaders in a statement which said that the election 'would be a test of Christian responsibility and political maturity'. A few days before the poll the third inter-church meeting was held at Ballymascanlon and adopted a report calling for the end of internment. [23]The election returned forty-six representatives of the loyalist groups of parties (UUUC), and twenty-two representing parties that had supported the power-sharing Executive of the previous year. There was immediate fear in Dublin and elsewhere that the British would give way to the loyalists, and Mr Cosgrave took steps to remind them of their pledges. At this point the Revd. William Arlow, first in America and subsequently on RTE, alleged that the government had given the Sinn Fein representatives in February an undertaking of ultimate withdrawal. [24] This was firmly denied by the Northern Ireland Office. It would seem that the Sinn Fein representatives had drawn that conclusion, perhaps from some vague comment on a hypothetical situation. Mr Arlow has since said that he was led to make the statement at this time because the Provos needed something tangible to hold their volunteers to the cease-fire, which was beginning to crumble; and that he thought some of Mr Rees's advisers would not be averse to the announcement as an indirect warning to the loyalists not to be too intransigent. Naturally the statement caused much alarm. Steps were taken by loyalist paramilitaries to prepare an 'army' that would hold the province against the IRA and/or the Republic, if the British withdrew, and the case for independence began to be canvassed vigorously in some quarters.

The Convention met and set up a rules committee, which in

its turn drew up rules that facilitated a majority report rather than an agreed one. This was to frustrate from the start any genuine attempt to find the greatest possible measure of agreement. The validity of these rules was contested, but the Chairman of the Convention, who was after all the highest judicial officer of the Province (Sir Robert, now Lord, Lowry, Lord Chief Justice) ruled that they were not incompatible with the act which set up the Convention. The constitutional body had got off to a bad start, accentuated by the news that seventy people had been killed during the three and a half months of cease-fire.

When the Presbyterian Assembly met in June, the Moderator appealed to the Convention members to 'stop bickering', and the Assembly passed a resolution calling on the Convention 'to show statesmanlike leadership in seeking to devise meaningful and acceptable ways by which the political majority and minorities can effectively participate in public life and in government'. For a time it looked as if this, and similar admonitions from the other Churches, might have an effect. It was agreed that inter-party talks should be held during the summer recess, and a conciliatory debate took place in the Convention before it adjourned. When it resumed in October, the proposals of each party were debated in turn; but then, instead of looking for common ground, it voted through those of the UUUC as the Convention's report to Parliament. Needless to say Parliament rejected the report, which did nothing to fulfil the purpose for which the Convention had been summoned.

Direct rule continued, and no further attempt to resolve the constitutional deadlock was made until the winter of 1979–80.

7   Prisoners and Peace-Makers

After the failure of the Convention the possibility of an early political solution in the Northern Ireland crisis disappeared. The government concentrated on containing and reducing the inevitable violence. Those who had striven for a new order, in which the two communities could live together in justice and peace while actively co-operating in the government of the province, had been greatly disheartened by the events of 1974–5. The remaining year of Mr Rees's service as Secretary of State was a time of disillusionment and loss of hope. Because people felt that way, a radically new peace movement in the autumn of 1976 evoked a startling emotional response.

The feeling of frustration that was to pervade the Churches during this period had already been foreshadowed in 1975 by a dispute in the Roman Catholic diocese of Down and Connor. On 16 June it was reported in the press that Father Desmond Wilson, a well-known and popular priest who had been in the van of ecumenical relations in the sixties, had resigned his curacy in the parish of St. John's in west Belfast. Father Wilson had long felt dissatisfaction with his priestly role, and had been critical of what seemed to him a paternalistic approach by the Church to the problems of the people. He had written, for example: 'If the institutions of our society, the courts, the police, the universities and the Church, had given the same measure of recognition and protection and a sense of dignity to those people as the small guerrilla groups have given them, then they would have as much loyalty to those institutions.'[1] This was to come very close to identifying himself with the propaganda, though in no way with the activities, of republican paramilitary groups. If by his resignation, which caused a short-lived stir in the press and among the people, Father Wilson had intended to raise a major challenge to the Church's policy, he failed; but in making a personal identification with the underprivileged, among whom he now serves as a community worker, he had borne witness to an aspect of the Christian message which should not be neglected. His misfortune was that others had made that identification whose actions that Church could in no way condone.

The 'cease-fire' petered out as 1975 drew on towards autumn. Undoubtedly the government hung on to the pretence of it long after it had ceased to have any meaning. They wanted to phase out internment, and they recognized that this would become impossible politically if the campaign of IRA violence were openly renewed. Another factor was the hint that seems to have been conveyed in the talks that followed the Feakle encounter, of massive attacks on the London Underground, if hostilities between the IRA and the British army were renewed. Protestant responsibility for the gradual renewal of violence must not be minimized. When, on 2 April, the first IRA bomb for seven weeks exploded in Belfast, it was stated to be in response to the assassination of Catholics; this had been going on since the renewal of the cease-fire in February, and by the end of May seventy had been murdered. On 31 July the UVF killed a minibus-load of popular musicians (the Miami Show Band) as they were returning to the Republic after an evening performance in Banbridge. A month later, in acknowledged retaliation for this, eleven Orangemen were killed at a meeting in Tullyvally Orange Hall, Newtownhamilton, and the southern part of County Armagh began to sink into the condition of near banditry from which it has never wholly emerged.

In reaction to these horrors, the Presbyterians of Newry called for enforcement of the rule of law on both sides of the border, and the four church leaders called on people in both states to support their governments and to let no one take the law into their own hands. The SDLP, Alliance, UPNI, and NILP parties called for impartial enforcement of the law, and were not supported in this by the dominant UUUC.[2] Since the cease-fire, Mr Rees had been steadily releasing internees, and the loyalist coalition wanted the statement to condemn this policy. In October, just as the Convention was voting through its one-sided report,[3] the UVF was proscribed by the government. It was alleged that consultations took place before this was done, in which the UVF asked to be incorporated in the security forces of the state, an interesting indication of the difficulties confronting a government anxious to maintain impartiality. Protestants, however far outside the law they act, still believe that they are the state and that their opponents are the enemies of the state.

Internment without trial had now been practised for four years. The internees, not having been convicted of any offence, were treated more or less as prisoners of war. They lived communally in huts under the command of their own officers. They were not required to wear prison clothes or to do prison work. When Mr Whitelaw granted special category status to those convicted prisoners, whose offences were politically motivated, they were held under similar conditions. Free association and choice of how to pass the time could easily turn the prison into a school of terrorism.

On 9 November 1975 Mr Rees announced that the last internee would be freed by Christmas and that special category status would not be granted to any person convicted of any offence committed after 1 March 1976.[4] Thus he struck two blows at the 'prisoner of war' concept. None would now be held simply because they were 'the enemy' and those held because of what they had actually done would be regarded unequivocally as criminals. This change of policy was made possible by the completion of new cell-blocks, built to an H-shaped plan, which supplied the nick-name by which they were to be known throughout the subsequent controversy. They were in fact the most up-to-date and best-appointed prison accommodation in the United Kingdom, until reduced to squalor by their inmates.

Pope Paul VI's new year message for 1976 referred to 'festering centres of armed conflict',[5] and Cardinal Conway was not slow to apply these words to Ireland. On New Year's Day, 15,000 people signed a declaration for peace organized by the Churches and trade unions of Derry to show the opposition of society at large to the sectarian assassinations on both sides. On 3 January five members of the SDLP were shot in Armagh, and two days later ten Protestants were murdered in an ambush at Kingsmills in direct retaliation. At this point Rory O'Brady called for a move on the part of the Feakle group to halt the assassinations. The group met and replied that 'killings can be stopped if all paramilitary organizations decided they will not be party to any such activity . . . We see no purpose in attempting private negotiations where the onus is on others to call off the killings.' A day or two later the Armagh Presbytery asked the Feakle group not to renew contacts but to give time for government security measures to take effect in south Armagh; but the UUUC refused to participate in a conference on security called by the government. The leaders of the four Churches held a vigil in the market-place at Armagh which was attended by

1,200 people, including 200 clergy. Early in February, a 'day of reparation' was observed in all Roman Catholic churches in Ireland. Cardinal Conway said that violence was crime against humanity, against Ireland, and against the majesty of God. The whole Irish people should seek to make reparation.

In the spring of 1976 controversy arose in the Republic concerning the kind of changes necessary there to make any hope of ultimate unity realistic. Dr Conor Cruise O'Brien, at that time a member of the government, spoke of the need to change the law on contraception[6] and Dean Griffin, preaching at St. Patrick's Cathedral (C of I), Dublin, called for a new policy on mixed marriages, integrated education, and inter-communion. Dr O'Brien was summarily rebuked by the Roman Catholic Bishop of Limerick, Dr Newman, who developed his attack in a long address on 'Church and State' delivered at the end of May.[7] The bishops, he claimed, had been right in the notorious case of Dr Noel Browne.[8] 'In our struggle for Irish unity we must not sacrifice our spiritual heritage.' 'Catholic people have a political right to the provision of the kind of social framework that supports them in the living out of their moral and religious principles.' He attacked Dr Garret Fitzgerald, another Cabinet minister, who had referred to 'the Catholic proclivity to enforce private morality by the State'. The close link adduced by Dr Newman between the teaching authority of the Church and the legislative authority of the state provoked much opposition in certain Dublin circles, and was strongly criticized in a leading article in the *Irish Times*.[9] In June the Episcopal Conference gave an assurance that the bishops had never suggested that the state should impose their moral theology on all; but Dr Newman had already provided further fuel for Protestant intransigence in the north.

It was to these exchanges that the Presbyterians were referring when the General Assembly welcomed 'current debate within the Republic on questions that would arise in a pluralistic society'. The Church of Ireland at its General Synod welcomed 'the noticeably increased sensitivity and realism of recent pronouncements by leading political figures in the Republic of Ireland'. All the church gatherings were concerned at the failure of the Constitutional Convention: the Methodists called on community leaders to create conditions in which 'a government may be formed to which all citizens of goodwill can give their allegiance'. At this juncture private talks were going on between

John Hume of the SDLP and the Revd. Martin Smyth of the OUP, a Presbyterian minister and Grand Master of the Orange Order. They were trying to explore confidentially the possibilities of agreement in spite of the failure of the open Convention. It was to these that the Presbyterians were alluding when they welcomed and encouraged 'talks between political parties in an attempt to overcome the political impasse and find a way out of our despair and a way to an acceptable form of government for our country which appears to be drifting more and more towards total collapse'. The Anglicans welcomed 'considerable agreement on greater participation by the minority'. It will be seen that as far as their official governing bodies spoke for them, the Protestant Churches did not share the intransigence of the UUUC coalition, but it remains an inescapable fact that the members of that coalition had been elected by voters, who for the most part professed a link, whether close or more tenuous, with one or other of these denominations. The church leaders were inclined to blame the impasse, and certainly the violence, on those whose connections were slight; two of the annual gatherings deplored the identification of victims and the attackers as 'Catholic' or 'Protestant', implying, as the Presbyterians expressed it, 'an affiliation that very often does not exist'.

That summer of 1976, two very different tragedies occurred which had a marked effect on the emotional climate. On 22 July, near Dublin, a land-mine destroyed the car of Mr Christopher Ewart-Biggs, British Ambassador to the Irish Republic, killing him and a secretary. There was, as in the later case of Lord Mountbatten, a strong revulsion of feeling in the Republic. At a memorial service in Dublin, the Foreign Minister, Dr Fitzgerald, made a noble pronouncement on the relations between the two countries. So far from driving a wedge between them, the event, he said, had brought them closer together in the face of a common threat to their security and well-being. Three weeks later three young children from one family lost their lives in Belfast, when a car, driven by a terrorist under fire from the army, crashed into them. A spontaneous protest from women in the Andersonstown area led to the rise of the Peace People, whose remarkable movement is described in chapter 11. The two incidents were linked when Mrs Ewart-Biggs, who might well have detached herself in disgust from Ireland's problems, threw in her lot with the new movement and became its principal representative in England.

During the autumn there appeared a paperback volume of some 128 pages entitled *Violence in Ireland: A Report to the Churches*.[10] It was the work of the Joint Group on Social Questions, set up in 1970 by the Roman Catholic Hierarchy and the Irish Council of Churches. The report was sympathetically received, but action was slow to follow. The whole episode illustrates the difficulty of moving from words to deeds, when the decision-making processes of the respective denominations are cautious, slow-moving, and different in method.

In September 1976, as the peace movement seemed to be gaining ground, Mr Merlyn Rees was appointed Home Secretary and was succeeded in Northern Ireland by Mr Roy Mason. As he arrived at Stormont, the first terrorist prisoner not entitled to special category status entered The Maze prison. Whether acting on his own initiative or obeying instructions from the Provisional IRA, he refused to wear prison clothing and, having been deprived of his own, went 'on the blanket'. He was soon joined by others, and before long there were public demonstrations in Belfast at which relatives of the prisoners, men and women, appeared wearing nothing but a blanket. After a few months the internal protest was intensified: prisoners refused to wash, and instead of 'slopping out', daubed the walls of their cells with excrement and urine. By evacuating the cells in rotation and cleaning them with high-pressure steam, the authorities managed to stave off the threat to health and so to make this new form of prison protest less sinister than the classical Irish weapon of the hunger-strike. Concern mounted, however, as the evil conditions continued month after month and then year after year. To the self-inflicted squalor was added the disciplinary loss of privileges, reducing visits and letters to the statutory minimum of one a month, and denying exercise and association outside the cells.

The Protestant Churches for long had little to say about this festering sore. They were not the voices to which the republican prisoners would listen; and they felt inhibited from addressing the government on the subject because the hardships were self-inflicted and could be ended by action on the part of the prisoners. Later the Roman Catholic episcopate would make a notable intervention, but for a year and a half no voice was raised on the matter save that of the terrorist organizations and the prisoners' relatives.

The logic of the campaign for political status destroyed the case for the previous campaign against internment. If members of an organization claim 'prisoner of war' rights because they consider themselves belligerents and not criminals, they cannot complain if they are not tried before imprisonment. For who ever tried prisoners of war? The truth of the matter is, of course, that the IRA must always have a propaganda weapon against the authorities to maintain its influence in Catholic quarters. When internment ceased to be the obvious grievance, the status of convicted prisoners took its place; and at times, when the pressure was high, prison officers became targets for gunmen. Nineteen lost their lives betwen 1975 and 1979, invariably when they were off duty, and sometimes in their own homes before their wives and children. Against these murders all the Churches spoke out many times; but endlessly repeated condemnations lose their force, even as endlessly repeated horrors leave the heart numbed and almost indifferent.

A similar campaign was conducted simultaneously against the RUC in connection with interrogation at Castlereagh holding centre. To understand the background to this problem, it is necessary to grasp the difficulty of securing evidence in court when witnesses are subject to intimidation. With the dropping of internment, it became all the more necessary for the police to secure convictions for specific offences. The police had by now excellent intelligence and were, in fact, able to identify to their own satisfaction the perpetrators of many politically motivated outrages, going back in some cases for five or more years. But there is a difference between intelligence and evidence that can be produced in court. In the absence of witnesses willing to testify openly, reliance had to be placed on confessions. Confessions were obtained by holding suspects under the emergency laws for up to seven days and confronting them with the intelligence. A high degree of mental pressure was clearly involved in this process, and the borderline between severe interrogation and actual ill-treatment—'torture' to the propagandist—was an ill-defined one. As more and more of their men went behind bars for long periods, convicted of specific crimes by their own statements, not only IRA propagandists but defence lawyers and doctors began to allege that the methods used to extract confessions were improper.

The Churches were more active in their reaction to this problem than to the situation in the Maze prison. They called for a thorough investigation and for a reliable and open complaints procedure, as much for the protection of the police from misrepresentation as for the protection of the suspects from ill-treatment. For example, in 1977 the General Assembly resolved:

In calling for support for the police forces north and south and paying tribute to their courage, efficiency and devotion, the General Assembly, disturbed at recent allegations of brutality in the treatment of suspected terrorists, supports the demand for investigation and, if the allegations are proved, that reparation be made and assurances given that generally accepted standards and conventions in regard to interrogation be adhered to strictly. At the same time the Assembly deplores attempts to blacken the good name of the police force.

It is worth noting that an amendment was lost which would have expressed the current loyalist view on these matters, namely to add the words 'by deliberate provocation and false accusation and, recognizing the strain, frustration and danger of their work, calls for greater freedom of action in dealing with terrorists'. The Chief Constable, Sir Kenneth Newman, repeatedly denied that anything improper was occurring. However the government set up a committee under Judge Bennett which made various recommendations for the better conduct of interrogations, and most of these were accepted. Incidentally, in a very similar situation in the Republic, the government declined the recommendations of a committee under Judge O'Briain. At its spring meeting in 1979 the Irish Council of Churches called on both governments to implement in full the recommendations of the respective committees.[11]

8   New Faces—Old Problems

The loyalists saw in the appointment of Mr Roy Mason, who had previously been Secretary of State for Defence, and so in charge of the army, a shift of emphasis on the part of the British government from trying to 'solve the problem' to compassing the defeat of terrorism. They were elated, and they were not far wrong. As time went on, there was a marked increase in the number of convictions for terrorist offences, some relating to events that had occurred several years before. For many people life was becoming more normal than in the early seventies. Car bombs became fewer, and so did 'proxy bombs', when a driver was compelled to drive his own vehicle loaded with explosives to some sensitive point while his wife or workmate was held as a hostage. Towards the end of the decade, anxiety about economic prospects overshadowed in most areas the lessening fears about security; but an end to the troubles in terms of a solution seemed to be as far off as ever.

On 22 December 1976 Mr Mason stated flatly that Britain's political role would be passive until parties reached a sufficient degree of agreement to warrant a change in the direct rule system. This was disappointing to nationalist opinion, which looked to Britain to reverse the outcome of the loyalist strike and the collapse of the Convention by imposing on the unionists institutions which seemed to the nationalists to be just. This point of view was vigorously advanced by Bishop Cahal Daly, who said in January 1977 that the political vacuum left by Britain in Northern Ireland was unpardonable.[1] Politicians should exploit quickly the conditions created by the peace movement. It was insufficient to have security operations without a policy. The *Irish Times* replied in a leading article that 'the peace movement's influence is least where it is needed most. Its contribution is to sentiment and morale. It is not an instrument of politics.'[2] RTE broadcast a discussion[3] between the Bishop and Dr Garret Fitzgerald, in which the latter insisted that power-sharing could not be enforced, that the British government must act in the way most likely to produce agreement, and that too much pressure would give weapons to extremists on both sides. The Bishop continued to maintain that the Irish government should keep on pressing the British to break the deadlock; at least the British should maintain a forum in which the politicians could operate. Dr Fitzgerald retorted by asking what the Churches had done about implementing the recommendations of their own working party in the report *Violence in Ireland*. It was perhaps naïve of the Foreign Minister to expect action from the Churches within three months; but a year later the Churches' response could only be seen in endorsement of words rather than implementation of proposals.

In February the Church of Ireland's Role of the Church Committee issued a report, subsequently endorsed by the General Synod, which emphasized, as Bishop Daly had done, the dangers of a political vacuum, but which put the onus not so much on the British government as upon the Northern Ireland parties to reach a measure of agreement on partnership. 'Partnership is essential but it cannot be imposed.' It went on to say that partnership in Northern Ireland was impeded by the 'absence of a positive, realistic and honest approach by the Republic of Ireland to the issue of unity . . . The stark fact is that the great majority in Northern Ireland will not be absorbed in the Republic of Ireland as it is.' (This, it should be remembered, came from a Church with nearly half its clergy serving south of the border.) In the same month, a working party of the Churches suggested that the Convention might be allowed to resume, with an 'executive' that would monitor the government's programme and advise the Secretary of State.[4] Nothing came of this suggestion, which would have turned a constituent assembly, elected to devise a constitution, into a representative parliament, debating, though not yet controlling current affairs.

The general public in the spring of 1977 was less concerned about the political vacuum than about the security situation. Before the Churches gathered for their annual meetings in the summer, Dr Ian Paisley had attempted to exploit this feeling by calling another general strike. This time the organizing body styled itself the Ulster Action Council, and the ostensible aim was to press the government into a more vigorous and more Draconian security policy. Whether the underlying aim was to replace Mr Mason with a provisional government led by Dr

Paisley is another matter. Certainly the situation was very grave, and a repetition of the success of the 1974 strike was expected by many. In fact, the strike failed for a variety of reasons, ranging from a determination at Stormont Castle to defeat it greater than had been apparent in 1974, to a much less whole-hearted support by the loyalist population, and in particular by the electricity workers whom Dr Paisley could not persuade to join it. The strongest support came from farmers in Dr Paisley's parliamentary constituency of North Antrim, who blockaded the town of Ballymena with tractors, provoking a confrontation with the police in which Dr Paisley submitted to arrest. This he achieved with some dignity, calling upon his followers not to resist the police, for the object of their demonstration was to strengthen, not weaken, the security forces. He was released after a few hours, and a few days later called off the strike. Farmers who attempted a similar blockade at Toomebridge had their tractors thrown into the River Bann; but the population there is predominantly Catholic. Dr Paisley had said during the strike that if it failed he would retire from politics; in fact he refrained from attendance at Westminster for seven months, saying he would only go if his vote would bring down the government. In December he made his first speech in the Commons since May, and thereafter appeared to forget his threat—or was it a promise?

Ironically enough, the government's success in defeating this pro-security strike marked the turning-point in security. The Catholic population began to take a more favourable view of the RUC, which had been seen to act against loyalists. Without adopting the measures the strikers had called for, the police and the army, with enhanced morale and developing skill, began to show ever more visible results in tracking down offenders. Whether judged by the increase of arrests and convictions or by the decrease of lethal incidents, the next three years saw a marked improvement,[5] which included considerable relaxation of the physical barriers and other restrictions that had curtailed commercial and social life for so long. Car bombs became almost a thing of the past. Attacks with incendiary devices and shootings of individuals continued, but not at the level characteristic of the early seventies, and now affecting mostly police, soldiers, and prison officers. In spite of a number of major outrages, such as the slaughter of fourteen people at the La Mon restaurant near Belfast in 1978, life became more normal for the great majority of the population.

This trend, however, had not become fully evident when the Churches passed their annual observations on the situation in the summer of 1977. The Presbyterian Assembly saw 'little to encourage hope', but affirmed 'its faith in the Sovereign Lord of history'. It acknowledged the generosity of the Westminster government in its financial support for services in the province, but all this was 'no use without law and order'. So it implored the government 'to heed the calls of the people for more adequate protection.' At the same time it condemned the 'recent political strike . . . as a denial of personal liberty and constitutional authority', and 'paid tribute to those who courageously withstood the call'. (How many 'Presbyterian' tractors had blockaded Ballymena?) It is interesting that an amendment calling for greater freedom of action to be given to the security forces in dealing with terrorism was rejected by the Assembly.

The Methodist Conference received a report from its Council of Social Welfare which condemned 'the use of violence to attain political ends', and, perhaps rather naïvely, urged 'the security forces to do all in their power to control it'. 'The only way finally to defeat the terrorists is for all people of goodwill to come together to work for the good of the community. The Churches have a particular responsibility to co-operate with one another in setting up a government in Northern Ireland that will have the whole-hearted support of the large majority of our people.' The Church of Ireland Synod adopted the report issued by its committee in February and quoted above.

While these statements may seem platitudinous, it is important to note that they are calling precisely for the things that the elected Convention had rejected. Those elected or appointed to leadership in the Churches were still seeking some form of 'partnership' or 'power-sharing', when those elected to represent the people had rejected it. A majority of those who elected UUUC members to the Convention must have been members or adherents of the very Churches whose supreme courts now continued to seek what the UUUC had declared unacceptable and had rendered unattainable. Christian leadership failed to bring along with it a sufficient body of electors willing to follow its lead; and there can be little doubt that the principal reason for that failure lay in the continuance of violence by republican groups; yet these claimed to be acting for the community that had most to gain by the acceptance of the principle of partnership.

The strike of 1977 had split the UUUC. Henceforth the Democratic Unionist Party, led by Dr Paisley, would go its own way, a thorn in the flesh of the Official Unionists, who were however before long to receive back into the fold Mr William Craig and others from Vanguard. The dwindling remnant of Brian Faulkner's following was dispirited at his retirement from politics, and still more at his accidental death just twenty days after accepting a life peerage.[6] Apart from them all types of unionists were together in their rejection of the principle of shared power that had underlain the Executive of 1974. The result of this attitude was to strengthen support within the SDLP for an all-Ireland solution, and to provoke among loyalists, especially among paramilitaries, a movement in favour of independence for Northern Ireland. By their refusal to accept the conditions attached to the union by Britain, the unionists had made the ultimate dissolution of the Union, in one way or another, much more likely.

On 18 April 1977 William Cardinal Conway died. Born in 1913 in Dover Street, one of those Belfast streets running between the Falls Road and the Shankill Road that were to be dissected by the Peace Line in 1969, he understood at first hand the social situation that underlay the rioting with which the troubled decade opened. As a former Professor of Moral Theology and Canon Law at Maynooth, he was well versed in the ethical issues involved. Raised to the archbishopric of Armagh in 1963, he had participated in the later stages of the Second Vatican Council and had taken to himself its generous approach to other Christians. By his firm and repeated condemnations of violence, coupled with strong appeals for reform and for justice to the minority community in the North, he earned the respect and gratitude of many Christians on both sides. He advanced with circumspection, but not without warmth, towards closer relations with the other Churches. The joint statements of the four church leaders, the establishment of the Joint Group on Social Questions, the inter-church dialogue at Ballymascanlon, and the concerted peace campaign of the church leaders in the winter of 1974–5; all these derived from initiatives or from responses made by Cardinal Conway of a kind that would not have been expected from any of his predecessors. But his influence on the violent men of the republican tradition was small. His repeated condemnations of violence were rejected as 'judgemental', and he was seen by priests and people sympathetic to the republican cause as in league with the state to suppress their aspirations. Ironically, this view is a mirror image of that held by many Protestants that his declarations were often veiled support for the IRA.

Cardinal Conway was succeeded by Dr Tomàs O'Fiaich, President of St. Patrick's College, Maynooth. He had also been born a northerner, but in the border town of Crossmaglen in south Armagh. Here there had been little opportunity to meet the typical northern Protestant, and every opportunity to imbibe the republican tradition and anti-partitionist sentiment. He had no previous episcopal experience, and not much parochial; and the death, shortly after he took office, of his auxiliary Bishop, Dr Frank Lenny, who was not replaced until August 1980, left him without the support of a colleague in his own wide diocese. In January 1978 the new Archbishop startled the northern public by advocating in an interview given to the *Irish Press* the withdrawal of the British from Northern Ireland. 'I think it is the only thing that will get things moving. I regret that it didn't happen after the fall of Stormont.[7] (The 'fall' of Stormont, it will be remembered, was an assertion of power by Britain, not likely to be immediately followed by an abdication!) Six bishops of the Church of Ireland said of the Archbishop's statement 'Stability comes from recognizing that there can be no constitutional change in the status of Northern Ireland without the consent of the majority of her people. Uncertainty on such issues will only increase suspicion and division.'[8] The General Board of the Presbyterian Church said that 'calls for "British withdrawal" are taken by many of our people as directed against them and an attack on their historic heritage and identity . . . Political and religious slogans, used from one point of view and taken from another, exacerbate our differences . . . and encourage men of violence.'

In that same January 1978, Archbishop O'Fiaich paid the first of many visits to the Maze prison. In August he spoke vehemently about the appalling conditions there—'worse than Calcutta slums'[9]—without mentioning the responsibility of the prisoners themselves for the filth and stench. There was a natural feeling in Protestant circles that they had no friend in the Archbishop. It was some time before an opportunity occurred to raise Dr O'Fiaich to the Cardinalate, and rumours circulated that the British government was exercising influence at the Vatican against his promotion on the grounds of his nationalistic views. This was firmly denied in December 1978, and shortly afterwards Pope John Paul II included his name at a

consistory. When the time came for the ceremony of instal-
lation, Cardinal O'Fiaich invited the Revd. William Arlow, at
that time Secretary of the Irish Council of Churches, to be his
guest in Rome. This and other gestures of goodwill, together
with the evident personal friendliness of the new Cardinal, have
helped to reassure Protestant Church leaders, but among the
wider Protestant community the view that he is a threat to their
position is by no means dispelled.

In June 1978 one of the few cases of physical violence against
a clergyman occurred. A policeman had been abducted by the
IRA in south Armagh, and it was not known whether he was
dead or alive. Loyalists in County Antrim seized Father Hugh
Murphy and held him hostage for the constable's safe return: in
whatever condition the policeman was found, the priest would
be found also. Pressure from Protestant organizations led to
Father Murphy's release the next day after a terrifying ordeal.
The constable was subsequently found dead. It turned out that
the priest's captors were two RUC men, one of whom is now
serving life imprisonment for the murder of a Catholic. A
banner presented by this man to the Cullybackey branch of the
Apprentice Boys was carried in that organization's 1980
demonstration in Derry, amid widespread protest that this was
condoning murder. The other was converted in prison.

During the late 1970s there was an increasing feeling among
the Catholics of Northern Ireland that a solution of the political
impasse was only possible in the context of the whole island.
Reunification again became the primary aim, rather than one
deferred to the indefinite future while reform within Northern
Ireland was achieved. For example, in November 1978 the
SDLP proclaimed at its annual conference that British withdrawal was inevitable and desirable, and demanded a quadri-
partite conference of Britain, the Republic, and the two sides in
the North. There was also an increasing realization in the South
that union would necessitate as big a change in the character of
the Republic as in that of Northern Ireland. Dr Noel Browne
pointed out that De Valera's constitution of 1937 was a sectarian
document which betrayed the principles of Wolfe Tone, a hero
of Irish nationalists who nevertheless stood for the equal
partnership of Catholics and Protestants in an independent
Ireland. Dr Garret Fitzgerald, now in opposition, set about
compiling a policy paper for Fine Gael which attempted to
specify changes that would be needed to accommodate
northerners, and proposed a federal structure. Meanwhile the

new government under Mr Lynch set about reforming the law on contraceptives. Whatever the merits or shortcomings of the bill introduced by Mr Charles Haughey, Minister for Health, the attitude of the Hierarchy, revealed in April 1978, is relevant here: the bishops declared that although contraception was morally wrong, it was not necessarily the state's duty to prohibit the sale of contraceptives. Explaining this decision, Dr Murphy, co-adjutor to the Bishop of Cork, said contraceptive legislation was a matter for the government, and the bishops' view was that the Church did not need the state to bolster up its teaching.[10] In the face of the persistent Protestant belief that the Church was constantly using the state in southern Ireland for precisely that purpose, this is a significant utterance. If events could show over a sufficiently long period that the bishops really meant what Dr Murphy said, a big step forward towards the long-term solution of the Irish problem might have been taken. A single state would only be possible on the basis of pluralism, with responsibility resting with the Churches for their respective moral disciplines. In 1977 the Presbyterian General Assembly had received a detailed report entitled *Pluralism in Ireland,* of which the gist was contained in a paragraph which read: 'Churches must cherish and express the basic truths on which they are founded. At the same time they must take their place alongside other churches on the one hand and political and social institutions on the other, with tolerance and respect for their aims and objectives, where they are not in conflict with loving God and neighbour.' In previous years the Assembly had received major reports on *Republicanism* and *Loyalism* in Ireland[11]. Together with that on *Pluralism* these reports constitute a notable analysis of the realities of the Irish situation. If they reflect, as they are bound to do, a Presbyterian viewpoint on those realities, they display an objectivity and fair-mindedness which is an example to those who write and speak on the subject.

In 1979 it was the Methodists who produced a major document. Theirs was entitled *The Current Situation in Ireland,*[12] and was the work of a committee which had been meeting for two years. Although much briefer than the Presbyterian studies, it displays a similar desire to reflect rationally on the experience of the decade. The report recognizes that no superficial measures can do much to ameliorate the crisis: a new society needs to be created on the basis of 'a love that cares for the well-being of friends and enemies alike; a justice which is the other side of love and demands that all be treated fairly; and a concern that reconciliation should be sought between all who are estranged from God and from each other . . . All the Churches should press for a social and political order that offers freedom and justice for all its citizens.' In accepting this report, the Conference asked that a small deputation should wait upon the political leaders in Belfast, London, and Dublin to present the detailed findings, and this was done.

The impact of this report was overshadowed by two major events which followed quickly on its publication: the murder of Lord Mountbatten, and the visit to Ireland of Pope John Paul II. The former, occurring on 27 August 1979 and coinciding with an IRA ambush at Warrenpoint which cost the lives of eighteen British soldiers, the heaviest casualties on a single occasion since the Korean war, was a sharp reminder that the diminution of violence was reversible. Churchmen and church bodies expressed their sympathy and their indignation in predictable fashion, but the most direct relevance of that tragic day to the story of church relations in Ireland was that it finally dissuaded the Roman Catholic authorities from bringing the Pope to Northern Ireland.

The possibility of a papal visit to mark the centenary of the Marian shrine at Knock in County Mayo had been mentioned by Archbishop O'Fiaich before the election of John Paul II. In the summer of 1979 it was announced that the Pope would come at Michaelmas for two and a half days. The announcement provoked two controversies: should he visit Northern Ireland, and should representatives of the Protestant Churches meet him? Dr Paisley had recently topped the poll in the election for the European Parliament, Northern Ireland voting as one large constituency, but his first-preference votes numbered little more than one-eighth of the electorate. Claiming now to be the unquestioned spokesman of the Ulster Protestants, he took up the traditional cry of 'No Pope in Ulster'; but the Irish Council of Churches, followed by other bodies, hastened to assure Cardinal O'Fiaich that, provided the protocol for a visit to the United Kingdom was observed, the Pope would be welcome north of the border. (The importance of the proviso was that the Pope must not appear to be treating Ireland as one country, though it was, of course, ecclesiastically one.) In fact preparations to receive him at the Primatial See of Armagh were already being made when the assassination of Lord

Mountbatten and the eighteen soldiers, by emphasizing the security problems that would be posed, led to their abandonment. When it was certain that the Pope would not visit Northern Ireland, the Orange Order invoked its principle of civil and religious liberty to say that it would have raised no objection.

The Pope's general message to the Irish people and his contacts with the other Churches are discussed in the chapter on the ecumenical movement.[13] Here we must record what he said about the Irish political situation and the troubles in the North. This he did at Drogheda, a town chosen, with its history of persecution and martyrdom and as being in the Archdiocese of Armagh, as the point at which Catholics from Northern Ireland should assemble to meet him. Before 300,000 people, with prominent northern politicians in the front row and with a lesson read by John Hume, the Pope called for justice and peace. He expressed gratitude for invitations from other Churches to go north, and saw in them 'a truly fraternal and ecumenical act', and:

a testimony that the tragic events taking place in Northern Ireland do not have their source in belonging to different churches and confessions . . . On the contrary, Catholics and Protestants, as people who confess Christ, taking inspiration from their faith and the Gospel, are seeking to draw closer to one another in unity and peace . . . Christianity does not permit us to neglect and refuse to see unjust social or international situations. What Christianity does forbid is to seek solutions to those situations by the ways of hatred, by murdering of defenceless people . . . We must call by name those systems and ideologies that are responsible for this struggle. We must also reflect whether the ideology of subversion is for the true good of your people, for the true good of man. Is it possible to construct the good of individuals and peoples on hatred, on war? . . . The moral law, guardian of human rights, protector of the dignity of man, cannot be set aside by any person or group, or by the State itself, for any cause, not even for security or in the interests of law and order.

That last sentence roused the ire of Dr Paisley and his political party. It was the nearest the Pope got to a reference to the controversies surrounding police methods and the deadlock in the Maze prison. What he said about the state would have been universally applauded had he applied it to Russia or South Africa. To say that in applying it to Ireland he gave comfort to the Provisionals was to overlook the far stronger things that the Pope went on to say:

Peace cannot be established by violence, peace can never flourish in a climate of terror, intimidation and death . . . I pray with you that nobody may ever call murder by any other name than murder . . . let us remember that the word remains for ever: 'All who take the sword shall perish by the sword.'

The Pope then addressed directly the men and women engaged in violence:

I appeal to you in language of passionate pleading. On my knees I beg you to turn away from the paths of violence and to return to the ways of peace. You may claim to seek justice. I too believe in justice and seek justice. But violence only delays the day of justice.

And then to the political leaders he said:

Never think that you are betraying your own community by seeking to understand and respect and accept those of a different tradition. You will serve your own tradition best by working for reconciliation with others . . . You must show that there is a peaceful, political way to justice . . . Violence thrives best when there is a political vacuum and a refusal of political movement.

'I came to Drogheda to-day', the Pope concluded, 'as a pilgrim of peace . . . May no Irish Protestant think that the Pope is an enemy, a danger, or a threat. My desire is that instead Protestants would see in me a friend and a brother in Christ.'

What can be said, a year on, of the results of these moving appeals? It is believed that secret contacts were made with the Provisionals before the Pope spoke in the hope of eliciting a positive response. However that may be, none came. Interviewed in 1980, two Roman Catholic bishops, while regretting that the Pope's words had had no apparent effect on the leadership, claimed that many young people had probably been dissuaded from joining the movement, and that, to their certain knowledge, a number of men had withdrawn from the movement and been reconciled with the Church. The obvious dangers to such men preclude any attempt to verify or document this statement.

As for the appeal to Protestants, there is no doubt that in the immediate wake of the Pope's visit many were deeply impressed. Any lasting effect, however, is bound to depend on the extent to which some of the outstanding problems, especially those relating to mixed marriages, can be resolved. And there remains a considerable section of Protestant opinion to which soft words are simply another cunning device of the old enemy, who exercises naked power when he has it and subtle temptation when he has it not. Others draw a distinction between his attractive and friendly personality and the doctrinal claims he continues to make.

There remains the appeal to politicians. They had been complaining ever since the closing of the Convention at the political vacuum to which Mr Roy Mason condemned them by declining to try any more approaches to self-government, unless the local parties could first agree among themselves. But now there was a new government. Airey Neave, the prospective Conservative Secretary of State, had been murdered in London before the election by the Irish National Liberation Army. The new Secretary was Mr Humphrey Atkins, hitherto little known in Ulster. He took, in the autumn of 1979, a new initiative in inviting the political parties to confer with him on possible forms of devolved government. Here was the chance to put an end to the political vacuum, but the Official Unionist Party declined the invitation. Dr Paisley, however, attended for the Democratic Unionist Party, as did members of the Alliance Party and the SDLP. So tightly had the agenda been drawn to try to secure Unionist participation that the SDLP had to meet the Secretary of State in parallel talks outside the conference to express their full views to him. Eventually the government issued a Green Paper[14] proposing two alternative constitutional schemes, the one very similar to that tried in 1974, the other a slightly liberalized version of the Convention report of 1975. For a time these were the subject of desultory and unenthusiastic discussion, but by the end of the year they were a dead letter.

The Churches encouraged parties to participate in the conference and expressed hopes for its success. Little enthusiasm was apparent in church circles for either of the proposals that emerged, largely because it was believed that one would prove unacceptable to one side and the other to the other. There is little doubt that the majority of church members, concerned to keep violence to a minimum and to see a measure of fair play in social affairs, support for the time being the continuance of direct rule. As we write in 1980, however, the growing industrial depression and the deliberate cuts in the social services imposed by the present government are creating a general atmosphere of gloom and discontent which might well produce before long a reaction against government by Englishmen. When benevolent, it is tolerated; but if it begins to appear harsh, what then?

'Harsh' is the last word anyone would think of using to describe Dr George Simms, who early in 1980 retired from the Primacy of the Church of Ireland. Throughout the years of controversy and of physical conflict his had been an irenical presence. His first weeks as primate had been spent in the riot-torn streets of Belfast in 1969. His brotherly approach to the other Churches helped to calm the atmosphere and made a very positive contribution to the joint action of the four church leaders which developed so markedly, as we have seen, during the decade. Naturally the two archbishops of Armagh, being permanent in their appointments, had more capacity to make or break this relationship than the succession of annually appointed Moderators and Presidents who shared it with them. Some thought Dr Simms could have exercized a more positive leadership, but it was quite unjustifiable for someone to say that it was 'pathetic' that at such a crisis the Primate should go around lecturing on the Book of Kells. More and more it has become apparent that the maintenance of ordinary activities and interests is in itself a positive contribution to sanity and goodwill in a time of stress; the sheer continuance by the Churches of their 'ordinary work' amid considerable difficulties and dangers is something not to be overlooked in the story of Northern Ireland's ordeal. But in his steadfast refusal to countenance, not simply violence, but intolerance and harsh judgements, prejudice, and injustice, Dr Simms did indeed exercise a leadership all the more effective for its gentle manner and its avoidance of the trenchant, assertive, and all too often self-righteous utterances to which some Ulster clergy are still prone.

Dr Simms was succeeded at Armagh by Bishop John Armstrong, previously Bishop of Ossory and Cashel. It is too early to assess the impact he will have on the situation, but it is perhaps worthy of note that leaders of the Dublin government, Roman Catholic though they are, came north to his enthronement as they had to that of Dr O'Fiaich, and that the Taoiseach, Mr Charles Haughey, gave a reception for him in Dublin Castle, as his predecessor had done for the Cardinal. These gestures reflect a progress in relationships since the days when Primate D'Arcy could write his memoirs without mentioning a Roman Catholic. And yet one must sadly reflect that those who view such gestures as sinister have still a determining political strength in Northern Ireland.

As 1980 drew to a close, the republican protest at the Maze prison, which had by now been dragging on for four years, took on a new intensity, and anxiety was felt that it might incite a new outbreak of communal violence. During 1979 and 1980 the

Churches had at long last made some moves towards finding a solution for this problem. In February 1980 the Irish Council of Churches issued an interim report by its Advisory Forum on Human Rights, and this was followed later in the year by a more widely circulated final report.[15] This expressed very tersely the aim of the protest as outsiders saw it: 'A primary objective of the Provisional IRA, and of others who may engage in acts of violence for political objectives, is to justify or excuse such violence as legitimate acts of war, not criminal acts. The H-block protest, make propaganda out of the largely self-imposed conditions of the prisoners there, is part of this wider campaign.' The report went on to maintain that the government could not possibly concede a special status to these prisoners, both because the claim is ill-founded and because it would exacerbate 'strong feelings within the community about the horrific nature of the crimes committed by many of the men in the H-blocks'. The report did, however, recognize that the application over a long period of disciplinary rules designed for occasional use helped to create a degree of hardship not envisaged in the original framing of the rules, and concluded by recommending 'that an official study of prisons, the methods of prison discipline and prison rules for all sorts of prisoners should be undertaken as a matter of urgency'. During the summer an answer was received to an appeal made on behalf of the prisoners to the European Court of Human Rights at Strasbourg: this confirmed unequivocally that the prisoners had no right to political status, but it did suggest that a certain inflexibility on the part of the authorities had aggravated the effects of the protest.

Meanwhile a determined effort to solve the problem was made by Cardinal O'Fiaich and Bishop Edward Daly. Between March and September 1980 they made several visits to the Maze and Armagh prisons (in the latter a smaller number of women had by now embarked on a similar protest). They had five meetings with the Secretary of State, three other meetings with officials of the Northern Ireland Office, discussions with the prison Governors and with the Chairmen of the Boards of Visitors, and numerous meetings with parents and other relatives of prisoners on protest.[16] Men of goodwill can do no other than commend their strenuous efforts to find a way out of the impasse. Consistently with the Roman Catholic Church's condemnation of violence, the bishops made no plea for the restoration of special status for these prisoners, but did explore very thoroughly the possibility of changes in the general prison regime that might persuade the prisoners to give up their protest. So far from doing a 'deal'—that ugly word always used by the intransigent in Northern Ireland to smear every attempt at mediation—the prelates said clearly that they could not affirm that the prisoners would in fact respond to any particular steps that the authorities might take. They did, however, assert that: 'The overall conviction which has been borne in on us in the course of these meetings is that the H-block impasse could be solved in the context of a general prison reform in Northern Ireland regarding prison dress and prison work.'[17] The government did not entirely fail to respond to this appeal. After their first visit to him, the Secretary of State announced that the rules about letters and visits would be relaxed, and that the men might exercise in shorts and plimsolls, a costume not specifically prison garb. In August, after further visits from the Cardinal and the Bishop, it was announced that these prisoners would be eligible, like the rest, for compassionate parole in the event of the death or serious illness of a near relative. So far from these concessions resulting in any reduction of the protest, the prisoners made it known in October that a number would embark on a hunger-strike on 27 October. On the eve of this date, the government announced that all male prisoners in Northern Ireland would be allowed to wear civilian-type dress. It was at first thought that this meant their own clothes, but that was not the case. The concession was treated with contempt, and seven men began the hunger-strike. At the same time, a further 142 prisoners joined the 350 already on the 'dirty' protest.

Cardinal O'Fiaich and Bishop Daly expressed disappointment that the government had not found it possible to meet more of the recommendations they had made; but at street demonstrations in support of the hunger-strike the emphasis remained on political status; many people hitherto not unsympathetic towards what the prelates were seeking to achieve, found the response of the prisoners to any concessions disappointing, and were forced back to the view that only a formal restoration of special category status would end the protest. In standing firm against this, the government had the support of the overwhelming majority of the population. Any other position would legitimize murder as a form of political activity.

The Protestant Churches were in full agreement with this

position, and Archbishop Armstrong issued a long statement referring back to the report of the Advisory Forum and other documents. So did the Presbyterian General Board. The Methodist Council on Social Welfare put out a statement which included the words: 'The Council urges the Government not to allow the issue to drift and urges it to consider again what ways and means may be to hand of defusing this dangerous situation, short of granting the political status demanded'. There was immediate protest from some within the Methodist Church that this was to advocate giving in to the prisoners, and the President (the Revd. Sydney Callaghan) thought it wise to state 'that Methodists had always been actively involved in reform of the prison system, but it must be clearly understood that any such reforms must have application for the entire prison population'.

As Christmas approached, three women in Armagh gaol and a further twenty men at the Maze joined the hunger-strike. The condition of the original seven was now becoming critical. Street demonstrations in support of their claim were held in many parts of Ireland, and the fear grew that their deaths would be followed by calamitous violence.

Meanwhile a group of UDA men in prison started their own hunger-strike, demanding segregation from republican prisoners. After a week, the UDA leadership sought the advice of the Anglican Bishop of Down, Dr Robin Eames, and after their discussions the prisoners abandoned their action. The Secretary of State made repeated efforts to assure the republican prisoners that, if the protest ended, certain practical reforms, applicable to all prisoners, would quickly be made, but he remained adamant on the issue of any status different from that of other convicted criminals. On 18 December the original seven hunger-strikers gave up and were quickly followed by the others. Sinn Fein claimed the government had conceded the substance of their claims, but there was no grant of special status.

Intense relief was felt throughout Northern Ireland at this outcome, although loyalist leaders accused the government of a secret deal. Christmas passed quietly and statistics published at the end of the year showed casualties in 1980 were the lowest for ten years, being only one-third of the number caused by road accidents. Rumours circulated of an IRA cease-fire, and the end of the mass 'dirty protest' in the prison was confidently expected. By the last day of the year, however, neither of these hopes had been realized, and a wrangle was going on between the authorities and the prisoners about the conditions on which the hunger-strike had been abandoned.

POSTSCRIPT

Dramatic events followed in 1981, and agents of the Roman Catholic Church were actively engaged in trying to solve the resultant problem.

The 'dirty protest' ended but on 1 March, 1981 Bobby Sands, leader of the Maze Provisionals, claiming that the prisoners had been deceived, commenced a new fast. Others followed at regular intervals to ensure a 'succession' of men at the point of death. Cardinal O'Fiaich appealed for concessions regarding clothing and work. A country-wide 'anti H-block' campaign called for 'political status'. The government repeatedly indicated that reforms were possible but could not be introduced while the strike lasted. The sudden death of the sitting member caused a Parliamentary by-election in Fermanagh—South Tyrone. Sands was a candidate and was elected. Some days after the election, he died having rejected a number of appeals to call off his fast, including one involving a two-day visit from Father John Magee, the Pope's Irish private secretary. Nine more hunger strikers died during the summer. Each death was followed by a massive and widely publicized funeral and by outbreaks of rioting which, although sixty people were killed, progressively diminished in scale. A delegation from the Irish Justice and Peace Commission, led by Dr O'Mahony, Auxiliary Bishop of Dublin, came North to 'shuttle' between the government and the prisoners in an arduous but unsuccessful search for a solution. Eventually, when the prisoners stated that they sought no privileges that would not be accorded to all prisoners, the demand for 'political status' was played down. The families of dangerously ill or unconscious fasters began to call for medical attention for them. In early October the relatives of the remaining hunger-strikers announced they would follow the same course and the strike ended. Father Denis Paul played a large part in enabling the families to decide. The newly-appointed Secretary of State, Mr James Prior, announced changes in the regime and the 'blanket' protest ended as the prisoners began to receive their own clothing. In November, however, some prisoners were still losing remission through refusal to do prison work. Loyalists protested at the 'concessions' and also that some Catholic apologists had refused to brand the dead prisoners as having committed suicide.

9 Ecumenism 1969–80

In chapter 2 we described the hesitant, yet hopeful, beginnings of ecumenical encounter in Ireland. We must now consider how the movement faired under the stress of civil strife.

When the delegation went to see the late Cardinal Conway in connection with the New University, they found him careful and wary, though not suspicious.[1] Catholic–Protestant encounter of this kind was a new experience for him as well as for his visitors. But dramatic changes were on the way. The sixties had produced the *Declaration of Ecumenism* of Vatican II. Its reverberations were already being felt in Ireland. By 1969 Glenstal and Greenhills were already established features of the unofficial ecumenical scene. The School of Ecumenics was on the drawing-board. The New University approach on a united basis to Captain O'Neill, and the 1968 New Year call to prayer were history. The time was ripe for an articulation of Irish Catholic attitudes to ecumenism. Indeed, taking into account that the Vatican II *Declaration* was nearly six years old, it could be said that an Irish statement was long overdue. Few could have foreseen the community and political scene into which it would be launched.

As the storm clouds gathered in the autumn of 1968, the Churches were more ready than the political parties to stretch out hands of friendship. It was well that they were in the light of all that lay ahead.

Early on New Year's Day 1969, the People's Democracy started its march from Belfast to Derry. The last day of that eventful journey was marked by the bloody encounter at Burntollet. During the following week, a scheduled meeting of the ICC Executive Committee was due to be held in Aldersgate House, Belfast. The Primate, Moderator, and President were invited to attend. The combined groups took three decisions that afternoon. They wrote, as we have seen, to the Prime Minister asking for some form of judicial, or other, inquiry into the causes of the current unrest and the way it was being handled. They wrote to the daily papers and put their disapproval of

Burntollet on public record. They also wrote privately to Cardinal Conway suggesting the time was ripe for some form of continuing consultation regarding the developing unrest, with its implications and opportunities for the Churches. The Prime Minister's reply came within a day or two.[2] The letter was a support in his struggle with a reluctant Cabinet for the decision to set up the Cameron Commission. The Cardinal's answer took some days longer.[3] He was in England on a speaking engagement. He wrote saying that he had been deeply moved to hear, and read, the 'courageous' declaration of the Protestant leaders. He would be pleased to discuss the possibility of joint consultation.

The Cardinal's positive reaction was gratifying and a bit surprising to the ICC side. When they decided to write to him, they did not know that he and his colleagues of the Hierarchy were about to release a document that was destined to have a profound effect on Irish Catholic relationships with Protestantism. It was the *Directory on Ecumenism*, which was published within days of the Cardinal's reply.

The other Churches have long been accustomed to conducting their affairs, and holding their debates, with the eyes and ears of the media attentive to every word and move. Not so, then or now, the Hierarchy. In the circumstances of the time, there was no way the ICC could have known when or how far the Hierarchy was likely to respond to Protestant overtures. In the after-light, sufficient land-marks are now visible to distinguish the route Irish Roman Catholics have taken on their ecumenical pilgrimage.

The new *Directory* had, of course, been prepared before the events of early January, and consequently there are no topical references such as were to appear in its 1976 successor. Professor Michael Ledwith of Maynooth is secretary of the Commission on Ecumenism. Commenting on the *Directory*, he has said 'It was basically geared only to presenting those parts of the Roman Directory which had appeared up to date.'[4] It was a short document of twenty-four paragraphs. Four of them dealt with the conditions in which the Roman Catholic Church could recognize the 'validity of Baptism conferred in Christian communions separated from the Apostolic See'. There were ten paragraphs setting out conditions in which Catholics were, or were not, allowed to share in prayer and worship with separated brethren. Generally this was encouraged. A short section dealt with sharing by Catholics in the liturgy of the Eastern Orthodox Churches.

From our immediate point of view, the 1969 *Directory* is significant for two reasons. The first is its only Irish reference: 'There is in Ireland a new endeavour among Christians of different denominations to live in harmony and peace. It is to be devoutly hoped that this movement will grow and become even more profoundly permeated by the love and truth of Christ.' The bishops acclaimed the influence of Glenstal and Greenhills, and the participation of Irish Catholics in the movement they represented. The other matter of significance is the explicit statement of their understanding of what ecumenism meant to them and to the Catholic Church. 'It is the will of God that all Christians should come together in one flock and that the Holy Spirit has deepened the desire for unity in the hearts of all followers of Christ.' This reference to the work of the Holy Spirit was taken up again in the fifth paragraph, which quoted the Vatican declaration, 'the ecumenical movement must be promoted without obstructing the ways of Divine Providence and without prejudging the future inspiration of the Holy Spirit'. Lest, however, there should be any doubt about the roads along which the Spirit might lead the faithful, they saw fit to add to the same paragraph a salutory warning: 'Catholics are reminded that they must remain fully loyal to the truth handed down by the Apostles and professed throughout the centuries by the Catholic Church, for it is through Christ's Catholic Church alone, which is the all-embracing means of salvation, that the fullness of the means of salvation can be obtained.'

To the discerning, the goal of Catholic ecumenism was clear. Many non-Catholics, however, who in the coming decade were to welcome increasing ecumenical involvement, did not fully appreciate the different shades of meaning attributed by Catholics and Protestants respectively to the word 'ecumenism'. 'ecumenism'.

Burntollet, however, and its consequences, gave a new urgency to the situation. The new Irish *Directory* had made quick action possible. Thus the semi-official Ad Hoc Committee emerged in the spring of 1969.[5] It was composed of six clerics, two nominated by the Cardinal, one each by the Moderator, President, and Primate, and one by the Executive of the ICC. Its terms of reference were to study the developing situation and its underlying causes. It was, further, to advise the Church leaders whether or not they should meet together specially and issue joint statements during any crisis. Its members were, on the Catholic side, the Revd. Fathers Patrick Walsh, then Chaplain at Queen's University and now President of St. Malachy's College, and Denis Faul of Dungannon, and, on the ICC side, the Revds. Harold Allen, Canon Eric Elliott, Eric Gallagher, and John Radcliffe. The committee had a short, eventful, and occasionally tempestuous history. It was in almost continuous session during the traumatic weeks of August 1969. It discussed many issues, including what was then unheard of, the setting-up of a police authority. It voiced its concern to Brian Faulkner about the treatment of arrested suspects. However, it soon became redundant: its advice and the developing catastrophe persuaded the four church leaders to engage in the joint meetings which, in spite of problems in 1979, were to become regular features of their relationships. During those nine years the ecclesiastical scene at that level was transformed. Joint statements, meetings, and television appearances became commonplace.

Meanwhile the tripartite discussions had taken the place of the original separate sets of negotiations. Their progress, or lack of it, attracted little secular attention, and only the naturally suspicious inside the Churches involved showed much interest. The negotiators issued a 'Declaration of Intent' and persuaded their respective church courts to endorse what they had done.

The high point was reached in 1973, when the tripartite negotiating committee produced a report entitled *Towards a United Church.*[6] It contained agreed statements on the Divine Revelation and the Scriptures, the Church, the Sacraments, the Creeds, and later Historical Statements of Belief. On the thorny issue of these historical statements, meaning, in particular, the Thirty-Nine Articles and the Westminster Confession, the report limited itself to a description of their status in the respective Churches and a discussion of the implications of subscription. Whether they were to be retained in a united church, or by what they were to be replaced, was left vague. On the other hand, the chapter on the ministry was remarkably specific: 'The United Church will begin with an ordained Ministry of Bishops and Presbyters . . . It will also begin with a commissioned ministry associated with the ordained ministers in spiritual oversight and pastoral care, embodying, for instance, Deacons, Ruling Elders, Class Leaders, Local Preachers and Lay Readers.' There followed descriptions of the functions of these officers, continuing, in large part, their role in the denominations that already had them, and some proposals for the territorial organization of the united church.

The report was received, with varying degrees of approval, by the governing bodies of the three Churches at their summer meetings in 1973, and was sent down by all of them for consideration in their local church courts. The outcome was disappointing. While the specific points of objection raised were predictable, and could probably have been overcome if the will had been present, the local debates revealed either a profound apathy or a deep-seated suspicion about the whole matter. The conversations have continued, but the heart has gone out of them. Some measures of practical co-operation have been suggested, and even achieved. In 1978 the Joint Committee asked the three governing bodies for instructions. Was it to be organic union, federation, or mutual recognition of ministries? The Church of Ireland voted overwhelmingly for organic union and ignored the alternatives. The Presbyterian and Methodist bodies by their votes placed these options in reverse order of preference, putting mutual recognition in the forefront. The supporters of organic union were in a minority in the Presbyterian Assembly. The goal of union seems far off. The Methodist Conference of 1980 hesitated before reappointing its negotiating team, and only did so on condition that the team should alert the other negotiators to Methodist disenchantment at the lack of progress. Yet slow progress in this respect can hardly be said to be peculiar to Ireland; and the days when the Protestant Churches bitterly competed with each other, for example, over the appointment of teachers to schools, have given way to a measure of common endeavour, sustained at the centre, if somewhat spasmodic in the parishes.

But to go back to Roman Catholic–Protestant relationships: the setting-up of the 'Joint Group' in 1970 was the first action taken officially by the member Churches of the ICC and the Hierarchy. It was a natural and quick development from the informal Ad Hoc Committee and the church leaders' meetings, which were becoming an accepted part of the way of life. The group consisted of Roman Catholic members both lay and clerical, led by Canon Robert Murphy, and an equal number of representatives of the member Churches of the ICC. Its terms of reference were to advise the Hierarchy, the member Churches, and the Council with regard to the 'role of the Churches in Irish society with special reference to such matters as alcoholism, drug abuse, unemployment, housing, world poverty etc.' The inclusion of the 'etc.' was to be important. The group has operated by setting up working parties to consider and report on given issues. To date several reports have been published. The first, on drug abuse attracted widespread notice. Others have followed on teenage drinking, housing in Northern Ireland, under-development in rural Ireland, pollution of the environment,[7] and violence in Ireland.[8] At the time of writing, others are awaited on housing in the Republic, development in the west of Northern Ireland, and retirement problems. Of them all, the report on violence has attracted most attention. It has appeared in two Irish editions and one German. The decision to set up the working party was reached only after special authority was given by the Hierarchy and for Roman Catholics to participate in it. The 'etc.' had been justified.

The working party had as joint chairmen Bishop Cahal Daly of Ardagh and Clonmacnois, and the Revd. Eric Gallagher. Dr Stanley Worrall was responsible for most of the final text. This was unanimously agreed on after fourteen difficult plenary sessions and innumerable smaller groups and subcommittees. Those who reached this unanimity were not only Catholic and Protestant but also clerical and lay, northern and southern, pacifist and non-pacifist. The leading Irish, and some British, dailies gave generous coverage to it on publication, and its findings were widely acclaimed. Regrettably the response to it from the Churches has been less than enthusiastic. Indeed, one could be forgiven for concluding that the secular world took more notice of it than did the Churches for whom it was commissioned.

New possibilities opened up in youth work, which have not fulfilled early expectations. Joint church adventure youth camps were held in 1970 and 1971 for boys from 'ghetto' areas on each side of the Belfast Peace Line. In 1971 an ecumenical all-night vigil, led by Michel Quoist, was held in Stranmillis College, Belfast. By this time, mutual trust and respect had developed between the Protestant Youth Officers on the one hand (the Revds. Gordon Gray, Presbyterian, Cecil Hyland, Church of Ireland, John Knox, Methodist, and Mr Albert Wall, Salvationist), and on the other the Revd. Father Colin Campbell, who had youth responsibilities in the Diocese of Down and Connor. The years 1971–3 were marked by vigils and joint conferences for young people, some sharing in the training of youth workers, considerable consultation about the role of the Churches in the youth service, and eventually the publication of a joint church youth-leaders' manual *Together*

with Youth. The year 1973 was the high-point of their relationships. Changes in personnel took place, and the tempo of
co-operation slowed down. An ecumenical youth workers'
consultation was held at Ennis, County Clare, in 1974. The
Catholic youth officers from Dublin and Wexford in the South
were reported to be more open than their Northern colleagues,
and a new caution was noticed among the Protestant personnel.
Nothing positive emerged from the consultation, and, with
little or no progress since then, one can only report a sad
conclusion to what could so easily have been an exciting
development.[9]

One very successful venture, however, has been the working
of the Inter-Church Emergency Fund for Ireland. It was set up
in response to generous financial aid for reconciliation coming
mostly through the Conference of European Churches (whose
interest has sprung from the deep personal concern of its
Secretary General, Dr Glen Garfield Williams) and the
European Catholic Episcopal Conference. This fund has had a
twofold effect. It has enabled over £150,000 to be funded to at
least 165 youth clubs and organizations, community
associations, and reconciling agencies. The sum includes major
grants made to the Corrymeela and Glencree Communities and
the Irish School of Ecumenics. It has, with at least equal
significance, facilitated developing mutual trust among the
members of its committee drawn in equal numbers from each
side.[10]

It has been convenient to discuss the work of the Joint Group
and other developments before reporting on 'Ballymascanlon'.
'Ballymascanlon' is shorthand for what the daily papers called
'summit conferences' held at Ballymascanlon Hotel near
Dundalk. John Cooney, at that time religious affairs corres-
pondent of the *Irish Times*, in an article in the September 1973
issue of *Doctrine and Life*, a publication of the Dominican
Order, described the origin of the conference vividly. He wrote:
'The road to Dundalk began in effect in the spring of 1972 at the
biannual meeting of the Irish Council of Churches. It was
reported at this meeting that the organizing secretary of the
Council, the Revd. Norman W. Taggart, had written to and
subsequently met Cardinal Conway, to discuss the possibility of
setting up a working party which would discuss joint pastoral
problems, including mixed marriages and violence in Ireland.'
It was also reported that Cardinal Conway had said that he
would consult with his fellow bishops about such a proposal.

The Council was therefore awaiting a reply.

Cooney was not the only one to be surprised at the reply and the manner of its publication. In the midsummer of 1972 the Hierarchy 'went public' over their response. 'Making', to use Cardinal Conway's phrase, 'the ICC a "post-box",' they issued an invitation to the member Churches to take part in a Conference at which 'the whole field of ecumenism in Ireland would be surveyed'. Indeed, through a press conference, the public knew about the invitation before the letter containing it had been received by the ICC.

The timing of the invitation very quickly exposed a problem inherent in different forms of church government. It was a problem that was to reappear in connection with the papal visit to Ireland in 1979. There was no difficulty for the Church of Ireland in registering an immediate acceptance. The Presbyterians and Methodists were impeded by the need for a decision of such significance to be made by their supreme courts. In the event the General Assembly of 1973 had a 'cliff-hanger' debate which turned a virtual refusal into a qualified acceptance by means of an amendment won by 288 votes to 217. The eventual resolution stated that the Assembly would not agree to a discussion of the 'whole field' of ecumenism, but would be willing 'to discuss matters of Church and community relationships especially the problem of mixed marriages and the proclamation of the gospel in Ireland but excluding the question of Church union'. The Methodists and other member Churches also accepted the invitation, though in some cases with no great enthusiasm.

Thus the scene was set for the first Ballymascanlon meeting on 26 September 1973. The *Irish Times* had earlier welcomed the Hierarchy's move: 'The occasion should give the adherents of the ecumenical movement in Ireland an opportunity to put an end to a decade of timidity—a timidity which the opponents of ecumenism have fastened on as a sign of weakness and lack of conviction. If the situation in the North does not now provide the necessary degree of conviction and sense of urgency, nothing else will.' Against a background of intense media interest and the inevitable Paisley protest, the eighty-three delegates, lay and clerical, met under the co-chairmanship of the Cardinal and Archbishop Simms (in his capacity as Chairman of the ICC). Papers were read by Archbishop Dermot Ryan of Dublin on 'Church–Scripture–Authority', with a response by the Very Revd. T. N. D. C. Salmon (Church of Ireland); on

'Social and Community Problems' by the Revd. Eric Gallagher (Methodist), with a response by Bishop Eamonn Casey, then of Kerry; on 'Baptism–Eucharist–Marriage' by the Revd. Professor J. M. Barkley (Presbyterian), with a response by Bishop W. J. Philbin of Down and Connor; and on 'Christianity and Secularism' by Bishop Cahal Daly of Ardagh and Clonmacnois, with a response by Bishop H. R. McAdoo, then of Ossory (Church of Ireland). Bishop Cahal Daly also contributed a paper on the position of the Irish Episcopal Conference with regard to inter-church marriages. All these papers were subsequently published in *The Furrow*.[11]

The conference set up a number of working parties to pursue the issues raised in the papers. Reports from these groups were discussed at two further all-day plenary sessions in 1974 and 1975. The work of the three conferences and the working parties has been described in *Ballymascanlon*, compiled by Bishop Cahal Daly and Stanley Worrall.[12] Most attention has been given to the reports coming from the group dealing with mixed marriages, an issue which in the succeeding years became one of increasing controversy. As a result of the plenary discussion on the mixed marriage issue, the Churches appointed a standing committee to monitor and report on cases where violation or harsh application of the regulations was alleged.

Later reactions of the Churches which accepted the Hierarchy's original invitation have been mixed. The continuing unrest in the North, the ongoing debate about ecumenism, with the WCC at the centre of it, made many Protestants hesitant. The reluctance of the Hierarchy to enter into debate on certain issues, and especially those associated with mixed marriages and aspects of family planning, contributed to a mood of, at best, qualified approval. Most criticism came from the Church of Ireland. This was surprising enough, and yet understandable in view of its long-standing sense of grievance over mixed marriages.[13] Over and over again Church of Ireland bishops at diocesan synods and elsewhere were publicizing their criticisms and strongly felt objections regarding the Hierarchy's refusal to move on the issue. It was no surprise that, at the spring meeting of the ICC in 1976, Mr Barry Deane, a well-known and highly articulate Church of Ireland layman, spoke of 'soft words at Ballymascanlon and hard lines at the grass roots'. He complained that a document presented in his home diocese by the Catholic authorities to young people contemplating a mixed marriage was a 'use and abuse of authority'.[14] Incidentally at the same meeting the Presbyterian Revd. (later Principal) J. M. Barkley claimed: 'In the ecumenical movement the one essential thing is that every question is open for discussion and no Church nor Council of Churches has the right to veto a topic or a problem.'[15] Later the same month the Church of Ireland Standing Committee, while agreeing to the continuation of the Ballymascanlon meetings, affirmed that there was 'a widespread consensus of opinion coupled with genuine concern that the Ballymascanlon meetings were seen as irrelevant by many clergy and many laity, and perhaps even dangerous, as leading to suspicion and misunderstanding in the views of some'. The committee demanded that participants should be committed to 'discussing all issues, no matter how sensitive and that there should be no papering over the cracks'.

The Church of Ireland voiced its concern again at the beginning of 1977. On 2 February the influential Role of the Church Committee most unusually went public. In the course of a long statement it said:

The Churches must engage in an open, honest and courageous examination of issues such as Church/State relations, law and morality, mixed marriages, experience in integrated education, freedom of conscience and basic human rights. We are bound to say that the unreality of inter-Church dialogue hitherto e.g. the Ballymascanlon meetings, as illustrated by an apparent inability to come to grips with these moral, social and practical issues which affect the lives of ordinary people and contribute to the maintenance of divisions based on suspicion and fear. . .

Clearly as far as the Church of Ireland was concerned there was a growing disenchantment with Ballymascanlon.

The Hierarchy issued in 1976 a *Directory on Ecumenism in Ireland*, which superseded the *Directory* of 1969.[16] Naturally they took into account the ecclesiastical developments, inside and outside Ireland, since their previous document. The issues already raised at Ballymascanlon could not be ignored. Neither could the thoughts and interests reflected in the Catholic journals. The *Irish Theological Quarterly* had carried major articles during the preceding five years on Anglican teaching on authority, divorce and remarriage in early Christendom, the New Testament and divorce, and the Church as an ecumenical problem. *The Furrow* had published a number of articles dealing with the current religio-political questions, including one in 1973 entitled 'The Abortion Dossier'. *Doctrine and Life* in November 1973 had a most interesting article on 'The Protestant and the Priest' from the pen of Samuel Smyth, a well-known loyalist later to be assassinated. In August 1975 the same journal dealt at length with 'Ecumenical Collaboration at the Regional, National and Local Levels'. Clearly the stage was more than ready for the new *Directory*. Taking into account all that had happened since 1969, the length and content of the new document came as no surprise. It had seventy-six paragraphs, with a three-page appendix on the Ballymascanlon meetings. The background against which the bishops had been thinking was clear. Again there was the emphasis on God's will that 'all Christians should come together in one flock' and the sincere hope expressed that certain forms of ecumenical activity would flourish and grow. The emphasis on the work of the Holy Spirit and the unique nature of the Catholic Church were repeated. Recognition was given to the fact that other Christian Churches and communities enjoy a significance and a value in the mystery of salvation being endowed with many elements of sanctification and truth. Paragraph eleven makes clear the conditions on which Catholics can participate in ecumenism. It also reveals the Hierarchy's fears about current issues.

It would not be a correct understanding of the principles of ecumenism if Catholics, with the aim of drawing closer to other Christians, were to neglect any part of the truth and integral tradition of Catholic life and worship . . . It would be wrong to imagine that Catholics are acting in the true spirit of ecumenism if they minimize the importance of the Sacrifice of the Mass, or if they neglect such precious Catholic traditions as adoration of Christ in the Eucharist, devotion to our Blessed Lady and the Saints, reverence and loyalty towards the Vicar of Christ on Earth, prayer for the faithful departed, esteem for the religious life and priestly celibacy. Neither should they let themselves be persuaded to underestimate the beneficial effects on social and community life of the Catholic witness to certain fundamental and Christian values e.g. the sacredness of unborn life, the indissolubility of marriage, the essential unity of the interpersonal and procreative ends of married love. To seek to promote the unity of Christians by attempts to weaken this Catholic witness, so far from acclerating the progress of ecumenism, would place grave obstacles in its path.

That paragraph encapsulates the Irish ecumenical dilemma of negotiating with regard to the apparently non-negotiable.

The second part of the 1976 *Directory* elaborated a diocesan structure for promoting ecumenical activity. It was followed by a section recognizing Church of Ireland, Presbyterian, Methodist, and certain other forms of baptism and shared worship. Then came the section on education (treated in chapter 10), and finally one on the pastoral care of mixed marriages. The latter called for charity and clarity. It set out the current attitude and spelled out the dangers. Where 'one party cannot in conscience respect the conscientious obligations of the other party, efforts should be made to convince the parties that the proposed marriage should not take place'. Paragraph 64, if allowing for some flexibility, sets out clearly what was expected:

In Ireland the declaration by the Catholic, normally in writing, should take this or similar form: I declare that I shall remain steadfast in the Catholic faith and that I shall guard against all dangers of falling away from it. Also I sincerely promise to do all in my power to ensure that all children born of the marriage will be baptized in the Catholic Church and carefully brought up in the knowledge and practice of the Catholic religion. The declaration should be explained to the other party by the priest, or by the Catholic party.

Normally the canonical form was to be used in celebrating mixed marriages, but in exceptional cases this could be dispensed with. 'In this case the marriage is valid in the eyes of the Catholic Church.' Significantly the *Directory* quoted from 'Matrimonia Mixta', an encyclical of Paul VI, 3 March 1970. In the interests of the pastoral care of mixed marriages it called for 'relationships of sincere openness and enlightened confidence with ministers of other religious communities.'

Perhaps the most pointed comment on the new *Directory* was from a Catholic pen—not surprisingly that of Father Michael Hurley, S.J. By then Director of the School of Ecumenics, he wrote from his 'marginal position', in the August issue of *The Furrow*: 'many will be disappointed that the 1976 *Directory on Ecumenism* opens up so few new horizons and new possibilities for the ecumenical apostolate . . . The sad fact is that the great majority have not yet become concerned for the unity and joint mission of the Churches so that the world in Ireland can believe.' He spoke nothing but the truth.

Father Hurley had by 1970 become sufficiently well known on the Irish ecclesiastical scene as to be able, almost alone, to launch the Irish School of Ecumenics. The school, with patrons drawn from the mainstream bodies, had to struggle hard for survival in its early days against what at times could only be termed, at the most charitable, official apathy, and, from the traditionalists on each side of the divide, extreme hostility. Its achievements so far may be short of its foundation aims. But the story is far from being one of failure. At the end of its first decade, before handing over the leadership to Dr Robin Boyd, his Presbyterian successor, Father Hurley said:

I have to admit that the country has not yet made the kind of ecumenical progress one would like to have seen. On the other hand, the school itself has, I think, made quite remarkable progress in building itself up for the task of ecumenical education. It has achieved academic status by its affiliation with the University of Hull and acquired a certain stature by its International Consultations.[17]

Those consultations have included one on mixed marriages and one on human rights. Each was of significance in itself, and both had implications for the Irish Churches.

Cardinal Conway died on 17 April 1977.[18] His untimely death created a vacuum in inter-church relationships, especially when difficulties regarding mixed marriages were becoming increasingly acute. Dr Dermot Ryan, Archbishop of Dublin, became co-chairman of the Ballymascanlon Steering Committee. To the Protestant members, he seemed not so fully versed as the late Cardinal had been in northern problems and thought-patterns.

Naturally speculation regarding a successor was rife. The appointment of Monsignor Tomàs O'Fiaich of Maynooth surprised many but arrangements for his episcopal ordination on 2 October 1977, and preoccupation with the deaths of two popes and the election of their successors, postponed the date of the next Ballymascanlon. The visit to Ireland of Pope John Paul II in September 1979 prolonged the vacuum.

The appointment of Archbishop O'Fiaich and his elevation to the Curia brought a new dimension to ecumenical encounter. He indicated at the time of his election that he favoured the eventual reunification, by peaceful means, of North and South in a Republic. At the same time, he expressed a wish to meet as many Northern Protestants as possible. His appointment was viewed with suspicion, if not alarm, by many Protestants. Subsequently *Irish Press* and Radio Telefis Eireann interviews[19] increased suspicion of one who seemed, and still seems, genuinely concerned to cultivate good relationships with his Protestant fellow-countrymen. Ecumenical discussion and co-operation take on a new meaning when conducted by people who may disagree profoundly on political issues. And that is no bad thing.

The deaths of two Popes and the election of their successors had taken attention away from Ballymascanlon. As far as the Presbyterians were concerned, there was another reason for it receiving less attention. For them the seventies were the years of the great debate. Shoutings without and fears within kept alive the embers of suspicion regarding the World Council of Churches. The 1969 Assembly had accepted without division Visser t'Hooft's dictum that a 'Christianity which would use the vertical dimension as a means of escape from its responsibilities for and in the common life of men is a denial of the Incarnation of God's love for the world in Christ'. By 1971 the mood had changed. An initiative from Brookside Kirk Session, in Ahoghill, County Antrim (incidentally the home village of Captain Terence O'Neill until his departure for England) had led to an instruction to the Inter-Church Relations Board to reconsider the Church's membership of the WCC. By 1972 the supporters and opponents of the Council were locked in conflict. The following year a twenty-page report on the WCC declared that a 'vote to discontinue membership was as divisive as one to remain in the Council'. The truth of that statement could be seen in the vote—219 for continued membership; 168 against. This time forty-three members wished to have their opposition recorded. In 1973 the hope was expressed that they would learn to live with this division of opinion. But grants from the Special Fund of the WCC's Programme to Combat Racism were causing misgivings in many countries. Naturally the misgiving was even greater in a country subjected to terrorism by the Provisional IRA. This greatly strengthened an opposition already growing on theological grounds. That opposition refused to be silenced. In spite of attempts by the Inter-Church Relations Board to describe and explain the varied work of the Council, in 1975 it was instructed to carry out another assignment—this time to prepare a major report—a critical evaluation of the grounds put forward for withdrawal. They reported in 1976 that 'membership is important for our Church. We can more easily discover the will of God for us if we remain close to other Churches.' A packed house decided by 481 to 381 to continue membership, and this time there were sixty-four recorded dissentients. It was clear that the fight was on, not merely about the WCC and the controversial PCR grants. It was the battle for or against ecumenism, and possibly more. In 1977 an *ad hoc* committee was appointed to monitor and study the work of the WCC. The Assembly of 1978 was peaceful. It passed, at the instance of the Inter-Church Relations and Evangelism Boards, an agreed resolution which encouraged 'ministers, elders and church members, as part of their witness to the Reformed faith, to be more outgoing in their association with the clergy and members of the Roman Catholic Church and encourage them where possible to study the Scripture together'. Those who thought the corner had been turned were in for a rude awakening. In the early autumn the announcement of further PCR grants to the Zimbabwe Patriotic Front synchronized with the murder of missionaries in Rhodesia, some of them from Northern Ireland, and other acts of violence. The Presbyterians were enraged to a degree that necessitated the calling of a special meeting of the General Assembly. Procedurally withdrawal required a duly submitted notice of motion, from one Assembly to the next. Temporary suspension pending eventual determination of the issue was the only possibility open to the vocal and still-growing body of opposition. They opted for suspension, by 561 votes to 393, pending procedural developments at the 1979 Assembly. The intervening months were ones of frenzied activity. The General Secretary and Clerk of the Assembly, Dr A. J. Weir, reported on a visit he had made with Eric Gallagher to Toronto to discuss the issue with the Chairman of the PCR, Archbishop Scott. There was a long report on a visit to London by an officially appointed delegation which met representatives of the WCC. There was another report on a meeting held in Dublin with Dr Philip Potter, General Secretary of the WCC. It was all to no avail. The Assembly passed the studied resolutions of the Inter-Church Relations Board welcoming increased sensitivity on the part of the WCC and regretting its failure to carry out a new examination of the nature and application of the governing criteria. But that action was not enough to deflect the storm. Several memorials were presented from Presbyteries. One coming from the Presbytery of Omagh was chosen for debate. It read:

That in spite of representation made by our Church, the World Council of Churches has continued its policy of making grants to terrorist organizations. That the theology behind WCC policies appears to be completely unchanged. The Memorialists therefore pray your Reverend Court (a) to accept notice of motion to the General Assembly of 1980 that the General Assembly rescind its former decisions in regard to our Church's membership of the WCC and terminate that membership (b) to renew suspension of our Church's membership of the WCC until the aforementioned General Assembly of June 1980.

An amendment was offered by the Revd. Donald Gillies and former Moderator, Dr James Haire. It was designed to accept the notice of motion but to reject the proposed suspension. Based on the Westminster Confession statement, it argued that all who profess to be united to Christ 'are bound to maintain a communion which, as God offers opportunity, is to be extended unto all those who, in every place, call upon the Name of the Lord Jesus'. Even the Westminster Confession was not good enough. The amendment was lost and the memorial was put to the vote. The result was a victory for the Omagh resolution— 421 for, and 248 against. The Moderator, Dr William Craig, who had been all along in the forefront of the battle against the WCC and who later in the year was to decline an invitation to meet the Pope, declared, as he was bound to do, the resolution passed.

The following week the Methodist Conference faced the same issue, but came to a different decision. The vote to with-draw was surprisingly small. By the end of 1979 it was evident that Methodist opposition was far from at an end, and equally clear, as the Conference had been warned during the debate, that what was at stake was something far more than any alleged acquiescence by the Irish Churches in the PCR grants. The issue was clearly 'the whole field of ecumenism', and that included any kind of relationship with Rome. A pressure group, largely but not altogether based on the Portadown area, was formed. It declared its concern to maintain traditional Methodist emphases, but its main aim was immediately clear. The real complaint was 'false ecumenical trends', a euphemism for WCC membership. It attempted to raise the issue at the Conference of 1980, without success because of procedural regulations. The Conference, in spite of what had happened the previous week in the General Assembly, took no action. But the problem remains.

Pope John Paul II visited Ireland at the end of September 1979. Cardinal O'Fiaich was anxious for an ecumenical dimension to the visit. But, as with the original invitation which led to the first Ballymascanlon conference, the circumstances surrounding the date of the visit made difficulties for the Presbyterians, and, to a lesser degree, the Methodists. The announcement of the impending visit and invitations to Protestant representatives to meet the Pope came after the summer meetings of the church courts. The Moderator of the General Assembly, Dr Craig, had earlier made known his unwillingness to meet Cardinal O'Fiaich. It was out of the question for him to meet the Pope. Eventually a discreetly chosen delegation led by the Clerk of Assembly, the Very Revd. Dr Jack Weir, met Pope John Paul II with other Protestant representatives in Drumcondra on the outskirts of Dublin. This action, coupled with the undoubted Marian overtones of the visit, led to renewed controversy in the Presbyterian Church which continued throughout the church year. An attempt to censure the Methodist President and Secretary, the Revd. Vincent Parkin and the Revd. Charles Eyre, and their colleagues, who had met the Pope, was successfully resisted in the Church's General Committee in October. Each of the delegations, and especially the Presbyterians, had been hopeful that they might symbolically open a dialogue with the Pope, by handing to him previously printed statements of their Church's ecumenical stance, with the spoken request that he should at some time make himself aware of the contents and that he should arrange for a reply from the Vatican to the points made in the statements. Last-minute arrangements cut across this expectation. Each of the delegations was informed that the crowded timetable would not permit of this. The various documents were now to be sent to the Papal Nuncio for onward transmission to the Pope at the Vatican. The meeting with His Holiness was to be very short and completely informal. The arrangement was understandable. The Presbyterians, although their documentation included a personal letter to the Pope setting out their desire for dialogue, were left open to further criticism from inside their own Church that they had not only undermined the Moderator but also failed to open a dialogue.

The visit was of course a great Catholic occasion. It could not have been otherwise. In a few crowded days, the Pope was greeted by Irish Catholics in overwhelming numbers. Few who saw or met him could have doubted the warm integrity and Christian love of this remarkable man. He spoke, as he was bound to do, as Pontiff and Chief Pastor to the members of his Irish flock. Indubitably he commended his faith and his Church to the hundreds and hundreds of thousands who journeyed by day and night to see him. But his visit had its significance for all the Churches and for many people other than Catholics. His warmth and compassion obscured for a time the inflexibility of the Catholicism he proclaimed. From the moment of his touch-down at Dublin Airport, when he spoke as Bishop of Rome, until the lift-off from Shannon with his injunction to the Irish people to be faithful to their Church, he made no apology for having offered the Roman Catholic faith in all its fullness.[20] And yet, with equal conviction, he was able to address his 'dear brothers in Christ' at the ecumenical meeting and say to them 'Let no one ever doubt the commitment of the Catholic Church and the Apostolic See of Rome to the pursuit of the unity of Christians. . . . I renew that commitment and that pledge to-day in Ireland where reconciliation between Christians takes on a special urgency, but where it has special resources in the tradition of Christian faith and fidelity to religion which marks the Catholic and Protestant communities.'[21]

In retrospect, an opportunity should clearly have been given for a longer and more relaxed meeting. A rushed informal encounter at the end of a long and tiring day is neither dialogue nor adequate preparation for it. The potential significance of this historic meeting was not fully grasped by those who arranged it. In any case, it was, though probably not on purpose, a unilateral arrangement, and unilateral arrangements are not calculated to make the most of ecumenical occasions, even of a papal visit.

The early months of 1980 produced a mood of uncertainty among the Protestant Churches regarding the future of ecumenical dialogue. In succession to Dr William Craig, whose refusal to meet Cardinal O'Fiaich, and later the Pope, had attracted a great deal of media interest, the Presbyterians nominated Dr Ronald Craig, a minister known to favour such contacts. The Clerk of the General Assembly, Dr Weir, had received a personally signed message from the Pope, indicating that the Vatican was giving attention to the Presbyterian document submitted through the Nuncio during the papal visit. At long last another Ballymascanlon had been arranged. The Steering Committee met in Dundalk in January, and arranged the details for the meeting in March.[22] There was a perceptible feeling of goodwill and gratitude at the prospect of renewed contacts. The ICC members were, however, unaware that their colleagues on the Mixed Marriages Committee were on the point of rocking the boat. On 17 January they issued a public statement revealing their frustration at their Committee's lack of progress and at the apparent or alleged difficulty the Catholic members experienced in agreeing to a date for a meeting. The release of the statement provoked considerable public interest and discussion. But it was quickly followed by an announcement that the Hierarchy were preparing a directory on mixed marriages and that the Cardinal would welcome evidence or communications from the Protestant Churches on the subject.

Against that background, a Ballymascanlon meeting took place on 6 March. In spite of all the warnings of doom, the meeting was well attended and harmonious. The format was changed, and the morning session spent almost completely in group discussion of the issues raised at previous conferences. By this arrangement it was possible for every single delegate at some time during the morning to participate actively in the discussion. In the afternoon a plenary session received two papers outlining the progress over the decade of peace groups, and other efforts, North and South, at co-operation. Reports from the morning discussion groups were approved and remitted to the Steering Committee for action. The day had brought new hope.

The Steering Committee met again in May to consider the recommendations of the conference. It authorized the formation of country-wide groups to study the fourth Gospel, making use of an outline study already prepared, and the creation of groups to: 1. recommend concerning the best way to encourage Irish Christians in the understanding 'of one another's faith'; 2. examine the implications of the unity 'that is ours already through baptism' with special reference to the consequences within the context of inter-church families; 3. the preparation of a study guide to draw out the implications of the Eucharist for the pastoral care and instruction of church members. (The Hierarchy and the ICC were to appoint representatives in each case.) It considered the time ripe for an examination in depth of the overall philosophy of crime and punishment, North and South, and consideration of the establishment of a joint pastoral ministry of the Church to help prisoners and their families—the Joint Group to be asked to 'make an initial response as to the steps to be taken in such an exercise'. It drew the attention of member Churches to the manifold problems of secularism, and agreed that representations should be made to the Departments of Education, North and South, regarding syllabuses and the teaching of history in both states. It considered that the terms of reference of the Steering Committee and the Joint Group should be discussed from time to time, and invited the Churches to appoint persons with responsibility for ecumenical activities in their local areas rather than the appointment of a person whose duty it would be to carry out the work of the conference.[23]

There were too many loose ends about these decisions to give the impression that the committee really meant business. The last two responses fell far short of what the conference had clearly asked for, and of meeting the real needs of the situation.

By June, however, the situation was different again. Peace of a kind had come in Zimbabwe. Yesterday's 'terrorists' were now in government, and showing goodwill. In the spring months, many people Presbyterians and others, hoped that the new climate and conditions might produce second thoughts about severing the link with the WCC. But, just a matter of days before the General Assembly met at the beginning of June, there was an outbreak of racial violence in South Africa. All the old fears and arguments were revived. A special resolution of the Church's General Board seeking Assembly approval for the action of the Clerk and his companions in meeting the Pope, and designed to outmanœuvre a possible vote of censure, was not put to the House. Later in the week the debate on the WCC took place before a packed house and against a background of intense public interest. Each side had its say, and each side was unmoved by the argument of the other. Battle lines had been drawn long before the session. The debate itself was almost a ritual prelude to the counting of the votes. In the event, 433 voted to leave the Council, and 327 voted in favour of remaining. The thirty-two, who had in 1964 asked for their names to be recorded as part of the minority against membership of the WCC, were now part of a victorious majority.

In the run-up to the Assembly, many had said that a vote to break the link would be the first step on the road to further ecumenical disengagement on the part of Irish Presbyterianism. Within days of the debate, Ian Paisley greeted the decision warmly. Never averse to writing an agenda for other people, he added ominously that the next battle to be fought would be for Presbyterian withdrawal from the British Council of Churches.

On the Catholic side, hierarchical positions seemed fixed and non-negotiable. And yet there were indications that not all Catholics shared the views of the bishops. Michael Hurley commented in an early 1980 issue of *Doctrine and Life:* 'Ecumenists ignore at their own peril that the basic aim is to reconcile and unite communities more than systems of belief or structures of government.' The comment was predictable, unlike one which was printed in the December 1979 number of *The Furrow*. It came from Father Peter R. Connolly, Professor of English at Maynooth. Writing on 'The Churches in Ireland since Vatican II', he referred to statistics from a Research and Development Unit exercise on Roman Catholic Church attendance in the Republic, which he quoted: 'Irish religious practice is sustained to an inadmissible degree by rule and law, social custom and a sense of duty, a framework of authority and sanctions rather than by a personal commitment of mind and heart, so that much belief or faith is extremely vulnerable in a rapidly changing society.' His own comment on churchmen is, to say the least, revealing: 'they must at some point face the fact of their own contribution to the present conflict'. He said:

the sectarianism they have allowed to flourish in the past and sometimes covertly encouraged: the violence of the language they have sometimes used in denouncing the authenticity of one another's creed: but above all the way these Churches surrendered in various degrees their independence to political ideologies—whether Unionist or Republican—forfeits their right to speak out prophetically in the name of Christ.

Father Connolly was sceptical about Ballymascanlon. He commented in the same article:

Such official encounters between prelates and theologians rapidly become institutionalized, and subject to strict ecclesiastical control. Such ecumenism is predictable and safe and can look all too like an exercise in public relations. We wait still for a genuinely mutual openness and generosity from those who are in charge, for the *political* gestures and moves which take risks—especially the risk of being misunderstood by the more conservative of their followers.

By September 1980 a new bishop had taken over in the Roman Catholic see of Cork in succession to the redoubtable Dr Lucey, whose application of the mixed marriage regulations had over many years caused so much distress. His successor, Bishop Murphy, made it clear that he would not require the Protestant partners to sign any undertaking about bringing up children of the marriage as Roman Catholics.

There the matter rested in the autumn of 1980. The end of the beginning or the beginning of the end? It is hard to say. Two developments in Ireland and one across the Irish Sea were bound sooner or later to influence the future of Irish ecumenism. One would be the degree to which Irish Presbyterians could or would contribute their great strength and deep convictions to future ecumenical dialogue. That in some degree would be influenced, though by no means altogether, by the Hierarchy's expected *Directory on Mixed*

Marriages. As 1980 came to a close, it was increasingly clear that no dramatic developments could be expected from that document. Indeed it was thought in some quarters that the new declaration could well mean a more uniform observation of Roman requirements from which no flexibility might be expected. Interviewed on BBC Radio Ulster on 2 November, Cardinal O'Fiaich said that the Catholic Church was increasingly taking a positive approach to mixed marriages and regarding them as making a notable contribution to breaking down the chasm between Christian communities. They were bringing the Churches closer together. Yet he was aware of the hurt to Protestantism arising from mixed marriages. He advocated joint pastoral care of those participating in such marriages. He spoke with understanding and compassion. But he said:

Obviously, from the Catholic point of view, there is the legislation of 'Matrimonia Mixta' and therefore there is no foregoing it. But I also can appreciate that the Catholic Church thinks that the duty of any of its members convinced that it is the Church of Christ is to hand on their faith to their children. Therefore it feels that by divine precept this is an obligation on the Catholic party. Now how perhaps to reconcile these two things—I think we should consider that again.

He went on:

We are drawing up at the moment in Ireland a new pastoral *Directory on Mixed Marriages* which I hope will be ready next year. As long as 'Matrimonia Mixta' of course as a document from Rome is providing the parameters within which we work, then the promise will have to be given in some form or other. But again all kinds of discussions are going on between Rome and the Protestant Churches on this issue. One of its purposes will be to enforce as far as possible uniformity in Catholic norms of mixed marriages throughout Ireland.[24]

Were his words ones of hope or warning? It all depended on what the uniformity he spoke about would be like. Across the Irish Sea, the outside factor for Ireland no less than for England would be the 1981 decisions to be taken on the Covenanting for Unity Report and the visit of the Pope to England in 1982. But above and beyond all else would be the response of the Irish Churches to the working of the Holy Spirit whose guidance they all claim to seek. One thing at least was clear. If in 1980 there were still many things to be done and others to be undone, far more had been achieved in Ireland than many could have thought possible in 1969. And perhaps more in Ireland than in many other places.

How much more was seen dramatically during the last two weeks of 1980. Cardinal O'Fiaich, Archbishop Armstrong, the Moderator (Dr Ronald Craig), and the President (the Revd. Sydney Callaghan) called for a week of prayer for peace and reconciliation. In preparation for it, they had participated in a programme of joint public visits to schools, hospitals, and charitable institutions, in both North and South. This was carried out against the background of mounting tension and unprecedented foreboding arising from the H-block hunger-strike. They announced their plans at a Belfast press conference on Tuesday 16 December. The journalists were there in strength. Their concern was not the week of prayer: they obviously were more interested in what the church leaders had to say about the seemingly inevitable calamity. The cynics were convinced that the week of prayer would be irrelevant, if not impossible. Two days later the hunger-strike had ended drama-tically. By the end of the same week, the Cardinal made history by inviting an Anglican clergyman, a Presbyterian, and a Methodist[25] to preach from his cathedral pulpit in Armagh during the forthcoming Unity Octave. Because they too were convinced that the Holy Spirit was still at work, they accepted his invitation.

10 Education

The government in the North had no need to apologize for its education system in 1969. It was comparable with any other in the United Kingdom, and it was arguably superior to anything in the Republic. Schools had been modernized or built on a lavish scale. There was simply no comparison between them and the ramshackle establishment that had existed in 1922.[1]

By and large the system that obtained in 1969 still exists. Education up to eleven years of age is free, except for those children whose parents send them to fee-paying preparatory schools. At eleven-plus, entrance to either grammar or secondary intermediate (equivalent to the English secondary modern) schools is determined by some form of attributable testing. Intermediate and grammar-school education is also free with one exception. Grammar schools may admit and charge fees in respect of a limited number of pupils who do not obtain sufficiently high standards at the eleven-plus test. The Local Education and Library Board pays the fees in respect of the others.

It is a dual system. As far as primary and intermediate schools are concerned, they are provided in one of two ways: either by the Education and Library Boards out of public funds, in which case they are known as 'controlled schools', or alternatively by the Roman Catholic Church. If the Catholic schools are prepared to accept a one-third representation from the Local Area Board on their management committee, they become 'maintained schools'. They can thus qualify for 100 per cent grants for expenditure on salaries and maintenance, and for 80 per cent grants in respect of approved building expenditure. Most of the grammar schools are under the control of 'voluntary' boards of governors, whether Catholic, Protestant, or 'mixed'. A few grammar schools provided by the Education and Library Boards are adequate to take the pupils for whom the voluntary schools have no room. Again, if the voluntary schools are willing to have one-third of their governors appointed by the minister responsible for education, they qualify for the generous building grants payable to maintained schools. In addition, they may negotiate a loan from the Ministry (now Department) of Education to cover their 20 per cent share of building costs. If they do this, they are allowed to charge a 'building' fee over a period of twenty years to cover repayment and loan charges.

This dual system applies throughout primary and secondary education. It would be hard to find a Protestant pupil anywhere in Northern Ireland enrolled in a Catholic school. The vast majority of Catholic pupils attend Catholic schools, though a relatively small number have in recent years been attending non-Catholic grammar schools. Effectively it is a case of schools apart and pupils apart. The only integrated education in the province worth talking about takes place in two areas. The first is the tertiary level of the universities and the Ulster Poly-technic: the other, the few institutions of further education and the small number of surviving technical schools.

Educational segregation, to be fair, is not in any way the result of deliberate government policies. Twice during the pre-ceding hundred years attempts were made by government to provide some kind of integrated schooling. Each time the attempt continued over a number of years. In the middle of the nineteenth century, the former Commissioners for Education launched an imaginative proposal for national and 'model' schools.[2] Again at the setting-up of the northern state, the Prime Minister, Lord Craigavon, a greater man incidentally than many of his critics have been ready to admit, and his Minister of Education, Lord Londonderry, made another attempt.[3] What is more, they were prepared to spend heavily on their proposal. The attempts failed each time. Although government could conceivably have done more, the real reasons lay elsewhere. They failed simply because neither Churches nor people would have them.[4] By 1922 the Catholic stance had not really changed in a hundred years. Michael Farrell, years later, put it bluntly: 'If the bishops had to choose between accepting the northern state and losing their schools, then they were going to keep their schools.'[5] And the Protestant Churches, while being ready to contemplate state schools, never had any other idea than that they would and should be 'Protestant' state schools. Their determination was strengthened by the prospect of the Roman Catholic Church getting away with its demands.

In the run-up to each attempt, political, community and religious temperatures had been high. Sectarian memories were long. The thinking of the educational planners no more coincided with the mood of the people in the mid-1850s and the 1920s than sociological thinking at government level did in the 1970s. The Churches and the people were content and convinced that children should live and learn apart. Segregation had become, and is today, a fact of life. Facts of life are no more easily altered in Northern Ireland than anywhere else.

The 'comprehensive' debate was still years away in Northern Ireland. Judged by the standards of the day, whatever might be said one way or the other about it sociologically and religiously, the system was good educationally. 'Oxbridge' had become more than a dream for many; it was now a reality. Curricular expansion was the order of the day in the intermediate schools. They had early learned the need for vocational training: the quality of their craft and engineering departments had virtually signed the death-knell of the technical schools. Some of them were rivalling the grammar schools in their success rate at the GCE A level examinations.

It was also a fair system. The late Cardinal Conway was heard to say at Major Chichester-Clark's peace conference that the Catholic community had been fairly treated by the higher civil service generally and by the Ministry of Education in particular. The financial assistance provided by successive Unionist administrations was far more generous than is realized outside the province. The Cardinal's remark was to be echoed in a completely unexpected quarter some years later. Michael Farrell, in his *Northern Ireland: The Orange State*, took many readers by surprise when he wrote: 'The one area where Craig's government had acted with a fair degree of impartiality was education.'[6] Throughout its history the Stormont Ministry of Education acted with that sense of impartiality. Paradoxically, the civil rights movement was a result of that policy. As greatly responsible for it as anything else was the frustration felt by many former grammar school pupils and university students, who found it difficult to secure the employment their qualifications had entitled them to expect. Without the system, the movement would never have had the leadership of people like John Hume, Austin Currie, Bernadette Devlin, or Michael Farrell. Its end-product was never better demonstrated than when one loyalist Convention member bitterly complained about what some called the star-studded front bench of university graduates sitting on the SDLP side of the House.

Taking one thing with another, each side was satisfied with what had been arranged. The Catholics had kept their schools and had moreover obtained almost unimaginable help to run them. The Protestants had succeeded in securing primary and intermediate state-provided schools, which nevertheless had church (or transferors') representatives on their management committees, in recognition of the transfer of former church schools to the public authorities.[7] This was assured by law, as was also non-denominational Bible teaching as the basis for obligatory religious instruction, to be given by the teachers and inspected by the clergy. The financial help available to voluntary grammar schools, whether Catholic or otherwise, was so generous that they are still more numerous than the provided grammar schools. The fact that children of different religions did not mix in the schools bothered very few. For the most part, segregated housing patterns did not make mixing on a large scale possible. It makes it less so today. In any case, neither side was rushing to have much dealings with the other. Gaelic culture and Gaelic games were of no interest to Protestants; yet most people were complacent about the long-term effects of these differences. But there was a price to pay: ignorance of each other increased suspicion and misunderstanding. If there was doubt in people's minds, and there is no great evidence to suggest there was, they felt there was more to be said for the arrangement than there was against it. Moreover, the educational product was both acceptable and marketable.

Shortly before the storm broke in 1969, two developments had a marked effect on educational thinking, although, as it turned out, not on practice. Each reinforced the attitudes of those who were to play leading parts in a debate that was just round the corner.

Vatican II issued its *Declaration on Christian Education* in 1965.[8] It was a lengthy document, but its message was clear. Every child has a right to a Christian education. All parents have a right to a choice of schools for their children. The state has an obligation to provide sufficient subsidies to make that choice possible. The Church, i.e. the Catholic Church, has the right to expect such subsidies to enable it to establish and run schools of every kind and at every level. Catholic parents have a duty 'to entrust their children to Catholic schools, when and where this is possible'. That became, and still is, the base position for every apologist for the Catholic school. The other factor was more

local. In 1967 and 1968 the *Belfast Telegraph*, the most liberal of
Northern Ireland's newspapers, commissioned two surveys on
Ulster youth. They provided a great deal of information, most
of it predictable, some of it very unexpected. Surprisingly,
there was reported to be a majority in favour of integrated
education. The figures quoted were more surprising still: 64
per cent of adults and 65 per cent of young people were alleged
to favour mixed schooling. Still more unexpected was the claim
that there was a Catholic lobby for it, and that the percentage
support was 69. No wonder, then, that around the same time
Bishop Philbin, the senior member of the Northern Hierarchy,
was quoted in the *Belfast Telegraph* as saying, 'In these days,
particularly when anti-religious influences are growing in
strength, we feel that we can protect the faith of the next
generation only through our schools.'

For all its tragedy and trauma, the summer of 1969 brought
exhilaration as well. Reform and change were in the air. Sociologists, peace programmers, and political observers flocked into
the province. They homed in on every sociological or other
factor worth looking at. When it came to education, they were
like wasps in a honey-pot. Supported by a limited number of
indigenous reformers, they began, almost with one voice, to
advise British Home Secretaries, and their successors the Secretaries of State for Northern Ireland, to look carefully at the
education system. It was all so clear to them: much of the
trouble starts in the schools. The equations were quickly and
simplistically stated. Segregated education equals ignorance
and strife; integrated education equals understanding and
reconciliation: *ergo* integrate, and the sooner the better.

To take but a few examples: the Ministry of Community
Relations and the Community Relations Commission were the
ace cards in the hand played by the Cabinet in its attempt to
promote better community understanding and respect. People
consequently began to take notice when the Commission in its
report on its first year's work (1970) stated: 'It remains to be
explored how far a more integrated schools system is either
desirable or acceptable. There is a great need for research and
explorations into such questions as the sort of schools system
which would be acceptable, the sort of 'integrated' schooling
that is envisaged, the method of organization and the mechanics
of implementation.'[9] The theorists were writing the agenda,
and they put integrated education high on the list. A year later
Mr William Moles, at that time head master of a large Belfast

controlled grammar school, wrote an impassioned article critical of segregated education in *Community Forum*, a publication of the Community Relations Commission. He said: 'I can see very little difficulty, other than the proverbial Irish lack of goodwill, in starting to mitigate the sinfulness of segregation.'[10] The phrase 'lack of goodwill' was to prove prophetic. In 1973 Mr A. E. C. W. Spencer, of the Queen's University of Belfast and an English (to be distinguished from Irish) Catholic, writing in *The Month*, was critical of Catholic clerical control over the Catholic education system in the Republic and Northern Ireland. He argued that Church control ensured 'that the culture transmitted from one generation to the next not only protects the power of the Church over its members but also its very strong solidarity and its concomitant ethnocentricity and xenophobia.'[11] He asked for a joint Protestant–Catholic commission to suggest a modification in the system. He argued that long and difficult discussions would be required to achieve the needed fundamental changes. Instead of clerical control of Catholic schools, he advocated the development of ecumenical management. In 1974, the Social Studies Conference (described in chapter 11) sponsored a well-attended residential seminar on sectarianism. Its findings included a section on education. It argued: 'Within the educational structures, the attempt should be made to create an understanding and acceptance of varying religious traditions and cultures and a recognition of the validity and positive value of plurality in society.'[12] It also recognized 'that the educational structures themselves may be inimical to this purpose and they should be examined to see how they ought to be developed to facilitate and encourage the understandings referred to'.

Among the observers and commentators, special mention must be made of a group led by General Sir John Hackett, Father Ray Helmick, an American Jesuit, and Mr Richard Hauser. The National Westminster Bank, the Esmée Fairbairn Charitable Trust, and the Waites Foundation were among their sponsors. They reported that:

The ecclesiastical leadership may personally deplore extreme outrages as going too far, producing a bad image for their establishments, but it is not at all clear how far, while disliking the image of conflict, they dislike the conflict itself. . . . What these divisive leaders have produced and maintained to a surprising degree is a division of living that in many cases goes far beyond that of blacks and whites in the United States. The whole impact of the divisive forces is seen in practically every action; in nurseries, in schools, so that the young hardly ever see each other except across barriers or come to know each other.[13]

One further illustration may be quoted. Dr. F. S. L. Lyons, the Provost of Trinity College, Dublin, himself a product of Ulster Protestantism, delivered the W. B. Rankin Memorial Lecture in the Queen's University in December, 1978. He spoke of 'the local manifestation of Gaelic-Catholic culture, as represented by the nationalists of Northern Ireland. In many respects this community seems faithfully to mirror the native culture in the rest of the island to which indeed it has contributed much.' He went on to notice 'the familiar marks of identification—the prominence of the church in education and in other aspects of social life, the deep attachment to Irish games, all given the intensity that comes from the consciousness of existing under the shadow of what has generally been felt as a hostile or suspicious majority'.[14]

Many at the time were feeling and saying much the same things: the push for integrated education seemed to be gathering momentum. The polls pointed the same way. A survey carried out by *Fortnight*, published in Belfast, claimed that the *Belfast Telegraph* statistics of 1967 and 1968 had not altered substantially. Sixty-two per cent of parents were claimed to be in favour of integrated schooling, and of the remainder 24 per cent would accept it without undue protest. Only 13 per cent were listed as 'against'. More Catholics than Protestants were said to be in favour of change. In 1977 six staff members in the New University of Ulster were to publish a study of education and community, *Northern Ireland—Schools Apart?*[15] They referred back to another survey carried out about the same time. Again the result had indicated a similar trend. This time it was claimed that 81 per cent of parents questioned would wish their children to attend a neighbouring integrated school, if one were available.

All the figures produced by the polls are impressive. Yet at no single time during this period or since was there anything in the nature of a strong ground swell actually attempting to alter the *status quo*. Perhaps a survey carried out in the Republic during 1973-4 reflected Catholic opinion in the North more accurately than did the northern investigations. It was carried out by the Research and Development Unit of the Catholic Communications Centre of Ireland, and was entitled *Attitudes to the Institutional Church: A Survey of Religious Practice, Attitudes and*

Belief in the Republic of Ireland 1973–4.[16] One of its well-documented findings dealt with attitudes towards continuing involvement of priests as managers of primary schools, and clergy and religious as managers of secondary schools. Fifty-four per cent agreed with such managership in primary schools, and 62 per cent in secondary schools. Those who disagreed with the system were 34 and 23 per cent respectively. The 'don't-knows' were about 12 per cent in each case.

Whatever the truth of the polls, there were however some in Northern Ireland actively seeking and working for change. They were more articulate than numerous. In the early seventies the diocesan authorities in Down and Connor became aware that a relatively small number of Catholic parents were, as an act of deliberate policy, sending their children to controlled primary schools in Belfast and its environs. Considerable publicity was given to allegations that confirmation had been refused in a number of cases despite their parents' wish that they adhere to the Catholic faith. As so often happens in Northern Ireland, the truth was blurred by what many thought to be the truth. In point of fact, the Bishop had postponed confirmation until acceptable catechetical arrangements had been made.

Mr Basil McIvor, who had been Minister of Community Relations in the former administration, was responsible for education in the power-sharing Executive. In late April 1974 he was ready to lead a brief foray into the educational minefield. Although it was obvious that the Executive would not last much longer, he had the courage to introduce suggestions for legislation on 30 April designed to open up the way for shared Protestant–Catholic schools. It was clear that he had listened to the arguments for integration. His proposals were tentative, but he made his own position clear. He said, 'I must declare my basic belief that the mixing of school children would contribute to the reduction of community tension in Northern Ireland.'[17] He recognized the hesitation of the Churches arising from 'understandable anxiety about the religious upbringing of their children in schools not under their management'.[18] Nevertheless he asked 'them earnestly to consider the very special needs of Northern Ireland and to join with a power-sharing Executive in a constructive approach to meeting those needs'. He had in mind the possibility of a new management arrangement, which could be accepted by either 'controlled' schools or 'maintained' schools.

I think we could consider the possibility of changing the law to facilitate another class of school, which we might think of as a 'shared' school and in which the two groups of churches would be equally involved in management. Obviously the details of this suggestion will have to be worked out in consultation with the interested parties before practical proposals for legislation can be formulated. I approach these at this stage with a very open mind and I shall wish to obtain the views and assistance of the two groups of Churches, the Area Boards and other interested bodies, especially the teachers' organizations and the bodies representative of parents.[19]

How open the Minister's mind was became apparent next day, 1 May. His Ministry's letter to the 'interested bodies' requesting their views demonstrated, if proof were necessary, his good faith. It was clear that no well-prepared and secret plans were in existence. In fact, it would appear that Mr McIvor and his Ministry had at that stage no formulated plans whatever. His letter did, however, indicate that 'shared schools should be financed 100% from public funds, and therefore provided by the Education and Library Boards'. A shared management scheme was obviously required. He said there were many possibilities and 'one arrangement favoured by some is a committee consisting of representatives of transferors (Protestant) and trustees (Catholic) in equal numbers; of the parents and the Area Board'.[20] He contemplated the possibility of new schools, particularly in the nursery sector, all presumably in the new mixed areas of which the planners were still dreaming. The lack of detail was further demonstrated in the section on religious education. 'Not all the provisions of the Education and Libraries Order regarding religious education seem to be appropriate for shared schools; instead it could be left to the school management committee to determine the arrangements for religious education'.

In the event, the Executive had been hustled out of office before Mr McIvor could assess the reaction of the Churches and the public, let alone frame and pilot through the necessary legislation. He did have time, however, in the thirty-minute debate which took place on 30 April, to assess the reaction of the House. Hansard vividly records the cool and suspicious reception his remarks received among a group of SDLP members particularly. It was all too clear that in any future division some members were likely to divide on the traditional sectarian lines. The proposals, such as they were, were killed by the demise of the Executive in the historic and dramatic events of the next three weeks.

Ulster's 'No' was not, however, the end of the matter. Reference has already been made to the Hauser report, which had mentioned the confirmation controversy. Parents of children involved in that issue and others were active founder-members of 'All Children Together', a movement designed to intensify the pressure for integration. Their organization gathered strength. They held public meetings, but their more important work was done almost unobserved. Perhaps their most publicized activity was when several of their members took part in a conference on 'Segregation in Education' arranged by the New University of Ulster and held in Londonderry in May 1978. Prior to that, they had been busy behind the scenes. What Stormont had failed to provide, they were determined to secure from Westminster. They were party to a bill sponsored in the House of Lords by Lord Dunleath, a prominent member of Northern Ireland's Alliance Party. The bill became law and is now 'An Act to facilitate the establishment in Northern Ireland of schools likely to be attended by pupils of different religious affiliations or cultural traditions'. Its date is 25 May 1978. The act and its subsequent regulations provide cumbersome and not very satisfactory machinery whereby a transferred school may become 'a controlled (i.e. statutory controlled) integrated school', managed by a joint or integrated committee on which Protestant transferors and Catholic interests wil be represented in equal numbers.

There has been no rush to make use of the new act. Indeed, the Department of Education was caught out when in 1980 a request reached it for the act to be applied. It had no regulations ready. The request, when it did come, had little to do with conviction regarding the merits of integration. The move came from the transferors' representatives on the committee of a steadily declining school in north Belfast. The act permitted them, without consultation with their Church Boards of Education, to initiate a request for the school to be accorded 'integrated status'. They did just that, their clear purpose being to keep the school open at all costs. Supported by a number of Unionist City Councillors, with little previously known interest in integration, they persuaded the Belfast Education and Library Board to request the Department to operate the new act, although there was no support of any kind from the trustees of neighbouring Catholic schools.[21] In fact, there was recorded unwillingness: there was also no indication of local Catholic community support. It was like arranging a wedding with the

likelihood that the bride would not turn up and in the knowledge that, even if she did, her parents would refuse to attend
the wedding, let alone give her away. In 1981 the Department
approved and the school became 'integrated' without Catholic
participation in management, staff and enrolment.

The reluctance to take advantage of the Dunleath Act rein-
forces the questions already raised about the dependability of
the opinion polls. In 1971 Professor Richard Rose was arguing
that to introduce integrated education 'would literally take
generations before the bulk of the adult population had been
exposed to the weak ameliorating influence of a mixed
education'.[22] Had his thesis sunk in, or was it that the con-
tention of the 1977 study of the NUU (already referred to) was
nearer the mark? It stated that many who favoured integration
had not thought out 'the massive administrative, financial,
religious and political problems involved'.[23] J. J. Campbell, a
noted Catholic educationalist and member of the Cameron
Commission, had considered in 1947 that many Protestants had
the sincere though naïve belief 'that Catholics ought to be able
to accept conditions that were acceptable to the various
Protestant denominations: that in satisfying the Protestant conscience, and changing the state system of education to do so, the
government had thereby satisfied all Christian consciences'.[24]
In the 1960s Mr Frederick Jeffery, Vice-Principal of Northern
Ireland's largest grammar school, confirmed the continued
existence of this conviction. He noted that full integration
would involve accepting Roman Catholic teachers, including
members of the teaching orders, for Protestant pupils, as well as
Protestant teachers for Roman Catholic children, but claimed
that 'when this is indicated, it becomes apparent that their idea
is not simply integration, but rather more like forcing Roman
Catholic children to attend "Protestant" schools'.[25]

The situation did not change between 1978 and 1980. The
total result of all the pressure was one enabling act, which has
had only one very doubtful taker. Significantly, over the years,
the Local Education Authorities and their successors, the
Education and Library Boards, have been careful not to get
involved. They have made no effort to discuss the issue, let
alone take any initiatives.

How did the Churches react to all that was going on? One way
or another they could not avoid coming out into the open; the
Roman Catholic Church least of all. The message of Vatican II
had to be spelled out in and for Ireland, irrespective of whether

politicians and theorists were busy. In addition, they were increasingly under pressure from the media. The politicians and the sociologists were anxious to know where the Church stood. The Protestant Churches had not been under the same duress, and had been content to allow the Hierarchy to make the running. If Rome was not pushing for integration, they did not need to defend segregation. They did not have to do anything as long as there were no proposals on the table but could afford to wait and that is what they did until the McIvor proposals lured them out of their corners.

Vatican II had enunciated the principles of Catholic education for world Catholicism. Would they hold in an Ireland of communal strife and social pressures? The answer came well within a year of the McIvor initiative. On 16 February 1975 the *Sunday Press* of Dublin carried a long interview with Bishop Philbin. He was quoted *in extenso*, and the subject was Catholic education. Not surprisingly, there was no ambiguity about what he said. 'We cannot act on an understanding of education as dealing chiefly with such matters as knowledge of the world around us and ourselves, the gaining of skills and completeness, going through a curriculum of studies that lead to good employment and attractive incomes.' He claimed that the great majority of Catholic parents in his diocese regarded Catholic schools as a necessary part of the provision for their children. Proof of this, he said, could be seen in the 'fact that ninety-nine per cent of the Catholic children of Down and Connor are attending Catholic primary and secondary schools. A tangible indication of the effectiveness of these schools is the discharge of the Church's law of Divine worship on Sundays by about ninety-five per cent of our population.' He recognized that in recent years 'children from Catholic schools have been involved in activities that were anything but good and moral', but he argued that 'things would have been worse' without the influence of Catholic schools. 'The idea that there would have been less civil disturbance had there been a monolithic educational system is the reverse of the truth.' He contended that the schools were essential to the very survival of the Catholic faith. 'Short of banning religion completely, there is no greater injury that could be done to Catholicism than by interference with the character and identity of our schools.' Those trenchant words from the acknowledged strong man of the northern Hierarchy chilled any hopes of Catholic participation in shared or integrated schooling.

The Hierarchy issued their new *Directory on Ecumenism* the following year.[26] In it they gave unexpected prominence to education. They spoke about the necessity of Catholic schools and the role of the Catholic teacher. They were at pains to take note of the challenge presented to their schools by the ecumenical movement and 'the tragic conflict which is now rending society in Northern Ireland'. But they said that 'care must be taken not to detract from faith in the Catholic Church, in which the sole Church of Christ subsists'. A special paragraph followed on the teaching of history and the need to instil in pupils 'a profound love of justice and a firm determination never to resort to unchristian methods in pursuit of it'. They claimed that Catholic schools are not a divisive element in society.

There is now abundant sociological research to indicate that, on the contrary, Catholic schools promote tolerance and peaceful inter-community relations. The replacement of Catholic by inter-denominational (multi-denominational, non-denominational) schools in Ireland would not contribute to overcoming the divisions in our midst. . . . We must point out that in such schools the full Catholic witness is inevitably diluted, and that the compromise which this entails is not conducive to the development of a secure and strong Christianity in those who experience it.

Thus, having stated their position without ambiguity, the bishops did not miss the opportunity presented to them by Protestant insistence on the need for denominational schools in the Republic. 'Members of other Christian denominations including Church leaders can be counted among those, who agree with our convictions regarding the value of denominational schools, and have pronounced them as necessary for the Christian formation of their children and youth.' It was a shrewd though polite warning to Protestants that they could be hoist with their own petard, if they were to say anything rash about shared schools.

Bishop Cahal Daly came back to the issues in the 1978 series of the *Irish Theological Quarterly*. He gave almost nine pages of a twenty-four-page article on 'Ecumenism in Ireland' to spelling out the educational implications of the 1976 *Directory*. At the NUU conference in Magee College, Londonderry, already referred to, he and Father Michael Dallat left no doubt that, while they would welcome developments in certain common activities, the basic Catholic position was non-negotiable.[27] It was a diffferent line from that to be taken by the English

Hierarchy in 1980 after the National Pastoral Conference. It had asked that 'the possibility of establishing (shared) Christian schools should be carefully considered provided that they are based on sound principles of Christian education and are not proposed for merely pragmatic reasons'. To this the bishops replied in their post-congress message entitled *Easter People:* 'We wish to continue to investigate the possibility of further shared schools, not on a merely pragmatic basis, but in order to discover the potential that might lie in this for ecumenical and other reasons.'[28] Nor was the hierarchical line accepted by all Irish Catholics. In the Spring/Summer 1978 issue of *Studies*, a strident Jesuit voice was raised. Father John Brady, Director of the College of Industrial Relations, wrote: 'There are no insuperable difficulties about educating Catholic and Protestant children in the same school.' He said there was ample precedent for it, and advocated it strongly.

A response is called for from the Catholic Church in Ireland *vis-à-vis* the Northern Ireland situation. The needed response is a demonstration that the Catholic Church is prepared to pursue its legitimate interests in education through participative structures, at least in some instances and on an experimental basis. By collaborating in this way, the Churches would be saying in deeds rather than words that they do not wish to perpetuate the divisive social structures of Northern Ireland.

Over a year later, Professor Peter Connolly of Maynooth was writing in *The Furrow* about episcopal spokesmen on education in Northern Ireland who had a 'mental block'.[29] He declared roundly, 'They cannot see or will not acknowledge that segregated education in the North must be reckoned at least a contributory factor in the tragic divisions there.' He was perturbed at Bishop Cahal Daly's refusal 'even to envisage the possibility of a few experiments with inter-denominational schooling—showing its practical impossibility in Belfast but avoiding the question of alternative places where it might be practically tried out. This seems to be a firmly closed door at present and in the immediate future.'

What of the Protestant Churches? The Ulster workers' strike and the destruction of the Executive had to some extent let them off the hook. Nevertheless they were under obligation to reply to the Ministry even though the Minister, who had started the ball rolling, was no longer there. Their replies, such as they were, were mixed. The Presbyterians declared:

The General Assembly has on two occasions passed resolutions in favour of integrated education. Since education is a preparation for life, and since children have got to live together in mixed communities, they should therefore learn to learn together. Integration ought to take effect in four, among other areas, housing, work, leisure and schools. To have integration in some of these without affecting others is impossible.

These seemingly unambiguous words were followed by a declaration that integration should be initiated in sixth form colleges and nursery schools. There was insistence that 'integration of schools is a priority and that segregated religious instruction on a denominational basis should be available, if required'.

The Church of Ireland were faced with a dilemma. They had and still have a far greater stake than either of the other two Protestant Churches in denominational education in the Republic. Their spokesmen have consistently fought the battle to ensure the survival of these schools. An over-enthusiastic welcome for McIvor could consequently have proved a boomerang. None the less they welcomed the initiative and said they would 'be prepared to examine carefully and sympathetically the Minister's more detailed proposals'. They went on: 'It will be difficult for anyone who is sincerely concerned about growing understanding between our two communities not to wish the Minister well in an experiment, which demands of all participants the willingness to take a calculated risk for the possible greater good of the whole community.' Of the three responses, the Methodist one was perhaps the most conscious of the problems as well as of the opportunity. It saw:

many difficulties especially among the long established groupings in the Province. Careful working out of what is precisely meant by the theory and practice has obviously to be done. . . . The Board is convinced that the schooling of Roman Catholic and Protestant children together is but one step toward improved relationships. The community as a whole has to develop an atmosphere of better relationships which will in turn be reflected in schools.

As we have seen, none of the Protestant Churches was put to the test. Significantly, none of them has instructed any of their representatives on school committiees to make use of the provisions of the Dunleath Act.

The Church of Ireland response sets out clearly the hope that had been behind the McIvor offer. The advocates of integrated education have always worked on the assumption that it will promote reconciliation and that Catholic education is divisive. As we have seen, the *Directory of Ecumenism* challenged that assumption. Indeed the bishops had found strong support, and presumably those who favoured integration had been disappointed, in Professor Richard Rose's statement in 1971. 'There are sufficient persons with a mixed education to measure how much exposure affects political outlooks.'[30] He argues from the polls that the effect is only 'to a very limited extent', and he claims that his finding is substantiated by a 'variety of studies elsewhere of Catholic and state schools'. Rose's conviction is upheld to a surprising degree by the 1977 New University study.[31] Bishop Cahal Daly has pointed to the findings of this study in support of the traditional Catholic position. John Darby, the leader of the survey team, said:

The popular picture of Northern Ireland's dual educational system preserving and propagating different cultural heritages is far too simplistic. It is obvious that there are differences in cultural, religious and political allegiances between the two communities. More interesting perhaps is the evidence that both sets of schools accept some elements of a shared heritage. This covers a wide spectrum of school activities. School broadcasts and project materials, many of which deal with such value-laden areas as religion and history, are with very minor differences, used widely in schools of both religions.[32]

There are, of course, those who argue that the conclusions of Darby and company are in their turn too simplistic. That may be. It is wiser, however, to attempt conclusions on the basis of known facts than on surmise. They themselves claimed:

No investigation has ever been conducted into the similarities and differences in practices within the two sets of schools. There was no knowledge of a systematic nature . . . about the bread and butter organization of the schools. It would appear likely that the general woolliness which has characterized the segregation debate is not unrelated to simple ignorance of practices within the segregated system. It may indeed be the case that the very lack of research on the difference actually perpetrates and exaggerates the perceived differences themselves.[33]

The facts then emerging from the debate offer little comfort to the convinced integrationalist. Even if integrated schooling were to produce the better results hoped for, and if there were no support for Rose's comment on 'their weak ameliorating influence', the difficulties in the way of integration are immense. Leaving aside the generations claimed by Rose to be necessary for any worthwhile effect to be experienced, the financial, administrative, religious, and political problems mentioned by the NUU study remain. Large segregated estates are not the best material for integrated schooling. And so in many areas the busing factor would have to be taken into account. The political climate post-McIvor has, if anything, hardened, and gives little encouragement for radical change.

In spite of the various Protestant declarations, the matter has never been a live issue. In many ways Roman Catholic insistence on Church schools has seen to that. As long as Catholicism insists on its special role in education, the others are absolved from any requirement to develop their apparent or alleged call for radical change. To sum up, irrespective of the ideology, both in the short and foreseeable longer terms integrated schooling in Northern Ireland is 'not on'.

But one might ask, if integrated schooling is not possible, what about teacher-training? Two new institutions of higher education had emerged during the seventies. They were the New University of Ulster and the Ulster Polytechnic. Each has a teacher-training unit, and by the middle seventies it was becoming obvious that with falling school-rolls Ulster was over-provided in the area of tertiary education, and that in particular the long-established teacher-training colleges in Belfast were feeling the draught. The government appointed a commission under the chairmanship of Sir Henry Chilver to report and recommend regarding the situation. It issued an interim report in 1980, recommending that the two Catholic colleges of education in Belfast should be merged. Then the resulting college for both sexes, still under Catholic management, should share a site with Stranmillis College, the government non-sectarian college of education, which operates under a board of governors appointed by the Department of Education.[34] Chilver recommended that, while the colleges would retain their separate identities, and while the Roman Catholic Church would have the same rights and authority as it already had, opportunity should be taken from the new development to encourage a more economic use of resources by means of joint work, where it could be considered desirable and possible. Many felt that this in itself could have beneficial results. It was soon evident that Chilver found few takers in Catholic circles. For whatever reason, a seemingly orchestrated series of objections indicated both official and unofficial reluctance to accept the proposition. Evidently integrated teacher-training was also 'not on'.

What then can be done? The issue is too serious to be left in mid-air. The Churches, of all those engaged in the search for reconciliation, can least afford to neglect any opportunity for positive action. Whether or not one accepts the Catholic case, and let it be said that case is stronger than many of its critics admit, there are other inescapable facts. The community is not psychologically ready for integration, and, even if it were, the physical factors we have already noted would cause great problems. Furthermore, Professor Rose's warning about the generations needed for any worthwhile effect to be registered still stands. Time is short, however.

The NUU 1977 survey advocated a course of action for the Churches: it asked for the establishing of more fruitful and constructive relationships within and between both sets of schools. That was exactly what the Joint Churches Working Party had advocated a year previously in its report *Violence in Ireland*.[35] Those who produced the report discussed the issues regarding integration for a long time. The more they discussed them, the more they were aware of the pitfalls and difficulties inherent in a simplistic advocacy of integration. They were accused of cowardice and of shirking the issue, but they preferred realism to facile recommendations that had no chance of being implemented—and they were right. Later lack of desire to implement Dunleath demonstrates that the integrationists claimed by the polls had either disappeared, or, as is more likely, never existed. The working party saw what the theorists and idealists seem to have missed. They recognized, irrespective of the personal wishes of any of their members, that community attitudes are not changed by diktat. To impose integration on an unwilling or unconvinced community would be to hinder rather than help the cause. They could see no way to arrange a marriage without the bride.

The passage on education goes straight to the point:

The question of an integrated system of education is being increasingly canvassed and cannot be passed over in silence. Members of our Working Party are not agreed on this issue. We confine ourselves in this Report to conclusions in the matter of education on which we are agreed. We are in agreement that the Churches should produce pilot schemes and research projects to find effective ways of bringing together Protestant and Catholic young people at school level. Such schemes could include exchanges of teachers between Catholic and Protestant schools (particularly in sensitive areas of the curriculum, such as history, civics, Irish language and culture, history of the Churches in Ireland and in the promotion of joint projects and field work in the relevant subjects). Shared Sixth Form Colleges have also been suggested. Common nursery schools in suitable areas could be developed. This would give mothers opportunities of meeting which it would be otherwise difficult to bring about. Debates, cultural and folk-cultural activities can often be usefully shared. Games and athletics are also areas for sharing and this can be further developed. The different traditions in regard to games which have tended to characterize the two communities will need diversification so as to increase sharing.

The report went on:

> The teaching of religion in schools of both traditions must have explicitly and deliberately an ecumenical dimension. The stereotypes which each community may have inherited regarding the religious beliefs and practices of the other must be finally rejected and replaced by exact and sympathetic understanding. It will often be desirable to invite representatives of the other traditions to come to the schools to talk about their own traditions.

The Churches were asked for their responses to the report. The Hierarchy submitted a reasoned document, the other Churches replied less fully. None seemed to have made any major gestures. A year after its publication, Bishop Daly, who had been a co-chairman of the working party, said 'There are some worrying indications that this appeal of the inter-church Working Party may not yet have had the impact or the effect which we hoped it would.' It was an understatement. Three years on, there was still little sign of the movement asked for from the Churches or the schools.[36] Either the report for the most part had found few clerical purchasers, or it was gathering dust on its owners' book shelves. The Christian Education Movement had arranged for joint introductions of the report at some of its inter-church sixth form conferences. But there was no indication that any of the Churches, or their representatives on school committees and Education and Library Boards, were either concerned or convinced enough to do anything about the report's recommendations. None of them had started to think about the suggested pilot schemes or research projects. The shared nursery schools and sixth form colleges were no longer on any agenda. Everybody's business had become nobody's business. Indeed one wonders if the Churches were in any way convinced at a deeper level than that of a passing thought that the report was in fact their or anybody else's business.

Why? Was it inertia, lack of conviction, disapproval? Or was it that the 'business-must-go-on' treadmill left no energy and gave no room for experiment and manœuvre? For whatever reason, if they did not foment divison—and they did not—they did not see the vision and share the fulfilment of a joint search through the schools for reconciliation.

11   The Peace Movements

It was a Saturday afternoon in September 1976. For most Ulster towns and villages it was a normal Saturday. Belfast had its usual shopping crowds: so had the other towns. But there was a difference. There was unusually heavy traffic on the M2 and on the twisting stretches of the Glenshane Pass where the road snakes its way north to Derry. It was more than heavy traffic; it was an apprently endless convoy of buses. Not that there is anything unusual about buses on the Glenshane—it was the number of them. All of them were crowded. Thousands of women, and some men as well, were on their way to Derry. When at last they reached the east bank of the Foyle, just inside the city boundary, they stopped, and the passengers poured out on to the streets. They were joined and welcomed by still more thousands from Derry, from all over Ulster, and from the Republic too.

Long before the last of the buses had arrived, the milling crowd had somehow become a column, several columns, of orderly but expectant people. Apparently from nowhere banners appeared. There were all sorts, well made, home made, half made. They were hoisted every few yards along the ranks, which began to twist backwards and forwards for they had to make the most of all the space available. At last the head of the column began to move. Followed by a seemingly endless tail, it headed up and down the narrow streets on its way to Craigavon Bridge, Derry's only bridge across the Foyle. As they marched, they tried to sing. There was no common marching song. For some it was 'When Irish eyes are smiling' or 'We shall overome'. For others perhaps 'O God, Our help in ages past' or 'The Lord's my Shepherd'. And as they moved, the legends on the banners identified the places from which their bearers and the marchers immediately around them came.

The leaders stopped at the centre of the bridge. In any case, they would have had to stop for the way was barred. They were face to face with another crowd, this time from the west bank.

They too had their banners—the Bogside, the Creggan and many other place-names also.

As they stopped, they cheered. Suddenly the cheering gave way to something like a prayer. There was more singing, and then it was all over, long before many of the winding columns had ever reached the approaches to the bridge. Then came the newsmen, the photographers, the camera-crews. They were there from all over the world, and they had one target only, a small group of young and almost bewildered women standing in the centre.[1]

The Peace People, that new phenomenon in the Ulster story, were on the march, and they were news. The world was taking notice. Hard-bitten observers of the Ulster scene, mostly from outside, were beginning to say that this new movement was about to usher in a new day. This was people-power, and it was coming from where they said it should come, the 'grass roots'. They saw it as the beginning of the end of terror. The Provisionals were bound to take note, not only of that day's march but of all the others that went before or followed after.

That day there was euphoria, and it was repeated on every other march. But there were signs for those who had eyes to see that more was needed if Ulster's long night of suffering was to finish. There was a lack of organization; the meeting was over before many in the crowd had begun to move; a few duplicated sheets of paper were woefully inadequate even for those who reached the bridge. The new phenomenon had nothing like the broad base of support so many imagined. There was no common marching song or 'battle hymn'. There were strengths and weaknesses which the succeeding weeks and months were to make all too clear.

Yet nothing can take away the credit that is due to them. Whatever they achieved in the long term, at least, and it was a very big 'least', they were instrumental in helping untold thousands of Ulster women and men of every kind to register a visible protest at murder. But they were not Ulster's only peace movement. The outside world has been slow to learn that fact. They were the latest, and possibly not the last. The numbers and the names of Ulster's peace workers and organizations are legion. To attempt to list them all would be to share the failure experienced by the authors of the Fourth Gospel and the Epistle to the Hebrews. They are to be found in all sorts of likely and unlikely places, in long-established and recently formed organizations, in the statutory authorities, in government and its commissions, in this and that *ad hoc* group, and supremely among thousands of 'apostolics anonymous', whose identity will never be known. They jump almost at random out of the past, and, without trying to place them in any order of significance, they must include:

– Women Together,[2] People Together, and others like them; the Ruth Agnews and the indomitable courage and perseverance of the Saidie Pattersons[3] of the Ulster saga;

— self-help and community co-operatives and peace groups in places like Ballymurphy, Ardoyne, Whiterock, the Shankill and Ballymacarrett;[4]

– men like Dr Maurice Hayes, Catholic and one-time local-government official, and the late Mr Brian Rankin, Presbyterian solicitor and last Chairman of the Northern Ireland Housing Trust—in succession first and second chairmen of the Community Relations Commission—and the devoted staff who worked with them;

– the Ministers of Community Relations, and their successor, the Minister of State in the Prime Minister's Office: Dr Robert Simpson, Mr Basil McIvor, Mr David Bleakley, and Dr G. B. Newe;

– prestigious organizations like the Irish Association for Cultural, Economic and Social Relations, The British–Irish Association and Co-operation North,[5] with their participating peers and politicians, university dons and ecclesiastics, journalists and journeymen, communicators and critics, civil servants, and people of good will;

– Corrymeela in the North and Glencree, its counterpart in the South;[6]

– long-established youth organizations, the mushrooming youth clubs, senior citizens' clubs and the like;

– a Methodist President, the Revd. Robert Livingstone, speaking to a Sinn Fein conference;

– the unnumbered projects[7] which have appeared on the grant lists of Women Caring, the Inter-Church Emergency Fund, supported by the European Catholic Episcopal Conference (CCEE) and by money raised by Father David Bowman SJ, then of the Irish Desk of the National Council of Christian Churches in the USA, the Noord Irland Fund of Holland, the Blackburn Trust, War on Want, Save the Children Fund, and many others;

– well-organized agencies like Voluntary Services Belfast, Community Service, and International Voluntary Service on the one hand, and, on the other, the multitude of small groupings which find it difficult to complete grant application forms;

–the Samaritans, so universally trusted and dependable, that the illegal organizations would telephone bomb-warnings in the knowledge that police and security forces would certainly be alerted;

– the holiday schemes for old folk and children from the ghetto areas—many of them, like the Churches, in the business for years; others like the Harmony Trust and the Northern Ireland Children's Holiday Scheme recently emerged as a response to the needs of the seventies;

– courageous and effective bodies operating in and from Derry's Bogside, Creggan, and Waterside about whose work too little is known;

– social and community workers in the service of the Health and Social Services Boards and District Councils, whose contribution has often gone far beyond the demands of duty;

– groups like the New Ulster Movement and the Movement for Peace in Ireland that have reached out to politicians;

– the Northern Ireland Committee of the Irish Trade Union Congress with its Citizens United for Reconciliation and Equality and its Better Life for All campaigns; those like Mr Billy (now Lord) Blease, office-based, and the shop-floor man, Mr Sandy Scott;

– the Social Studies Conference, an annual event promoted mainly by Southern academics;

– local groups of clergy and laity, who have kept visions alive;

– the Women's World Day of Prayer reaching out across the divide, and smaller units like the one led in south Belfast by Mrs Mary Burrowes, which sponsors each year a moving ecumenical service, and many others like it;

– others like the Northern Ireland Mixed Marriage Association (NIMMA), Christian Understanding Everywhere (CUE), Protestant and Catholic Encounter (PACE), the Fellowship of Reconciliation (FoR), Good Neighbours, and Peace Point;

– Witness for Peace, which sought reconciliation out of the bomb-death of its founder's son and which was the subject of an Independent Television documentary, 'Revd. Parker says good-bye';

– the leaven of the university and hospital chaplains in their ministry to young minds and the suffering;

– the Quaker ministry to the relations of prisoners at the Maze;

– the Association of Peace Committees and the Churches'
Central Committee for Community Work;
– the Feakle churchmen and their meeting with the Provisionals, and the Church Leaders' Peace Campaign and their
1980 Week of Prayer for Ireland;
– all the others, known and unknown, for there are many of
them. Some have more than a local habitation and a name, and
some have had their day. Others struggle on with courage.
Everyone has played a part and, all in all, they make one thing
clear; they represent massive Christian concern and conviction
about Ulster's troubles.

It would be as tedious as it is impossible to chronicle all their
doings. But some require more than a passing reference because
of their impact on world opinion, their influence on political
thinking, or their effect on paramilitary activity.

But to return to the Peace People. Nothing in all the years of
violence did more to focus attention on Ulster. IRA propaganda
never attracted anything like the same interest over such a short
period. The story of their beginnings is simply told: a young
Catholic mother from west Belfast out walking with her
children on a summer afternoon, a runaway car with a wounded
Provisional at the wheel, an army patrol in pursuit, the inevitable, and three children dead and their mother at death's door
for weeks. The neighbourhood was roused: they had had
enough. One of the local women, Mrs Betty Williams, and Miss
Mairead Corrigan, the aunt of the dead Maguire children, had
launched the Peace People almost before they knew it. Before
many weeks were over, they were to lead mammoth protest
marches in Belfast's Andersonstown, Ormeau Park, the
Protestant Shankill Road, and the Catholic Falls. Each march
left its own memories: nuns being embraced as they made their
way up the Shankill; the incredulity of the Ormeau Park
marchers at what they saw; the success of Saidie Patterson,[x]
peace-warrior over the years, in neutralizing the flash-points for
the Shankill march; the viciousness of the Provisional supporters
on the Falls; the sheer fulfilment of the meeting on Craigavon
Bridge. There seemed at one time no limit to what could be
achieved, and they went on until the climax came on Sunday, 4
December 1976 on the banks of the Boyne, that most legendary
of all Ireland's rivers.

As we have seen, from the very beginning they captured the
admiration of even the most cynical of the press men and

women, who hoped they had actually found a 'grass-roots' movement. Tragically, the excitement disappeared and the momentum vanished. The later comment of Eamonn McCann, veteran of earlier civil rights marches in Derry, was to prove all too true: 'They were the expression of a mood, not a movement.'[9]

What went wrong? The two 'founders' were early joined in the leadership by an able Catholic journalist, Ciaran McKeown, who became the architect of their policy. They needed help, for neither had been trained or endowed for the role in which the media quickly cast them. Relatively soon after his arrival, they put out a statement of their campaign aims:

We have a simple message for the world from this movement of peace.

We want to live and love and build a just and peaceful society.

We want for our children as we want for ourselves, our lives at home, at work and at play, to be lives of joy and peace.

We recognize that to build such a life demands of all of us, dedication, hard work and courage.

We recognize that there are many problems in our society which are a source of conflict and violence.

We recognize that every bullet fired and every exploding bomb makes that work more difficult.

We reject the use of the bomb and bullet and all the means of violence.

We dedicate ourselves to working with our neighbour, near and far, day in day out, to build that peaceful society in which the tragedies we have known are a bad memory and a continuing warning.[10]

They were later to have some difficulties with a few of the Catholic leadership in Belfast, but initially they were given the approval of the Hierarchy, and various Protestant ministers made their support known. Though there was no actual church participation until the Boyne rally, when Cardinal, Primate, Moderator, and President were all present, or represented, their previous absence had not been caused by indifference. The Peace People seemed anxious to do 'their own thing', and, in any case, there was the suspicion that support from 'high up' could be regarded as an attempt at a take-over or a kiss of death.

The period immediately after the Boyne was one of 'make or break'. On 16 November Ciaran McKeown had challenged the 'just war' concept. At the Boyne, he adumbrated his political philosophy of power emanating from community groups, from the bottom up. It smacked of the original Soviet system. Before the week was over, the Revd. Martin Smyth was suggesting that the Peace People were being 'used by our enemies in the same way as the CRA in 1968–9'. In early January Father Desmond Wilson claimed that the Peace leaders were like the Churches, 'seeking peace without change'. The *Irish Times* stated: 'Its influence is least when it is needed most. Its contribution is to sentiment and morale. It is not an instrument of politics.'[11]

The Boyne rally was the last of the big Irish occasions. Betty Williams and Mairead Corrigan had become world-famous overnight. Invitations from Europe and America poured in to them; they were continually on the move. They were sponsored, too late as it happened, for the 1976 Nobel Peace Prize, though it came their way in 1977. Money came flooding in from all over the world, and the two women were awarded a further valuable Scandinavian prize worth many thousands of pounds. This they devoted to the emerging organizational structure. The following year they retained the money that went with the Nobel prize for their own use. It should be said, however, that at the same time they surrendered any claim they might have for the services they were giving.

Long before the two leaders received their Nobel award, the movement had lost its impetus. It was being said at an early stage that there was insufficient Protestant involvement, although they did endeavour to widen their base. Actually their first treasurer was the wife of the Revd. John Knox, now of the ICC. The way she was appointed is almost unbelievable, as told by Mrs Williams.[12] 'It was like monopoly. I'd open one envelope after another and out would come funny money, coloured bits of foreign paper. A Methodist woman called, looking to help. I made her treasurer on the spot. It was like Topsy, the movement just growed and very quickly too.' They also appointed Mr Peter McLachlan, former Unionist MP and supporter of Brian Faulkner, to a position of leadership; but his was not the authentic Belfast Protestant voice they badly needed, although there was no question regarding either his ability or integrity. They announced an 'escape-route' for those who wished to free themselves of paramilitary involvement; purchased a large house on the Lisburn Road, and made it their headquarters, sponsored training for community development work; and assisted community and other projects. But somehow the glory had departed. When the Nobel Prize winners returned to Belfast after receiving their award, there was no heroic welcome—just a small turn-out of the faithful, and no civic reception.

Public interest and support was waning. By the end of 1977, the movement was reported to be in financial difficulties. The original three leaders stood down officially, but quickly reappeared. In fact until 1980 they never were far from the forefront. Occasional reports of activity or dissension in the ranks fell on the ears of a none-too-interested public.

The Maguires with their one surviving child had emigrated to New Zealand, but found that the new start and the search for peace were in vain. The birth of another child failed to remove the memories of loss and horror. They came back to Belfast, and to further tragedy. One afternoon in January 1980 the older child returned from school to find his mother dead. She had taken her own life in the most harrowing of circumstances. Four years earlier the Peace People would have responded in their thousands; now the response was muted.

Obviously something had gone dramatically wrong. A month later there was a major rift. The leadership disintegrated, and the movement was in disarray. In August 1980, after another wave of assassinations, Mrs Williams was approached with a request to lead another campaign. Not surprisingly, she did not feel able to respond. Neither did anyone else. By the autumn of the same year their financial problems were worse than ever, and there was talk that their headquarters, Fredheim (*sic*), might possibly be sold.

What had happened? There is no simple answer. Clearly the two young women were swept up on a wave over which they had no control. They were projected from one situation to another almost without warning, continually at the mercy of the last telegram and the necessity to say something about almost every-thing that happened. They were not trained for it, and had not agonized for long years about what they should be doing. Their responsibilities had developed with devastating suddenness, and they were unprepared. However, nothing can take away from them the honour that is rightly theirs. For all too brief a period, their light shone with incandescent brightness in the darkness of Ulster. They inspired and enabled many thousands, who had never thought about it before, to make personal efforts at reconciliation. They planted seeds of hope in broken hearts and anguished minds, and for many that seed still lives. They focused world attention on Ulster's suffering. Peace-makers, politicians and those who had recourse to gun and bomb have much to learn from the events and efforts of these weeks.

We have given pride of place to the story of the Peace People, for it is necessary to consider some of the implications of what they and the others tried to do. A great deal of thinking still will be required before the final chapters of the Ulster saga can be written. Some of the lessons are to be found in the successes and failures of the multitudinous organizations which attempted, each in its own way, to make a contribution.

With the sole exception of the Peace People, no organization has attracted more attention than 'Corrymeela'. The word is shorthand for 'The Corrymeela Community', perhaps the best-known phrase in Ulster's peace vocabulary. It goes back to the visions of its founding fathers in the mid-sixties. Young graduates and professionals for the most part, inspired by the Revd. Ray Davey, then the Presbyterian Chaplain at the Queen's University, they had become increasingly aware of Ulster's underlying tensions. They wanted to do something, but they had also realized a need for some kind of life in community: their minds turned to the models of Iona and Agape.[13] They put it all on record some years later.

The community was started by a group of Christians who wished to express their belief in practical and contemporary terms. As the years passed the activities have more and more been directed to reconciliation. For us this means many things: the opportunity for people of different political and religious convictions to meet for rational and open discussions in relaxed and peaceful surroundings: the need to work together on the problems that concern us not only as citizens but as human beings. It means humbly and together seeking the will of Christ for Ireland to-day.[14]

The acquisition of a large house in south Belfast, and the purchase of a magnificently sited holiday chalet on the north Antrim coast, allowed them to set out on the adventure that Corrymeela has become. Its story has been well told by the Belfast journalist, Alf McCreary, in his widely sold book *Corrymeela*.[15] The community has since erected a complex of purpose-planned buildings: a conference centre, a building for worship, and holiday chalets on the hillside which bears the name Corrymeela, a Gaelic word popularly but erroneously thought to mean 'the hill of harmony'. Here and in Belfast they have sponsored impressive ventures in inter-church living. Its founders realized that far too often the participants in Ulster's religious and communal struggles have shouted from a distance to each other. Corrymeela has pioneered experiments in bringing them together face to face. It has arranged conferences and seminars for all sorts of disparate and important groupings:

politicians, paramilitaries, social workers, sociologists, clergy, teachers, journalists, economists, broadcasters, manual workers. The net result? No limits can be set to how far ideas circulated by person-to-person encounter may travel. Corrymeela has provided the environment for many encounters that have left their mark, but its work has not all been offering opportunities for sharing ideas. It has offered succour to the underprivileged, the handicapped, the families of prisoners and their victims. Its membership is mixed, though it probably has a Protestant majority.

What Corrymeela has been doing throughout the year, the Irish Social Studies Conference has done each summer through its residential meeting. Originally a Catholic organization, it opened its doors to a wider membership some years ago. To its credit is the invitation, accepted in 1958 by Dr G. B. Newe, to address its membership,[16] then probably altogether Catholic, at what was to be known as the Garron Tower Conference, on reasons why Roman Catholics should recognize and co-operate with the northern state. During the seventies Northern Ireland was to figure on the agenda more than once. Sectarianism, and a consideration, without prejudice, of negotiated independence, were topics for summer conferences, with speakers on the latter subject including Dr Garret Fitzgerald (leader of Fine Gael), Dr John Benn (former Ombudsman), and Mr Glen Barr (former Convention member and well-known member of the New Ulster Political Research Group, the body advocating independence). Their conferences have received outstanding press coverage in addition to the support of large numbers of participants.

No lasting peace will be possible without still more encounters of minds and spirits at levels only made possible by the residential settings.

There is a drawing-power in masses on the march, and a magic in meetings in Corrymeela, which camera-crews and newsmen find it difficult to resist. The issuing of political pamphlets, and discussions about the intricacies of old, but never changing, controversies are not compulsive news items. They may well be more significant, or at least every bit as important. Fortunately for Ulster it has not been without those who recognized the need for sowing seed in the barren soil of its political thought, and those who saw the urgency of doing something to improve the quality of that soil.

The long-established Irish Association for Cultural, Economic and Social Relations, the British–Irish Association, and PACE (Protestant and Catholic Encounter) are to be numbered among those groups which have tried to improve the relationships in which new thinking can be discussed. The Irish Association[17] would make no claim to be a peace movement as such, but throughout its history, which goes back to 1939, it has tried to promote better understanding among Irishmen, North and South. Long before the recent attempts at various kinds of cross-fertilization of political and social thought had been considered possible, it had recruited its membership of persons from both sides of the border and from each side of the religious divide. In recent years the British–Irish Association[18] has been doing the same kind of thing, with two important differences. It draws a considerable part of its membership from Great Britain, and its programme has been geared completely towards consideration of the Northern Ireland problem. One way or another, the conferences sponsored by the Irish Association, held for the most part in Dublin or Belfast, and the annual Oxbridge meetings of the British–Irish Association, have created new understanding and growth in mutual respect between politicians, civil servants, representatives of security forces, and those immediately involved in all that goes to make the Ulster problem. To succeed in developing such relationships and to do something to promote a new political vocabulary, where political slogans and catch-cries have altered little over a hundred years, is no mean achievement. PACE[19] is smaller, more narrowly based, and less well-known than the organizations just mentioned. But it deserves more than a mere passing mention, if only for the quality and the sense of urgency that surrounded its first meeting. That gathering was held in the home of a prematurely aged and incapacitated Professor of Orthodontics, James Scott, and his wife Olive. Born and brought up a Protestant, Professor Scott was by then a well-known and practising Catholic. What he lacked in mobility was more than compensated for by his frequent and very able contributions to the correspondence columns of the Belfast and Dublin papers. He had a consuming passion for understanding and reconciliation that illness and physical handicap could not destroy. The agony of the summer months of 1969 had persuaded him, and the others who gathered in his home, that time was short for Ulster. Perhaps he and some of the others who coined the name PACE that night, were conscious that time was running out for them as well. Within months, death had taken from a province that could ill afford to lose them, men of the calibre of Professor Scott himself, Dr Jack Sayers, former Editor-in-Chief of the *Belfast Telegraph*, one who had realized sooner than most the poverty of Ulster's political life, the Revd. Samuel Johnston, lately President of the Methodist Church in Ireland, and the Venerable John Mercer, a noted ecumenist and at the same time a member of the Orange Order. Some years later another of those founder members, Mr J. J. Campbell, the educationalist and member of the Cameron Commission, was also to die. The organization they launched still survives, with branches right across the province. In its own way, it has made a contribution to political discussion, and, more importantly perhaps, to bringing considerable numbers from both communities together for rational discussion of divisive issues.

The emergence in January 1969 of the New Ulster Movement (NUM) was one of the great signs of hope that a new day was about to dawn. Its declared purpose was to work 'to heal our historic divisions and especially between Protestants and Catholics, so that we may build a united community: to promote social justice and integrity in the political life of Ulster: to work for community peace through the democratic process'.[20] It declared as 'a first principle 'that it is equally legitimate for any citizen to support by non-violent means the continued union with Great Britain or to seek by non-violent means the unification of Ireland by the consent of the people of Northern Ireland'. In the early seventies, it poured out a flood of occasional papers which dealt with the continuing crisis, all of which were well thought out and presented. Their influence on political thinking, and especially the thinking of the British government, cannot be overestimated. The settlement of 1974, the Assembly, and the power-sharing Executive represented the achievement of policies advocated by NUM.

The destruction of Brian Faulkner's Executive left the NUM without alternative policies to advocate, and its advice to the Constitutional Convention in the pamphlet *A Challenge of Statesmanship* (1975) was a reiteration of a policy which at that time had no chance of revival. But, in the long term, Northern Ireland may have to look at that policy again. The organization was increasingly bereft of causes on which to fight and fighters to engage in campaigns. Many of its members became founder members of the Alliance Party, and the departure to England, on his appointment as Director of Oxfam, of its founder-

President, Mr Brian Walker, was a severe blow. He more than most had been responsible for the drive and insight which had made NUM unquestionably a force to be reckoned with. Finally dissension in its ranks over the Feakle initiative and the vacuum caused by continuing direct rule, coupled with diminishing resources, made its virtual disappearance inevitable.

One of the most significant, though among the shortest-lived, of the groupings, that came together was the Movement for Peace in Ireland. It originated in an idea, floated in the early autumn of 1971, of involving politicians of all Irish political parties with Church and community representatives, both Catholic and Protestant. In the event it was thought that the northern government would not agree to any meeting or discussion involving representatives of the government of the Republic, at that time the Fianna Fail party. It was consequently considered that it would be unwise to involve the SDLP in the absence of the Unionists. The final result was a series of highly constructive meetings between some leading members of the opposition parties in the Republic and persons appointed by the Churches and other organizations in the North. The southern representatives included Dr Garret Fitzgerald, later Minister of Foreign Affairs and subsequently Prime Minister, Dr Conor Cruise O'Brien, later a Cabinet minister and Editor-in-Chief of the *Observer* of London, Mr Declan Costello, later Attorney-General and now Mr Justice Costello, and the late Mr Michael McInerney, well-known journalist on the staff of the *Irish Times*.[21] The movement had an impressive constitution listing eleven objects, all designed to promote reconciliation and to eliminate recourse to violence. Dr Fitzgerald and Dr O'Brien, in their subsequent books on the Irish problem, refer to the meetings.[22] Unquestionably the northern personnel, who included well-known clerics, trade union and community officials, both Catholic and Protestant, gave their colleagues new insights into the intricacies of the Ulster problem, and, in particular, the Protestant mind. It is not too much to suggest that these meetings left their mark on subsequent government policies in the Republic.

The phrase 'charismatic renewal' has become part of religious jargon in Ulster as much as elsewhere. At first sight the phrase, and the expanding movement associated with it, would seem to have little to do with a study of Ulster's peace movements. But no survey dare neglect a phenomenon which regularly brings Protestants and Catholics together by the thousands. So much has this become the case that one can detect the Hierarchy endeavouring to guide the faithful along safe paths and away from dangerous influences. Official Catholic concern is more than matched by unofficial opposition from theologically right-wing Protestants, who are equally determined to steer their faithful away from danger.

Conferences and rallies attended by huge numbers are held from time to time in Dublin, Belfast, and elsewhere. Charismatic influence has become increasingly evident in congregational and parish life right across the divide. In 1974 a Christian Renewal Centre was established at Rostrevor, County Down. Its philosophy may be summed up in the words of one of its founders, the Revd. Cecil Kerr, one-time Church of Ireland Chaplain at Queen's University. He wrote in his *Power to Love*, 'a new way is being opened up through the hard soil of hatred and bitterness into the light of a new day of hope and brotherhood'.[23]

Judged by that criterion, one has to say, though with considerable reluctance, that the movement has not exercised the influence on political thinking, community attitudes, or paramilitary activity that could justifiably have been expected from such a widespread phenomenon. One wonders if many of those to whom charismatic renewal has brought an unquestionably real sense of liberation have yet fully grasped the inherent social and political implications of the gospel. Cardinal L. J. Suenens, world-famous as a leader of the charismatic movement, voiced his concern in 1980 about what was happening in Ireland to one of the authors. He drew attention to his own thinking set out in dialogue with Dom Helder Camara: 'the proclamation of the gospel permanently includes, for each and every Christian, the duty to contribute personally to that collective and essential righting of social injustice'.[24] The charismatics undoubtedly have the numbers and strength to achieve the goal, but there is no compelling evidence to suggest that they have the insight or will that would spring from deep conviction. They may yet see the vision. Who can tell?

The record of these organizations and of the others we have not described in detail is an honourable one. Long hours and nights, sacrifice, and danger, and with what result? The violence continued with its varying patterns. Sectarianism did not disappear. Politicians and paramilitaries have paid scant attention to what the many dedicated and courageous are doing, and polarization remains dominant.

Was all the effort wasted? By no means. There were great disappointments; there were also great rewards. In any case, several of the initiatives could only have been of local and short-term significance, and they helped to calm and stabilize in situations fraught with uncertainty and fear. They did something to build bridges across which people could and still do travel. If they did not produce answers, at least many of them made people realize the questions were more difficult than they had thought. They persuaded a far larger number than could have been envisaged in 1969 to 'stand up and be counted'.

But the haunting question remains: Why did they not succeed? Admittedly the preservation of peace, or its restoration after hostility has erupted, is more difficult than keeping the violence going once it has started. Also, of course, peace-makers may never resort to the methods used by mob orators or guerrilla movements to achieve their aims. But this is insufficient explanation, and it is also not enough to say that many of the attempts were not well enough organized, or that 'big money' and the media destroyed the Peace People. All along the Churches, the moderates, and indeed the leader-writers and the commentators, were claiming that the vast majority of the Ulster people wanted peace. Superficially then it could be argued that the peace movements should have done better.

Tim Pat Coogan in his monumental book *The IRA* states unequivocally that the Feakle initiative was the most successful and lasting peace movement of the decade.[25] Such a view may be questioned, but what is not in question is the fact that Feakle, NUM, MPI, and Corrymeela had one factor in common. They, of all the organizations mentioned and operating in Ulster, had most effect on violence and political action. The reason is clear. They endeavoured to make meaningful contact with either or both politicians and the para-military organizations. They were not deterred by the prevalent cynicism about politicians, and some of them deliberately defied the 'you don't talk to terrorists' view. They saw what so many others missed, that it is not enough to hope and sometimes work simply for 'peace'. Everyone wanted peace, but too many thought, and still think, of peace on their own terms only. There was all too little attempt to involve people either in the attempt to understand the conditions that make for peace or strife, or in the willingness to make the necessary compromises.

With hindsight, perhaps one can see here the real reasons for the disappointing results of the Peace People. Arguably Ciaran McKeown had his own political philosophy; the many thousands who joined or supported the movement either did not share it or did not understand it. They were obsessed, as were so many of the others, by the fear of party-political considerations introducing dissension into the ranks. Quite possibly the Peace People could have exerted a telling influence on events if they had, in the autumn of 1976 and succeeding months, persuaded their followers to deny their votes to candidates in local or other elections who were not prepared to make meaningful gestures and compromises for the sake of reconciliation, or indeed just for 'peace sake'. The effect of a Northern Ireland 'peace-pledge union', supported by the momentum of the marching thousands, could have been dramatic, but to create a lasting peace in any democratic society, there must be a political arrangement satisfactory to the vast majority of the population. In Northern Ireland, that means the majority of the majority as well as the majority of the minority. To have any chance of lasting, it must also be supported by an adequate economic and social infra-structure. All this adds up to an obligation on those who would be peace-makers to be involved in the political process. There is no substitute for the will, and the knowledge of the means, to achieve the conditions for peace. What is needed is not either a sustained and irresistible mass movement or the alternative of the 'right people in the right places'; it is both. It is not a choice between the NUMs of this world and others like the Peace People; each should be complementary to the other. It is not a case of either Protestant or Catholic effort; it is a need for both together.

Nell McCafferty recalled words written by Ciaran McKeown in 1977: 'If we fail to grasp the opportunity, we will have deeply depressed a world that dared to hope; and for good measure we will have nailed Betty and Mairead to a cross of wasted suffering.'[26] The cross and nails are now part of Northern Ireland's history not only for Betty and Mairead but for all the thousands who have suffered, and for everybody else. The suffering of one is the suffering of all. But there may still be time to make the suffering fruitful, if those who long for peace are ready to be involved in the far more arduous and costly business of being peace-makers.

Such is the story of some of the Ulster peace movements. Whatever may be deduced from their witness, whatever their successes or failures, one thing stands out. Christians in Ulster, in numbers far beyond popular conception, have been engaged in the search for peace. There may be far too many who have opted out, or rather never opted in. There may be questions about the record of the Churches as such. But the point must still be made: Christians, because of something their Churches had taught them, were searching and striving for peace, even if they did not always understand the implications of their search. Their record stands. At least they tried.

12 Churches on Trial

How will history evaluate the role of the Churches in this turbulent period of Northern Ireland's history? Any estimate at this date made by people who have themselves been closely involved with the events is bound to be subjective. It can only be put forward as part of the data on which an objective assessment may ultimately be based.

The present stalemate arises from the fact that the political problem *as posed by the protagonists* admits of no solution: that is, the respective aspirations are incompatible. If Ireland and Britain are two states wholly independent of each other, then the wish of one part of the population to be Irish is not compatible with the wish of the other part to be British. There is no possible line of geographical partition that would resolve this, and, even if there were, that would not satisfy a large element attached sentimentally to the dream of a united Ireland. The problem only admits of solution by a substantial change in the aspirations of one community or the other, or both. It seemed for a moment in 1968 as if that had happened on one side: that the nationalist population was prepared to put the idea of reunification on a very long finger indeed, in return for fair and equal treatment within the state of Northern Ireland. The reaction of the Minister for Home Affairs, of the Protestant mobs, and, we regret to add, of the RUC in Derry, soon put an end to that possibility. It is not the case that if both communities would be reasonable a solution satisfactory to all could be found; any solution will be in some degree less than satisfactory to one or both parties. Take for example the attempted solution of 1974. This was acceptable to those on the Unionist side who participated in it, because it retained the identity of Northern Ireland as part of the United Kingdom. It was acceptable to the SDLP because it combined minority participation in government and a measure of all-Ireland collaboration, and so could be represented as a first step in the direction of Irish reunification. Brian Faulkner and his colleagues did their utmost to deny that it had that implication; the bulk of the Unionist electorate showed in the February United Kingdom election that it believed it had. To eliminate the all-Ireland part might well have been to lose the SDLP from the coalition, because of the need to continue paying at least lip-service to the goal of Irish unity; to retain it was to ensure the overthrow of the coalition by popular pressure on the Unionist side. And failure to maintain, or to re-establish in the six years since this happened, a similar form of collaboration, has carried the SDLP further in the direction of insisting on an all-Ireland solution.

Politics has been called the art of the possible; and, when two programmes are incompatible, action has often succeeded in reaching a compromise which, while less than wholly satis-factory to either side, is seen as better than strife and the best that each side can expect. The difficulty of gaining acceptance for a compromise is much greater where a deep sense of national identity is involved; greater still when the use of phrases like 'no surrender' and 'not an inch' reveals a fear of psychological and social genocide[1] going back over many generations; and greater again when religious loyalty is held to be at stake as well. Roman Catholics in Ireland, reacting no doubt against long periods when the ruling powers despised their way of life and thwarted them, have expected that society in a free Ireland should exemplify, and therefore the state should uphold, the moral standards characteristic of Catholicism. They have accordingly built up in the southern state since 1921 a system that goes far to justify the fears that Protestants expressed in the phrase 'Home rule means Rome rule'. Thus to the Irish Protestant the reuni-fication of Ireland seems to be a betrayal not only of his British nationality but of his Protestant heritage: a person supporting that policy is both 'a traitor' and an 'apostate'. Likewise for the Ulster Catholic to forgo his aspiration to unite Ireland is not only to deny his country 'one of her four green fields' but also to continue forever living in what to him is easily made to seem a sub-Christian or non-Christian state.

It is this coincidence of political and theological factors that renders the issue so intractable. It demands both theological and political techniques for its solution. Ingenious con-stitutional schemes for ensuring fair treatment for the minority founder on the rocks of religious emotion, compounded by the indignation aroused by terrorism. Ecumenical endeavour to increase understanding between the Churches comes under suspicion because a political sell-out is feared. To the Ulster

Protestant, Catholics are seen at one moment as 'republicans' and at the next as 'papishes' (*sic*), with the connotation 'rebels' lurking just below each description, and 'Fenians'[2] available to sum up all the notions. To the Catholics, the Protestants are seen as clinging to the ascendancy, both political and religious, of days gone by, but giving this a cloak of respectability in the form of a demand for unqualified 'majority rule'.

We have seen in this book the extent to which Christians in Ireland have in the past few years risen above these simplistic concepts. The change has, however, been recent, and is far from complete. Too many have not yet been emancipated from the traditional dogmas that would exclude the other side absolutely from the Christian Church. The more charitable views that the main Churches now officially take of each other are of very recent growth. In Ireland they are held back by an inescapable conflict of interest in secular matters and the fact that this conflict has erupted into a violent phase in the very years, since Vatican II, when ecumenism has made notable progress elsewhere. Hence those among the clergy who have contacts with Churches in other countries, or who read about trends of religious thought outside Ireland, find themselves increasingly out of touch with the rank and file, both clerical and lay, who on both sides are still enmeshed in mental attitudes that were once widely encouraged throughout Europe. In days when acknowledged unbelief was rare, the deviant Christian rather than the outright pagan was felt to be a threat. In Ireland this is for many still the case.

There is on both sides of the religious divide in Ireland a theological conservatism and a puritanism of outlook that have been out of fashion in the English and European churches. One may note, however, in recent years a world-wide recrudescence of fundamentalism, observable in Islam as well as in Christianity. If this has tended to reverse the trend in many countries, it has reinforced what was already there in Ireland. Paradoxically this frame of mind results in a similarity between the two traditions, but makes no contribution to bridge-building. Alike to the outsider, they seem utterly disparate to those who belong. The conservatism hinders the impact of new ideas which might, without damage to basic Christian faith, act as a solvent to rigid preconceptions of the other side. The puritanism attaches great importance to certain aspects of conduct and tends to exaggerate the significance of the differences that exist. Neither characteristic is conducive to tolerance, whether in Ireland or elsewhere. Until quite recently social discipline in both communities was tight, and everyone knew just what the others did which 'we' did not do.

Ireland has not, of course, escaped the secularizing trend of the twentieth century, though its effects were felt more slowly. Today church attendance can no longer be taken for granted. The latest survey of attitudes towards religion in Northern Ireland, analysed by a member of the Political Science Department of the Queen's University of Belfast,[3] has produced some interesting results. Weekly church attendance over the years 1968–80 on the part of Roman Catholics had declined by 5 per cent to 90 per cent—still an unbelievably high figure, questioned by some Catholics. For Protestants over the same period the figure had gone down from 46 per cent to 39 per cent. The figures for Belfast are noticeably lower than for the rest of the province; Roman Catholic 82 per cent and Protestant 33 per cent. The outlook on morality is changing too. Television has been perhaps the most powerful influence in introducing young people in Ireland to the values—or lack of them—characteristic of British and American society today. British television, both BBC and IBA, is of course provided in Northern Ireland, and readily receivable in the most populous parts of the Republic. Radio Telefis Eireann rebroadcasts a fair amount of British and American material. The practices of the permissive society are disseminated, even though in the Republic Church and State combine to forbid them.

Despite these developments, indeed perhaps because of them, there are still many who take the view that Christian standards should invariably be enforced by law. Dr Paisley's party is as adamantly opposed to relaxing the laws on homosexuality in the North as the Hierarchy is to relaxing the laws on contraception in the South. But in the main this enforcement of morality has meant in practice the enactment, since the country was partitioned on a sectarian basis, of denominational morality. In the one state you could not buy contraceptives; in the other you could not swim in the public baths on Sundays. Slowly these taboos are being eroded, and the laws that upheld them amended; but always with strong rearguard action from some of the Churches. When it is remembered that every restriction of personal liberty in the name of religion intensifies sectarian feeling,[4] one is bound to ask how far some Christians consider these issues more important than life and death. Indeed one may note with misgiving that, while sex and nudity in films still raise an outcry, wounding and killing are—as elsewhere—regarded as a perfectly acceptable ingredient of popular entertainment. Secularization could be expected to lead to a clearer line between those matters which it is necessary for the State to enforce and those which it is the function of the Church to uphold. Ecumenism should encourage a clearer distinction between those beliefs which are essential to Christianity and those which are characteristic of particular denominations. Both these trends, which have begun to influence the Irish Churches, have yet to penetrate to the ordinary congregational level. Protestant ministers are always conscious of the loss that may result from an apparent sympathy with either of these causes. In most congregations the threat of secession to the Free Presbyterians or some fringe sect is never far away. And oddly enough, no doubt because of the communal conflict, some of the denominational characteristics are more stubbornly held by those who do not practise their religion than by those who do. 'Doggedly Protestant but totally irreligious' is not a meaningless description in Belfast. It is undoubtedly applicable to a proportion of those who belong to the traditional Protestant institutions, namely the Orange Order and its smaller partners the Royal Black Preceptory and the Apprentice Boys of Derry. It is more generally applicable to the new paramilitary bodies, the Ulster Defence Association, the Ulster Volunteer Force, the Ulster Freedom Fighters, and the Red Hand Commando.

The Churches, as we have seen from their official statements, have had little use for the latter type. Invariably they have maintained that none are entitled to take the law into their own hands, although sometimes they have warned that, if the state does not give full protection to its citizens against outrage, such action is understandable, if not justified. In relation to the traditional Protestant institutions the role of the Churches has been more ambiguous.

Rejuvenated but at times uncertain of itself, the Orange Order remains a constant reminder to every Protestant minister of what is expected of him. It is and always has been a curious amalgam of orthodoxy and the claim to individual judgement, of deep personal religion and rabid political Protestantism, of bigoted intolerance and a willingness to live and let live. It appeals equally to urban and rural workers, to small shopkeepers, to large and small farmers, and still to a number of landed gentry. Fiercely opposed to the ecumenical movement, if it embraces Roman Catholicism, no organization has done more to encourage interdenominational services and mutual exchanges of pulpits between the Protestant denominations. Up to the late sixties Orange membership was a *sine qua non* for aspiring Unionist politicians. This pattern was broken when Basil McIvor won the Larkfield seat in 1969 without having to join.

The voice of the Order may be more muted and uncertain than it used to be, but it would be folly to write it off. As we have seen, Ian Paisley was (but, long before the present troubles, ceased to be) a member. Many Orangemen reflect his views as he reflects theirs. Were he to renew his membership, the Order could become an even greater force to be reckoned with. Many clergymen belong, though not nearly as many as Roman Catholic apologists seem to think.

The qualifications of an Orangeman, as set out in 1970 by the scholarly Englishman, the Revd. Dr Michael Dewar, himself an Orangeman, read for the most part like the standards of a pietist society:

An Orangeman should have a sincere veneration for his Heavenly Father; a humble and steadfast faith in Jesus Christ, the Saviour of mankind . . . He should cultivate truth and justice, brotherly kindness and charity, devotion and piety, concord and unity and obedience to the laws; his deportment should be gentle and compassionate, kind and courteous . . . he should honour and diligently study the Holy Scriptures, and make them the rule of his faith and practice; he should love, uphold and defend the Protestant religion and sincerely desire and endeavour to propagate its doctrines and principles.[5]

The list of criteria goes on:

He should strenuously oppose the fatal errors and doctrines of the Church of Rome and scrupulously avoid countenancing (by his presence or otherwise) any act or ceremony of Popish worship; he should by all lawful means, resist the ascendancy of that church, its encroachments and the extension of its powers, ever abstaining from all uncharitable words, actions, or sentiments towards his Roman Catholic brethren.[6]

The third section reverts to personal behaviour and attitudes, concluding: 'The Glory of God and the welfare of man, the honour of his Sovereign and the good of his country, should be the motive of his actions.' Take the middle section out of the list and there remains a document at which few can cavil. Leave it in and you have a recipe for the religious apartheid that lies at the heart of so much of Ulster life. The veto on attendance at any act of Roman Catholic worship has caused incalculable heart-searching and heartbreak in the case of mixed marriages, and misunderstanding about non-attendance at funerals of friends, neighbours, and colleagues who happened to be Roman Catholics.

Given the fact that there is probably no Protestant congregation in Ulster without some Orangemen in its membership, the pressures on any minister who wishes to voice a word of criticism or judgement can easily be appreciated. There have been those who found it necessary to seek appointments elsewhere of a different character. It is no exaggeration to claim that criticism of one's own Church encounters less hostility than even the least critical word about the Order or its practices. Eric Gallagher recalls vividly the reactions in the highest echelons of the Order to something he had said about the creation of religious apartheid at a meeting in Edinburgh, under the auspices of the Royal Institute for International Affairs, in 1971. The Grand Master, Grand Secretary, and Grand Chaplain of the Grand Lodge of Ireland were deputed to convey to him personally the disapproval of the Order. The day of his visitation was arranged. The Orange hierarchy arrived, and within minutes a massive explosion was heard. Some seconds later a telephone call revealed that the Order's headquarters building, some three hundred yards away, had been blown up by the IRA. This news was not important enough to warrant the delegation curtailing their rebuke. It was sufficient for one to proceed to the scene of destruction while the other two continued the interview. This incident highlights the dilemma facing many Protestant ministers. So far they have failed to find the answer. If they are members of the Order, do they resign? And do they encourage Orangemen in their congregation to do the same? Or do they heed the point in a Quaker pamphlet:

There are undoubtedly some in the Orange Order who, while genuinely concerned for the Protestant faith and general well-being of Ulster, are also moderate and reasonable men. . . . It is not impossible that the Order, if successfully challenged by its own more moderate and far-sighted members, could respond to its own stated aims and ideals, in which case it might have had a useful part to play in a happier Northern Ireland.[7]

But the pamphlet goes on to point out the dilemma:

Some believe, however, that to imagine this is to misconceive the true nature and structure of the Orange Order, which, they say, already looks outdated and old fashioned, and which can only become more cantankerous and evil while it loses evolutionary purpose and effectiveness and finishes up as a brontosaurus-like relic of an incredible past.[8]

If any are tempted to poke fun at Orange ritual, regalia, and insignia, they would do well also to recall that Irish Protestantism is otherwise sadly lacking in the colour and ceremonial that make Catholicism (whether Roman or Anglo) so appealing to its rank and file. The Order answers the need for celebration, hierarchy, and public display. 'In working class communities like Sandy Row and the Shankill', as Frank Wright points out, 'it has become a central fact of social life: it is not merely a political institution but a community institution with social and religious significance.'[9] Again, if the critic is concerned at Orange reactionary attitudes and conservatism, he does well also to recognize that often, where there is no constitutional issue at stake, where the Faith or the Crown is not being called into question, working-class Orangeism can be as radical and as critical of the Establishment as anyone. The 1980 resolution[10] denouncing the government's policy on unemployment may have been unusual: it is not unprecedented. Politicians should never presume to count on the Orange vote.

Long ago a Dungannon magistrate is reported to have said: 'As for the Orangemen, we have a difficult card to play. They must not be entirely discountenanced. On the contrary we must in a certain degree uphold them, for with all their licentious-ness, on them we must rely for the preservation of our lives and properties, should critical times occur.'[11] 'Licentiousness' would not be the word used today by the Order's critics. Bigotry and obsolescence would be nearer the mark. Yet a majority of Ulster Protestants would still express in similar terms their belief that the Order is their ultimate bulwark. As Dr Dewar has written: 'Today the fact that all citizens in Northern Ireland have enjoyed their freedom, irrespective of their political party or religious affiliation, for nearly half a century, is in no small measure due to the upholding by the Orangemen of the principles of civil and religious liberty, which are symbolised by the open Bible and the British Crown.'[12]

The questions which such a claim begs are not questions which Protestants in Ulster ask. As a result, the belief con-stitutes a potent factor in the situation and an obstacle to understanding between the communities. The Orange Order is an obstacle to peace in so far as it ensures that the majority of the

majority, for which it speaks, maintain a rigid stance. It articul-
ates their underlying fears in such a way as to suggest that there
is only one way of guarding against the dangers: obstinate
resistance rather than mutual accommodation.

But a much greater obstacle to peace is the Provisional IRA.
For not only does it maintain a similarly rigid stance about the
visionary 'Republic'—a stance that sets it against both the
existing states in Ireland and against the material well-being of
the Catholic population—but it also has its share of guilt for
maintaining the physical-force tradition in Irish politics. One
notable contribution made by the Roman Catholic Church has
been its repeated reminder that in the liberation of most of
Ireland from British rule the part played by the physical-force
movement was limited, and that ultimate success depended just
as much on what had been done by parliamentary and constitutional means. In a notable pastoral statement relating to an
earlier IRA campaign the bishops set out in detail the fallacies
on which the IRA claim to be legitimately fighting for Ireland
was based: 'Sacred Scripture gives the right to bear the sword
and to use it against evil-doers to the supreme authority and to it
alone . . . We declare that it is a mortal sin for a Catholic to
become or remain a member of an organization or society which
arrogates to itself the right to bear arms or to use them against its
own or another State . . .'[13]

The Churches have consistently condemned violence on both
sides; and there is no doubt that the vast majority of their
practising members support them in this and sincerely want
'peace'. It is in the translation of this general will towards
reconciliation, which they have effectively fostered, into
practical steps that would be socially and politically effective,
that the Churches have so far failed.

On the social front we must ask: If the Churches care deeply
about reconciliation, what can they do without betrayal of
principle to mitigate communal separation, physical and
spiritual? Given the parameters set by the groups of extreme
Protestants who are unquestionably in the majority, what signs
are there that the Protestant Churches as such recognize the
complexity of the problem? Given the effect on Protestant
thinking of Catholic social teaching and the insistence on
Catholic education underlying its marriage regulations, what
can the Roman Catholic Church without betrayal of principle
do realistically to create the conditions of reconciliation?

In any case, whatever the limits set by the truth as each side sees it, and the degree of manœuvre set by those limits, the Churches must face the issues causing, and caused by, their adherence to historic dogmas. The factor of communal separation must be faced. Again and again calls have been made for communal acts of repentance. This was never more clearly articulated than by Canon Paul Oestreicher in his theological lectures at Queen's University in 1980, when he publicly regretted the absence of a symbolic foot-washing on the occasion of the Pope's address at Drogheda in September 1979. Frequently joint appearances and prayers by Church leaders meet the criticism 'They are not speaking for us'. Consequently those who are nearest to the action realize how false the kind of ceremony suggested by Canon Oestreicher would be. The representatives taking part would not be regarded as typical of the communities to which they belonged. What is needed is an all-out official endeavour to break down the communal separation. Do any of the Churches realize that absence of fellowship between Christians, let alone suspicion and division, is a threat to the credibility of the Faith? Whether they realize it or not, violence has its roots in attitudes of this kind, even if it is perpetrated by people whose Christian profession is minimal. In the long run the survival of any form of institutional Christianity is at risk. It is to their credit that in many of the most difficult and dangerous areas the Churches have succeeded in maintaining their week-by-week activities. But 'business as usual' is not good enough to meet, let alone to beat, the challenge of violence in Ireland.

In the search for an end to communal separation there are two uncertainties at the time of writing. One is how far the Presbyterian secession from the World Council of Churches presages a general retreat from ecumenism on the part of that Church; and the other is how far the forthcoming Roman Catholic *Directory on Mixed Marriages* will result in genuine freedom for the partners in such a marriage to reach with mutual integrity the decisions that need to be made.

On the political front we must ask: Why is it that the Churches, for all the good will they have mustered and fostered, failed to translate their members' longing for peace into coherent constitutional terms? It has been too easily assumed that peace could be got by persuading violent men not to be wicked; that peace meant a restoration of 'normality' i.e. going back to what people were used to on the Protestant side, or going on to the reunification of Ireland (the ultimate national 'normality') on the Catholic side; that peace could be got in fact without a radical readjustment of presuppositions. Thus at suitable emotional junctures vast crowds can be persuaded to march and rally 'for peace' and even to embrace their opponents in public; but when it comes to voting, nothing has changed.

Part of the difficulty lies in the natural unwillingness of church leaders directly to advise their members how to vote. The general arguments against party-political activity by clergymen are well known. They include the point made by the late Archbishop William Temple when he eventually renounced the Labour whip in the House of Lords: that party loyalty would sometimes require him to uphold stances at variance with his Christian convictions. Equally cogent is the argument that the Christian minister is or should be above all else a pastor to all his people. He has the obligation and privilege of sensitizing his congregation to the social, economic, and political implications of the gospel. Members of that congregation may with integrity see those implications differently and select their political parties accordingly. All of them have a right to expect spiritual and pastoral help and care from their minister. He should in a real sense be 'a man for others', irrespective of political creed or allegiance. The day he becomes a party-political activist, that minister places a barrier between himself and those members of his congregation who see things differently.

It may well seem to Christians elsewhere that these general considerations should in Northern Ireland be overridden by the paramount need for reconciliation between the communities. This would mean that in fulfilment of a ministry of reconciliation the leadership of the Christian Churches and the ministers of local congregations should openly give their support to those parties which seek their membership in both those communities. That, of course, is not how things look to the great majority of church members in Northern Ireland: they instinctively expect their ministers to support the traditional sectarian parties which on each side are supposed to give political expression to true Christianity as they see it. It is the conviction of the present authors that the tacit or active identification of religious denominations with fixed political attitudes has done very great harm in Northern Ireland and that, even in the interests of reconciliation, it would not be right to give a further twist to that particular phenomenon. And we think this view is held by most of the clergy who have been influenced by the ecumenical movement. The very fact that, in practice, voting in Northern Ireland has been sectarian makes those who would transform the political traditions less willing to use church influence to secure the transformation. The trouble is that so long as the church leadership refrains from declaring itself in party-political terms, the role of the Churches in directly bringing about the necessary political transformation is bound to be limited; and the ordinary voter is left thinking that if he goes on voting with his tribe, that is all right by the Churches. This restraint, necessary as it seems to be, on the part of the church leadership, is a limitation on the effectiveness of the Churches in achieving the reconciliation which, as we have seen throughout this book, they are visibly seeking.

A permanent solution to the problem of Northern Ireland can only come through political action, implying either a radical change of outlook by the traditional political parties or their displacement by new parties with a more pragmatic appraisal of Ulster's real needs. If for very good reason, the Churches disclaim any direct role in that process of political transformation, it will be slower in realization. It will come only through a gradual influencing of public opinion in the direction of reconciliation, with actual voting patterns always lagging behind the degree of common feeling that may be achieved between the communities. So long as direct rule continues, obsolete voting habits need not be disastrous. However direct rule, as we have seen, becomes less acceptable in times of economic depression and therefore may not last as a stabilizing factor as long as some expect.

The Protestants will always be a minority in Ireland as a whole. The time may well come when they will be at best a very precarious majority in Northern Ireland itself. It is therefore in their long-term interests to give in Northern Ireland an example of the fair treatment of a cultural minority in a pluralistic state; for, sooner or later, they will need that kind of justice for themselves. Their persistent claim for simple 'majority rule' is thus ill-conceived in the perspective of history. Majority rule in the sense that a party which has achieved a majority at the polls directs policy for the time being is one thing; majority rule in the sense that one community-of-identity permanently insists on monopolizing public life at the expense of a smaller community-of-identity is quite another. Without espousing party politics, the Churches could undoubtedly do a good deal more than they have done to clarify this distinction, to explore the kind of constitutional devices by which such a minority can best be facilitated within the structures of the state, and to pursue with determination the education of their own people in the meaning of justice for all in a mixed population. The Protestant Churches, having at present a substantial majority, have the responsibility of giving a lead in this; they would be noticeably helped if the Roman Catholic Church gave clearer evidence of having renounced the ambition to see every facet of their ethical system enacted as law of the state. As Father John Brady, SJ, has put it: 'The ultimate test of a new political order would be that it would not make any difference whether there was a majority or a minority of Protestants in Northern Ireland, precisely because the guaranteeing of vital interests and rights would be completely divorced from the counting of heads'.[14]

How much more, in spite of the obstacles that we have described, might the Churches have done during the 1970s to hasten the achievement of that new order? Part of the answer is bound to be that those leading the Churches in this generation have been inhibited by much of what their predecessors did, and even more by what their predecessors preached. Far too much of this preaching was preaching against other Christians. Protestants were taught for generations, and in some cases still are, that Roman Catholic theology and devotion are unscriptural and contrary to the gospel; and that, wherever it can, the Roman Catholic Church will persecute evangelical Christians. Roman Catholics on their side have been taught that Protestants are contumacious heretics destined for hell. These habits of thought cannot be eradicated overnight. Within the last year an intelligent polytechnic student asked one of the authors whether he thought that Roman Catholics had any chance of going to heaven, and a sixth-former at a Roman Catholic School warned the other author that his chances of getting there were negligible.

There is another aspect of past failure to be considered. It has been popular in many quarters to lay the charge of 'fifty lost years' against successive Unionist governments in Northern Ireland since partition. The accusation may well be justified, but Ulster Unionist governments have no monopoly of guilt in this respect. The years 1920–70 were lost by all involved in the Northern Ireland story. Neither London nor Dublin was faultless, and neither were the Churches. The late Cardinal Conway was once heard to say: 'Maybe we should have been raising our voices about unemployment and living conditions and ill-health and other social ills.' Truth to tell, there is little convincing evidence that during those fifty years any of the Irish Churches demonstrated much in the way of insight into the social and economic implications of the gospel. The failure of those years inevitably left its mark on their attitudes. They were relatively unaware of the winds of change that were blowing elsewhere in the world of Christian thought about the role of the Church in society. That ignorance was compounded by the violence and its pressures. Indeed the decision to set up the working party which produced the report *Violence in Ireland* was reached only with difficulty. In point of fact, it might not have been taken had Cardinal Conway and those who first suggested it not feared the judgement of history on failure to grapple with the problem.

Starting therefore from a position much less advantageous than it might have been, could the Churches have more effectively met the challenge of the years of strife? Looking back over the story this book has had to tell, it might be thought that there was too great reliance on the effectiveness of statements and appeals by church leaders and church courts. That reliance was not confined to the church authorities themselves. Those statements and documents were initially expected and sought by the professional communicators and the politicians. They seemed to think that the Churches could work miracles of which the secular world was incapable. In this expectation they were exaggerating the religious element of the conflict; they thought that, if Roman Catholic and Protestant churchmen said the same thing, there would be nothing left to fight about. But that was far from the truth, as we have seen. Internment day was not by any means the only occasion when Stormont sought a word or gesture from any or all of the Churches. It was in the early days common practice for editors to seek comment from the Churches on controversial issues and incidents, and their purpose was usually constructive rather than merely to seek news. Ulster Television openly claims that on occasion it initiated successful broadcasts by one or another churchman appealing for calm and restraint in a potentially explosive situation. Today, however, there is a cynicism regarding frequently repeated statements emanating from whatever quarter. It is not merely that repetition can be counter-productive. The sad fact would seem to be that the Churches have been learning the same kind of lesson that the producers of documentary programmes have done. No matter how well researched and objective a programme is, more frequently than not it has tended to reinforce rather than to remove prejudices. Too often the reaction to church statements has been to pick out and emphasize the element in the statement that is acceptable and to deplore the absence of something else, which, if it had been included, would almost certainly have been ignored. There is no better example of this than the joint communiqué on internment of 9 August 1971. Qualified support for internment was included because fault would have been found by loyalists had it been omitted. Its inclusion was hardly noticed by Protestants, but for Catholics it was vitally—and disastrously—important.

In conversation with one of the authors Ian Paisley said early in 1981 that many Ulster initiatives and happenings had suffered from instant comment. He recognized that, with others, he had on occasion been pressurized for quick reaction when silence might have been better. It may thus be contended that less reliance should have been placed on the instant statement and much more energy expended on the serious study of the underlying grounds of the conflict and on the education of church members in constructive thinking. The notable series of studies presented to the Presbyterian Assembly, *Republicanism, Loyalism and Pluralism in Ireland*[15] were not ready, respectively, until 1974, 1975, and 1977, i.e. from almost six to almost nine years after the outbreak of trouble. The joint report *Violence in Ireland*[16] did not appear until late in 1976. It can further be argued that even when these studies did appear, little was done to ensure their careful and prayerful study at congregational level, or any vigorous effort made to implement such practical recommendations as they contained.

It is perhaps worthwhile to consider the reaction of the Churches to some of the recommendations of this joint report, produced as it was by a working party composed of Catholics and Protestants from North and South. One clause supported the constitutional authorities, and went on: 'Where an individual has information about violent activities of paramilitary organizations he or she may be assuming a personal moral responsibility if, after taking account of all the personal, family and other dangers involved, he does not put such information before the authorities.' There has in fact been a considerably greater flow of confidential information to the police in recent years, leading to numerous convictions, some for offences committed five or six years previously; it is, of course, impossible to say whether the recommendation, which received wide publicity in 1976, contributed to this development. Two clauses proposing direct action by the Churches, centrally and jointly, namely to set up a Christian Centre of Social Investigation and to establish a joint committee to foster closer contact between Roman Catholic and other schools, have remained a dead letter. The call for 'a sustained and far-reaching programme of education within the Churches by which their members may be made more aware of the political and social implications of Christianity for Irish society' is reflected in the appointment by the Irish Council of Churches of the Revd. John Knox for a three-year project on 'peace education', which he is developing in close collaboration with Mr Jerome Connelly, director in Ireland of the Roman Catholic Commission for Justice and Peace. A series of study guides for use in the Churches is in course of preparation. The last of the recommendations may be thought by some to be naïve; but it goes to the root of the problem and has so far produced no visible result at all. It reads: 'We suggest that all political leaders should be encouraged to see their task as that of reaching a just agreement with their opponents rather than of achieving victory over them; and that to this end they should be open to any reasonable settlement proposed.' The reaction of most of the political parties to the initiatives taken in this field by Mr Humphrey Atkins in 1979 and 1980 indicates that little had been learned since 1968.

What more might the Churches have done? Might they not have adopted a more positive attitude to the process of secularization that is beginning to take root in Ireland as it has already done elsewhere? There is an irony about the situation in which some of the more positive results of the secularizing process—for example the principle of ignoring religious or political views in all contexts where they are irrelevant, such as employment, sport, social life—are just what Ireland needs to lessen its inter-communal tensions. Yet secularization is regarded as a menace by the Churches, which still largely seek to maintain their traditional rights and influence over all aspects of public life. Louis McRedmond has noted in the days of Cardinal Cullen and Henry Cooke 'a switch of emphasis' from the post-French Revolution concern for 'the rights of human beings to the rights of the Churches',[17] a switch the full impact of which has been felt throughout the twentieth century. We may quote in this connection Father John Harriot, who wrote in describing 'a long and thoughtful and intendedly eirenical address by one of the most sensitive and learned Irish Bishops, Cahal Daly' that 'there is evident drawing back from a substantial concession on every issue where an institutional sacrifice might be offered: schools, mixed marraiges, divorce, contraception. . .'[18] So long as a Unionist government ruled in Stormont the insistence of the Protestant Churches on their rights and privileges was not less marked. Even today it has been remarked that a debate in the General Assembly on a political issue will draw a much larger attendance of elders than one on spiritual or pastoral concerns.

Father Harriot's examples of institutional sacrifice are confined to what might be offered by his own Church. The most useful institutional sacrifices that could be made by the other Churches are, we think, of rather a different kind. They would consist mainly in bringing their own constitutional arrangements into line with the needs of an urgent and fast-moving situation. The need to wait until the meeting of an annual assembly or conference before any decision of substance can be made has gravely hampered the Presbyterian and Methodist Churches in dealing with developing events. A year's delay in accepting the Cardinal's invitation to the first Ballymascanlon conference, and a year's delay in formally responding to the report *Violence in Ireland* are examples of the price paid for leaving sovereignty in the hands of a body that meets infrequently. The Church of Ireland suffers less, as considerable power rests with the House of Bishops and the Standing Committee, and the Roman Catholic Church, where the Hierarchy has the first and last word, not at all from this inbuilt procrastination. It is a lesson that could be learned by similarly organized Churches elsewhere: it is possible in modern times to be confronted with a situation in which fundamental decisions have to be taken quickly, and better machinery for this needs to be devised before events become critical. Basic changes of constitution are difficult to effect when the heat is turned on. Another weakness needing correction in the same Churches is the practice of changing the leadership annually. A President or Moderator has scarcely got to know the two Primates when it is time to think of handing over to his successor. A serious breach in the continuity of relations can result: the supreme example came with the election in 1979 of the Revd. Dr William Craig as Moderator, when he declared that on principle he would not

meet Cardinal O'Fiaich in his official capacity. These constitutional traditions are tenaciously held by the denominations
concerned, but we believe that if they are to ask of the Roman
Catholic Church changes in fields that it considers as fundamental as education and mixed marriages, they must be
prepared to make changes that would facilitate continuing
relationships, i.e. a longer term of office for the leader of the
Church, and, on the part of the sovereign church court, either a
much greater delegation of real power to appropriate
committees or, as in the case with the Church of England
General Synod, a more frequent meeting of the court itself.

Nevertheless it would be easy to overestimate the effect of
such reforms. The difficulties of action faced by the Protestant
Churches are due less to the machinery of democracy than to the
fact of it. To a large, though perhaps a diminishing, extent, the
Roman Catholic Hierarchy can reach a decision in a relatively
small forum and expect it to be carried out by priests and people
on a basis of authority and obedience. (Events, however, have
abundantly shown that this authority no longer extends to
political action. The paramilitaries have ignored the bishops
consistently.) In the Protestant Churches leaders must gain the
support of the elected representatives of the whole body before
effective changes can be made. This is a principle that cannot be
jettisoned, although, in our view, the difficulties could be
greatly lessened by constitutional reform. The issue lies at the
root of a problem often noted in Northern Ireland, the problem
of leadership. Does the leader speak for or to his people? Does
he follow the light of his own insight and hope that he can
convince his membership? Or does he put his ear to the ground
and give voice to the murmurings he hears? From time to time
the cry goes up for a prophetic voice. In fact the authentic
prophetic voice has not been entirely absent; but to be
practically effective its deliverance must be endorsed by a
resolution of some democratically elected church court. It is
salutary to remember that in the Bible it was invariably the false
prophets who told the people what they wanted to hear.

Yet in spite of the unsolved problems the record of the
Churches in the current troubles is not wholly a negative one. In
the prologue we asked certain questions about the role churches
might be expected to play in a situation of conflict. Now that our
survey is concluded it seems right to test the record of the Irish
Churches against those criteria.

A 'Good Samaritan' role? A great deal has been done by the

Irish Churches, with generous support in money and manpower from Churches elsewhere, to alleviate the suffering caused by the civil strife. Temporary accommodation for those driven from their homes, opportunities for rest and refreshment for overburdened housewives and for children, comfort for the bereaved and injured, support for projects among young people: all these have been provided and a vast amount of voluntary service undertaken. The statutory services have continued to fulfil their work under very difficult conditions, and many devoted Christian people have been professionally engaged in their beneficent activities.

A 'blueprint'? We have indicated the great difficulty that Churches have in identifying officially with a political programme, though it is true that their traditional identification with political attitudes is part of the problem. The work carried out by various church committees, which have produced analyses of the situation departing in many ways from the established stereotypes, must not be underestimated. The personnel of such agencies as the New Ulster Movement, prolific in new political ideas in the early years of crisis, consisted largely of committed Christian laymen from all the Churches. The Churches possess in their well-attended Sunday services an unrivalled opportunity to disseminate new insights; yet they have failed to communicate the liberating ideas that have emerged and to get them accepted by the rank and file.

A 'shuttle diplomacy'? Our narrative has described a number of occasions on which church leaders, officially or unofficially, have tried to act as mediators in difficult situations. Among the more dramatic were the encounter at Feakle and the efforts made by Cardinal O'Fiaich and Bishop Edward Daly to defuse the H-block problems. Numerous deputations to governments, to political parties, and to paramilitary organizations have sought to lessen tensions and propose solutions. None has had a decisive effect on the general problem, but many have ameliorated particular issues.

We suggested in the prologue that deeper than all these roles lay the fundamental task of the Christian Church to offer salvation: this we defined as 'proclaiming the reality of God and promoting the fulfilment of individual and social life which God's grace in Christ makes possible'. In this connection it is important not to lose sight of the contribution made by the very fact that the Churches, in circumstances of grave abnormality, have maintained in large measure their normal work. Our survey has included words and action taken by the Churches as centrally organized bodies. It has also recorded words and actions for which individual church leaders, clerical and lay, have been responsible. What a narrative of public events fails to do, however, is to reflect adequately the part played at local level by numerous ordinary church members whose daily living is not 'newsworthy', but continually influences, indeed, to a considerable extent constitutes, the general situation. The journalists' question 'What are the Churches doing?' is not to be answered simply by recording what bishops and assemblies have to say. As Bishop Cahal Daly puts it, the tendency to think it can be so answered

implies that the Church is the clergy or the hierarchy. It suggests that action by the Church is action of an ecclesiastical kind by clergy or bishops in the domain of the spiritual and the canonical. It can thus be used as an alibi by laymen to escape Christian responsibility. It diverts the attention of laymen from the fact that they are the Church. It ignores the fact that temporal, social and even political action is Christian action.[19]

If the political actions of Christian people have so far failed to solve the problems, there is no doubt that the personal action of Christian people has done much to alleviate the results of the problems. Terrible as the ordeal of many sections of the population has been, Northern Ireland has so far always drawn back from the brink of open civil war. Things have not been as bad as they might have been or as many forecast they would be. A substantial reason for this has been restraint, and in particular a deliberate and expressed repudiation of revenge on the part of many of those who have actually suffered. To those living in the province this becomes apparent through numerous interviews on local television and in local papers, in which the severely injured and relatives of the dead have asked that there be no reprisals. In their manifest grief they have, over and over again, in a most moving way, excluded bitterness from their reactions and spoken particularly of forgiveness. Here we see at work the salt and the leaven of which Christ spoke; here are the 'People of the Way' showing the way, at least at a personal level. They may hold strongly to beliefs that are theologically divisive, but they hold even more strongly to the Christian love and forgiveness that are common to their differing traditions.

This spirit has been continually fostered by the work of the Churches which has continued amid every discouragement and difficulty. To gather children in a Sunday school, to run a Boys'

Brigade company, to visit the sick and lonely, to preach twice on Sunday, to hear confessions, to say mass: these things may seem undramatic, even tedious, when the foundations of society are being shaken. But to do so, year in and year out, in an atmosphere where political stances are expressed by bombs, bullets, and barricades is itself to make a substantial contribution to stability. It may be said that a response of 'business as usual' is an inadequate one in such a crisis; but it is the indispensable foundation on which further action must be based, and when the 'business' is continual witness to the Christian gospel it can act as a powerful antidote to the disintegration of society. Despite the sectarian element in the conflict, church services have been for the most part an oasis amid hostility. There have been Christians praying for their enemies—and in Northern Ireland that cannot be an abstract or formal activity—in every part of the province every Sunday for twelve years. Speaking in 1973 on an American network television programme, Cardinal Conway said: 'The Churches have helped to keep public opinion fair. They have spoken out clearly and unmistakeably against violence . . . Public opinion in this area is overwhelmingly opposed to violence . . . that essential attitude of public opinion does not come about by accident'.[20] That utterance would carry even more conviction in 1980. To translate this pervading Christian spirit into a political solution of the underlying conflict of interest has not so far proved possible. But to apply it to the situation in terms of restraint, fortitude, and goodwill is something that a vast number of Christians have tried, not without considerable success, to do. The results can only be measured hypothetically against what might have been; but they should not be ignored. Some words of Pope John Paul II at Drogheda are worth remembering:

I pay homage to the many efforts that have been made by countless men and women in Northern Ireland to walk the paths of reconciliation and peace. The courage, the patience, the indomitable hope of the men and women of peace have lighted up the darkness of these years of trial. The spirit of Christian forgiveness shown by so many who have suffered in their person or through their loved ones have given inspiration to multitudes. In the years to come when the words of hatred and the deeds of violence are forgotten, it is the words of love and the acts of peace and forgiveness which will be remembered. It is these which will inspire the generations of men.[21]

The corollary of this basic Christian charitableness has been a profound feeling of regret and shame at the continuing strife. In the early days of rioting and crowd conflict many Christians were more disturbed at the actions of those on their own side of the divide than at those perpetrated by members of the other community. Later, as popular violence gave way to the carefully planned campaigns of organized groups, it became more common to put all the blame on 'the others'; but usually this was mitigated by singling out the terrorist organizations for condemnation: there were 'plenty of decent people' in the other community. As we have seen, a number of movements have arisen whose aim was to establish contact among the 'decent people' and to build up an atmosphere of trust in which the perpetrators of violence would find that such support as they had, tacit or acknowledged, would wither away. Most of the movements have had no official link with the organized Churches, but the initiatives have been taken in most cases by convinced and practising Christians. At Christmas 1974 the church leaders as such launched a campaign on these lines, but for the most part the barricades, whether physical or psychological, have been crossed by Christians working in *ad hoc* organizations rather than by parishes or congregations.

The main thrust of the Churches' contribution has taken the form of greatly enhanced ecumenical collaboration at a time of increasing polarization between the communities at the secular level. In the sixties it seemed for a time as if the suspicion and hostility that divided Catholic and Protestant in the social and political spheres might be subsiding in the light of common interests. The resurgence of violence that followed the demands of the civil rights movement put an end to that, and revived the antagonism of the past. Nevertheless during the 1970s the organized Churches achieved considerable innovations and development in their relationships. There have been setbacks and disappointments in the ecumenical field, but they must not be allowed to obscure the fact that there is now more contact, more mutual respect and understanding, between the Churches than at any earlier period of Irish history. How far this will develop is very uncertain at the time of writing.

Ecumenism is of course a world-wide movement, and in many countries relationships have progressed beyond the point reached in Ireland; the point is, however, that what has been achieved in Ireland has been against the background of a conflict of nationalistic and material interests in which the two sides can be given a sectarian identification. In that lies much of the strength of the opposition to ecumenism; and by it also the dedication and effectiveness of those pursuing ecumenism must be measured. In this the Irish Churches have been greatly helped by Churches elsewhere. The fact that the main Protestant Churches are members of the British Council of Churches has enabled Irish representatives not only to receive from their British colleagues encouragement and comfort, but has also faced them with the challenge of independent judgement on their policies and achievements. The British Churches, and even more notably the European and American Churches, have given practical aid, making available funds which the Irish Churches have been able to administer in support of social activities among the old, the young, and the victims of strife. Conditions quite properly attached to these gifts have required them to be distributed with an impartiality that might otherwise have been difficult to maintain in the face of local pressures. The work of the Irish Council of Churches itself has been facilitated by the substantial financial aid given to provide it with headquarters and additional staff. Children for holidays, paramilitaries and politicians for conferences, have been received in British and European countries, particularly the Netherlands, under the auspices of Christian Churches.

This very real fraternal support from Churches outside Ireland has been deeply valued by the leadership of the Irish Churches. It has underlined the reality of the world-wide Christian community—even though, ironically enough, one Church in Ireland has broken its links with a major manifestation of that universality, the World Council of Churches. Ulstermen have sometimes been surprised at the degree of interest and concern evinced elsewhere in a small and peripheral province. Yet, though small in scale, the conflict is large in significance. Political conflicts abound within and between other countries. Christian unity, in spite of progress made in this century, remains an elusive goal. It is where Christian disunity helps to polarize a politically divided people that a very special kind of tension arises. Ulstermen may be forgiven for asking what would have happened in the United States if all the blacks had been Roman Catholics and all the whites Protestants; or what would be the religious position in Britain if all the coloured immigrants, instead of being Moslem, Hindu, Sikh, Buddhist, and Christian, had all held a common faith distinct from that of the indigenous population. Where would easy religious toleration have been then? There is still much apathy in those countries towards the quest for Christian unity.

If Christian disunity were identified with the racial problems of those societies in a direct way, there would be no apathy. Christians would fall, as they do in Ulster, into two kinds: those passionately seeking unity as an aid to the healing of society, and those deeply suspicious of it as some kind of surrender to the interests of the others. It is in this sense that Ireland brings into sharp relief problems that are less acute, but not less real, elsewhere. Ireland's cross is Christendom's cross. But, if Christian faith means anything, there will be resurrection. And, when it comes, Ireland's travail and its healing will be a sign that the Church is medium and message of God's reconciling love for the world He made.

Notes

The sources for all church statements and actions, and/or quotations from committee reports, not otherwise authenticated, are to be found in the first instance in the *Journal of the General Synod of the Church of Ireland*, in the *Minutes of the General Assembly of the Presbyterian Church in Ireland*, and in the *Minutes of the Conference of the Methodist Church in Ireland*; and, in the second instance, in the reports of the relevant committees and subcommittees to the supreme courts. All these documents are published annually by the respective Churches. The sources for specific references concerning the United Council of Christian Churches and Religious Communions in Ireland (later the Irish Council of Churches) are in the (unpublished) Minutes of the Council.

CHAPTER I

1. Fuller accounts of the general history outlined in the opening pages of this chapter will be found in standard histories of Ireland, e.g. T. W. Moody and F. X. Martin, *The Course of Irish History* (Mercier, Cork, 1967); J. C. Beckett, *The Making of Modern Ireland 1603–1923* (Faber & Faber, 1969).
2. Moody and Martin, *Irish History*, ch. 12; Beckett, *Modern Ireland*, pp. 43–8.
3. Moody and Martin, *Irish History*, p. 200; Beckett, *Modern Ireland*, pp. 82–3.
4. Moody and Martin, *Irish History*, p. 203; Beckett, *Modern Ireland*, pp. 102–9.
5. In general we use the expression 'Roman Catholic' to refer to that Church, its agents and agencies; and the word 'Catholic' to refer to the social community comprised of members of that Church. We use the word 'Protestant' to cover all other Churches, their members, and the community associated with them, knowing full well that some Christians who are not Roman Catholics would not apply the term to themselves.
6. The name Derry (Irish *Doire*, a grove) goes back to the days of St. Columba, and is the official title of the bishoprics, both Roman Catholic and Anglican. 'Londonderry' was coined at the time of the plantation, and is the official title of the municipality and of the county. Colloquially everybody calls the city 'Derry', except Unionists when consciously making a point. A loyalist organization calls itself the Apprentice Boys of Derry (not Londonderry). We accordingly use either name, and usually the shorter form.
7. Fenian, a name given to members of the Irish Republican Brotherhood, a secret society practising violence against the British from the mid-nineteenth century onwards. Also used generally by Protestants of Catholics as a term of abuse. (From *Fianna*, pronounced 'feena', a band or brotherhood.)
8. Moody and Martin, *Irish History*, pp. 209–16; Beckett, *Modern Ireland*, ch. 7.
9. The Revd. R. H. Gallagher, father of one of the authors, was among the few Methodist ministers who refused to sign. It took years of faithful ministry to live this down.
10. Moody and Martin, *Irish History*, chs. 18, 19; Beckett, *Modern Ireland*, chs. 19–22.
11. The Government of Ireland Act 1920, which provided for two equal and parallel parliaments and governments in Dublin and Belfast, each subordinate to the

Crown and Parliament at Westminster. This scheme was never implemented in the South, but the act was the Constitution of Northern Ireland until 1973.

12. See annual official publications as listed at the head of these notes.

13. *Irish Catholic Directory*, published annually. Census figures in 1971 gave in Northern Ireland: Roman Catholics, 477,919; Presbyterians 405,719; Church of Ireland, 334,318; Methodists 71,235; Free Presbyterians 7,337; others 80,601. In the Republic, out of a total population of 2,978,248: Church of Ireland 97,741; Presbyterians 16,054; Methodists 5,646. These may be compared with the figures for the same twenty-six counties before partition (1911): Church of Ireland, 259,533; Presbyterians, 45,486; Methodists, 16,440.

14. Information compiled by J. M. Barkley, and published in *Who are we? What do we Believe?*, ed. Stanley Worrall (Christian Journals Ltd., Belfast, 1977).

15. When Lord Erskine of Rerrick a member of the Church of Scotland, was appointed Governor of Northern Ireland, he caused adverse comment in the Church of Ireland by regularly attending the Presbyterian Church in Hillsborough. His action was, of course, quite correct.

16. Article 44 of the Constitution.

17. For details see J. H. Whyte, *Church and State in Modern Ireland* (Gill & Macmillan, 1971; Fontana 1973).

18. Prudence suggested that a reasonable number of Catholics should, if possible, be recruited to the RUC and other government agencies. Control was, however, kept in Protestant hands, and the Ulster Special Constabulary (the B Specials), a reserve force maintained to secure public order, was exclusively recruited from Protestants.

19. See below, p. 154.

20. See below, ch. 2.

21. F. S. L. Lyons, *Ireland since the Famine* (Weidenfeld & Nicolson, 1971; Fontana 1973). For a full exposition of this policy see D. P. Barritt and C. F. Carter, *The Northern Ireland Problem* (Oxford University Press, 1962).

22. A comment made after his resignation.

23. A doctorate of divinity conferred by the Bob Jones University, USA.

24. See below, pp. 35–7.

CHAPTER 2

1. Louis McNeice, *Selected Poems* (Faber & Faber, 1941), p. 28.

2. *Coleraine Chronicle*, 19 July 1980, and most provincial newspapers.

3. Ibid.

4. McNeice, *Selected Poems*, p. 39.

5. See, as examples, issues of 28 June, 10 September, 24 September 1969, 7 November 1970, 5 December 1970.

6. *Ravenhill Pulpit*, Numbers 15, 16; January 1964.

7. Published in undated booklet entitled *This We Will Maintain*, p. 2. It was Number 33 of *Ravenhill Pulpit*.

8. *Revivalist*, April 1966.

9. Ibid.

10. Michael Hurley, SJ, *John Wesley's Letter to a Roman Catholic* (Geoffrey Chapman, 1968).

11. The Furrow Trust, Gill & Son, Dublin, 1963.

12. Dr J. M. Barkley in a letter to the authors, December 1979. He was an original participant in both. The Revd. Ernest Gallagher of Dublin in a letter to the authors, 18 December 1979, regarding Greenhills, makes similar points.

13. Eric Gallagher was one of the group on each occasion.

14. Recounted by the Revd. T. C. Patterson to Eric Gallagher, November 1979.

15. 'We believe that the unity which is God's will and gift to His Church is being made visible as all in each place who are baptised into Jesus Christ and confess Him as

Lord and Saviour are brought by the Holy Spirit into one fully committed fellowship, holding the one apostolic faith, preaching the one Gospel, breaking the one bread, joining in common prayer, and having a corporate life reaching out in witness and service to all who at the same time are united with the whole Christian fellowship in all places and all ages in such wise that ministry and members are accepted by all, and that all can act and speak together as occasion requires for the tasks to which God calls His people.'

16. The Right Revd. Dr William Boyd, and Eric Gallagher.
17. The Revd. Fr. Hugh Murphy, OBE, and the Revd. Fr Desmond Wilson.
18. *Ravenhill Pulpit*, Number 33.
19. The Roman Catholic community favoured Londonderry for the site of the NUU. Coleraine was least likely to 'spark off' a united approach.
20. The Revd. Dr John Greer (C of I), the Revd. Dr Andrew Adams (PCI) and Eric Gallagher (MCI).
21. Eric Gallagher.
22. The background was an informal conversation between the ex-Moderator, the Very Revd. Dr Alfred Martin, and Eric Gallagher.
23. The Right Revd. Dr William Boyd, Eric Gallagher, and the Most Revd. Dr James McCann respectively.
24. Letter from Eric Gallagher to Cardinal Conway, 22 December 1967, and the Cardinal's reply, 23 December 1967.

CHAPTER 3

1. Belfast *News Letter*, 19 June 1968.
2. See British and Irish newspapers of the time.
3. Respectively Dr James McCann, Dr J. H. Withers, the Revd. Gerald Myles (of Dublin).
4. Belfast *News Letter*, 15 October 1968.
5. Ibid., 7 October 1968.
6. Ibid., 15 October 1968.
7. Ibid., 18 October 1968.
8. Minutes (unpublished) of the Irish Council of Churches.
9. Belfast *News Letter*, 13 November 1968.
10. Ibid., 15 November 1968.
11. Later himself convicted of corruption in London.
12. See above p. 39.
13. Terence O'Neill, *Autobiography* (Hart-Davis, 1972), p. 105.
14. Interview with the authors, June 1980.
15. Belfast *News Letter*, 14 January 1969.
16. Canon Arlow supplied in an interview the background to this paragraph.
17. Belfast *News Letter*, 21 January 1969.
18. *Irish Directory on Ecumenism*, issued by the Irish Episcopal Conference, 1969. See also below, p. 131.
19. Belfast *News Letter*, 21 January 1969.
20. *Disturbances in Northern Ireland* (Cmnd. 532) September 1969 (Report of the Cameron Commission).
21. Belfast *News Letter*, 3 February 1969.
22. See below, pp. 176, 184–5.
23. 17 January 1969.
24. This was disclosed by Cardinal Conway to Eric Gallagher.
25. Belfast *News Letter*, 26 April 1969.
26. Revd. J. H. Brown, reported in Belfast *News Letter*, 19 May 1969.
27. Minutes (unpublished) of the Irish Council of Churches.
28. Belfast *News Letter*, 3 June 1969.
29. *Orange and Green: Northern Ireland* (Northern Friends Peace Board, 1969).

30. Cardinal Conway *et al.*, *Statements and Joint Statements* (published privately, 1972).
31. See below, p. 52.
32. *Violence and Civil Disturbances in Northern Ireland in 1969* (Cmnd. 566) April 1972.
33. David Bleakley, *Peace in Ulster* (Mowbrays, 1972), pp. 89 ff.

CHAPTER 4

1. James Callaghan, *A House Divided. The Dilemma of Northern Ireland* (Collins, 1973).
2. Statements by Cardinal Conway, privately printed and circulated, 1973.
3. See above, ch. 1, n. 18.
4. Conway, *Statements*.
5. Belfast *News Letter*, 30 August 1969.
6. Ibid.
7. Ibid.
8. Callaghan, *House Divided*, p. 82.
9. Belfast *News Letter*, 30 August 1969.
10. Ibid., 1 September 1969.
11. *Disturbances in Northern Ireland*.
12. 10 January 1970.
13. See above, ch. 1, n. 18.
14. Belfast *News Letter*, 17 November 1969.
15. Ibid., 18 October 1969.
16. Ibid., 27 October 1969.
17. Ibid., 3 November 1969.
18. Ibid., 13 December 1969.
19. Ibid., 7 March 1970.
20. Ibid., 6 April 1970. For the Rising see above, p. 8.
21. Ibid., 6 April 1970.
22. 5 April 1970.
23. Belfast *News Letter*, 20 April 1970.
24. Conway, *Statements*.
25. Belfast *News Letter*, 30 May 1970.
26. See below, p. 134–5.
27. Conway, *Statements*.
28. Belfast *News Letter*, 10 August 1970.
29. 13 March 1971.
30. See above, p. 50.
31. Information supplied by David Bleakley, a cabinet minister at the time. Interview, March 1980.
32. Brian Faulkner, *Memoirs of a Statesman* (Weidenfeld & Nicolson, 1978), p. 120.
33. See below, p. 103.
34. Belfast *News Letter*, 27 August 1971.
35. Conway, *Statements*.
36. Belfast *News Letter*, 1 November 1971.
37. Ibid., 4 February 1972. The Moderator was Dr James Haire, the President the Revd. C. H. Bain.
38. Ibid.
39. On 4 March 1972.
40. 24 March 1972.

CHAPTER 5

1. R. Deutsch and V. Magowan, *Northern Ireland: A Chronology of Events* (Blackstaff, Belfast, 1974), vol. 2, p. 166.
2. Minutes (unpublished) of ICC.
3. Belfast *News Letter*, 25 March 1972.

4. Ibid., 4 April 1972.
5. See below, p. 105.
6. At that time chief of staff of the Provisional IRA.
7. O'Brady, President of Provisional Sinn Fein; Cahill, a well-known member of the Provisionals, subsequently imprisoned in the Republic.
8. New Ireland, a policy put forward by Provisional Sinn Fein, by which Ireland would be governed in a loose federation of the four historical provinces. *Eire Nua, The Social and Economic Policy of Sinn Fein* (Sinn Fein, Dublin, 1971).
9. Original duplicated document in the possession of Eric Gallagher.
10. Deutsch and Magowan, *Chronology*, ii. 193.
11. Belfast *News Letter*, 4 April 1972.
12. Ibid., 6 June 1972.
13. Ibid., 20 May 1972.
14. Ibid., 15 June 1972.
15. Ibid., 14 August 1972.
16. Ibid., 19 August 1972.
17. Minutes (unpublished) of ICC.
18. Belfast *News Letter*, 21 November 1973.
19. Ibid., 18 April 1973.
20. Ibid., 11 January 1973.
21. Details will be found below, pp. 133–4.
22. Details will be found below, pp. 137–8.
23. Total electorate: 1,030,000. For UK: 591,820; for Republic of Ireland: 6,463.
24. White Paper, *Northern Ireland Constitutional Proposals* (Cmnd. 5259, March 1973).
25. Minutes (unpublished) of ICC.
26. Belfast *News Letter*, 23 March 1972.
27. Ibid., 12 June 1973.
28. Ibid., 29 August 1973.
29. Dr Butler was born in Dublin and had previously been Bishop of Tuam, but he had worked in London, been a chaplain to HM Forces, and held the MBE.
30. There was also to be a consultative assembly.
31. Belfast *News Letter*, 14 December 1973.

CHAPTER 6

1. These were arguably the basis of SDLP participation.
2. Belfast *News Letter*, 7 January 1974.
3. Ibid., 22 March 1974.
4. Ibid., 30 March 1974.
5. Minutes (unpublished) of ICC, spring meeting 1974.
6. Belfast *News Letter*, 15 April 1974.
7. Ibid., 8 April 1974.
8. Ibid., 20 April 1974.
9. See below, p. 160.
10. *Reports of Northern Ireland Assembly*, 30 April 1974.
11. See below, p. 138.
12. Belfast *News Letter*, 22 April 1974.
13. For a full account see Robert Fisk, *The Point of No Return* (Times Books, André Deutsch, 1975).
14. See Fisk, *Point of No Return, passim*.
15. Belfast *News Letter*, 20 May 1974.
16. Ibid., 13 July 1974.
17. Ibid., 21 June 1974.
18. Ibid., 5 August 1974.
19. Ibid., 2 October 1974.
20. Ibid., 31 October 1974.

21. *Irish Times*, 27 January 1975.
22. Ibid.
23. Ibid., 26 April 1975.
24. Ibid., 26 May 1975.

CHAPTER 7

1. In an address to the Justice and Peace Conference, 1973, quoted in editorial in the *Month*, September 1973.
2. *Irish Times*, 4 September 1975.
3. See above, p. oo.
4. *Irish Times*, 5 November 1975.
5. Ibid., 1 January 1976.
6. Ibid., 31 March 1976.
7. Ibid., 1 June 1976.
8. See above, p. 11.
9. *Irish Times*, 1 June 1976.
10. Published jointly by Christian Journals Ltd., Belfast, and Veritas Publications, Dublin, 1976; revised edn. 1977.
11. Minutes (unpublished) of ICC, spring meeting 1979.

CHAPTER 8

1. *Irish Times*, 6 January 1977.
2. Ibid., 3 January 1977.
3. Ibid., 10 January 1977.
4. Ibid., 24 February 1977.
5. Total deaths in 1976: 297; in 1977: 112; in 1978: 81. *Chief Constable's Report 1979*, published by the Police Authority, Northern Ireland.
6. 4 March 1977.
7. 15 January 1978.
8. *Irish Times*, 19 January 1978.
9. Ibid., 4 August 1978.
10. Ibid., 6 April 1978.
11. Published as a composite pamphlet by the Presbyterian Church in Ireland, 1978.
12. Published, under the same title, as a pamphlet by the Methodist Church in Ireland, 1979.
13. The *Irish Times* published a supplement on 3 October 1979 giving the full text of all the Pope's addresses. They have since been published in an attractive illustrated volume, *The Visit. Pope John Paul II in Ireland. A Historical Review* (Veritas/A.C.W., Dublin, 1979).
14. *The Government of Northern Ireland* (Cmnd. 7950, July 1980).
15. Irish Council of Churches Advisory Forum on Human rights, *The H-Block Issue*.
16. Statement issued by Cardinal O'Fiaich and Bishop Edward Daly, December 1980.
17. Ibid.

CHAPTER 9

1. See above, p. 37.
2. There was an initial telephone response from the Cabinet secretariat followed by letters from Captain Terence O'Neill to Eric Gallagher, 14 and 17 January 1969.
3. Letter to Eric Gallagher from Cardinal Conway, 10 January 1969.
4. Letter to the authors from the Revd. Professor Michael Ledwith, 26 December 1979.
5. See above, pp. 44, 53: interview with Mr James Callaghan.
6. This was approved and published by the respective church courts in 1973.
7. All of these are available from the ICC.
8. Published jointly by Christian Journals Ltd., Belfast, and Veritas Publications,

Dublin, 1976. Revised edn. 1977.

9. Memo to Eric Gallagher from the Revd. John Knox giving details of the work accomplished by the ecumenical officers, 13 February 1980.
10. Details of the support given by the fund are to be found in the annual reports of the ICC.
11. January 1974.
12. Published jointly by Christian Journals Ltd., Belfast, and Veritas Publications, Dublin, 1978.
13. C of I press releases made frequent references to this issue.
14. *Irish Times* report, 3 April 1976.
15. Ibid.
16. *Directory on Ecumenism in Ireland* (Veritas Publications, Dublin, 1976).
17. Letter to the authors, November 1979.
18. See above, p. 117.
19. See above, p. 118.
20. *The Visit.* pp. 3, 109.
21. Ibid., p. 95.
22. Minutes of the Executive committee of the ICC (unpublished).
23. Ibid.
24. As recorded by the authors.
25. The Revd. Canon John Baker, Speaker's Chaplain, House of Commons, the Revd. Dr Ray Davey, and Eric Gallagher.

CHAPTER 10

1. Norman McNeilly, *Exactly Fifty Years: The Belfast Education Authority and Its Work (1923–73)* (Blackstaff, Belfast, 1974), p. 9.
2. Norman McNeilly, *Belfast Model Schools, 1857–1957* (Northern Publishing Office Belfast Ltd., 1951), pp. 12 ff.
3. *Public Education in Northern Ireland*, (HMSO, Belfast, 1970), p. 9.
4. McNeilly, *Exactly Fifty Years*, p. 9.
5. Michael Farrell, *Northern Ireland: The Orange State* (Pluto Press, 1980), p. 101.
6. Ibid.
7. *Public Education in Northern Ireland*, pp. 9–12.
8. Walter M. Abbott (ed.), *The Documents of Vatican Two* (Geoffrey Chapman, 1966), para 2, p. 640.
9. Northern Ireland Community Relations Commission, *First Annual Report*, 1971.
10. *Community Forum*, II, No. 1 (1972).
11. *The Month*, January 1973.
12. Social Studies Conference, *The Conflict in Ireland. A Religious Dimension?* (Action Committee on Sectarianism, 1974).
13. Richard Hauser, *A Social Option* (published privately, 1975), p. 34.
14. F. S. L. Lyons, *The Burden of Our History* (Queen's University of Belfast, 1979), p. 23.
15. J. Darby, D. Murray, D. Batts, S. Dunn, S. Farren, J. Harris, *Education and Community in Northern Ireland: Schools Apart?* (New University of Ulster, 1977), p. 11.
16. *Attitudes to the Institutional Church: A Survey of Religious Practice, Attitudes and Belief in the Republic of Ireland 1973–74* (Research and Development Unit: Catholic Communications Institute of Ireland. Report No. 4, 1976), tables 1–2.
17. *Parliamentary Debates*, Northern Ireland, 30 April 1974.
18. Ibid.
19. Ibid.
20. Letter to Belfast Education and Library Board, 1 May 1974.
21. Minutes of Belfast Education and Library Board, available in Belfast Central Library.

22. Richard Rose, *Governing Without Consensus* (Faber & Faber, 1971).
23. H. Sockett, *et al.*, *Segregation in Education* (New University of Ulster, 1978), papers read at a conference on the theme. The conference received reports of the project dealt with in Darby, *et al.*, *Education and Community in Northern Ireland*.
24. J. J. Campbell, *Catholic Schools. A Survey of a Northern Ireland Problem* (Fallon's Educational Supply Company, Belfast 1964), p. 16.
25. *Irish Christian Advocate*, 28 January 1971.
26. *Directory on Ecumenism in Ireland* (Veritas Publications, Dublin, 1976).
27. *Segregation in Education*, pp. 45 ff., 53 ff.
28. *National Pastoral Congress: Observers' Report* (British Council of Churches, 1980), p. 18.
29. *The Furrow*, December 1979.
30. Rose, *Governing Without Consensus*, pp. 336 ff.
31. Darby, *et al. Education and Community in Northern Ireland*, pp. 86 ff.
32. Sockett, *Segregation in Education*, p. 3, also Darby, *Education and Community in Northern Ireland*, p. 79.
33. Sockett, *Segregation in Education*, p. 1.
34. *The Future Structure of Teacher Education in Northern Ireland* (HMSO, Belfast, 1980).
35. Pp. 86–7.
36. Early in 1981 proposals were formulated and arrangements made by parents connected with the All Children Together Movement for the opening of a post-primary integrated school, to be known as Lagan College, in south Belfast.

CHAPTER 11
1. One of the authors was present.
2. The full story of Women Together and other early movements is told in David Bleakley's *Peace in Ulster*, pp. 82 ff. Had circumstances been different, Women Together could well have been The Peace People Mark 1.
3. See David Bleakley, *Saidie Patterson, Irish Peace Maker* (Blackstaff, Belfast, 1980).
4. The work of many of the groups mentioned has been examined and reported on by the Inter-Church Emergency Fund and in Bleakley's *Peace in Ulster*.
5. Based in Dublin.
6. Glencree operates in and from a former British military establishment in the mountains south of Dublin.
7. Information may be obtained from the Inter-Church Emergency Fund, ICC, 48 Elmwood Avenue, Belfast.
8. Bleakley, *Saidie Patterson*, pp. 83 ff.
9. Eamonn McCann, *War and an Irish Town* (Pluto Press, 1980), p. 153.
10. Ciaran McKeown, *The Price of Peace* (McKeown, Belfast, 1976), back cover.
11. The *Irish Times* and *Belfast Telegraph* gave considerable coverage to the Peace People during this period.
12. Reported by Nell McCafferty in *Magill*, August 1980.
13. The Revd. Dr Ray Davey in conversation with the authors, April 1980.
14. Statement of aims published in promotional literature.
15. Alf McCreary, *Corrymeela, The Search For Peace* (Christian Journals Ltd., Belfast, 1975).
16. Dr G. B. Newe in conversation with the authors, April 1980.
17. Bleakley, *Peace in Ulster*, p. 80.
18. Its meetings, though attended by journalists, are not reported. Eric Gallagher is a founder member.
19. Protestant and Catholic Encounter. Dr G. B. Newe and Very Revd. Dr Alfred Martin were prominent founder members. Both are now patrons.
20. As later reprinted in Articles of Association of NUM (New Ulster Movement Limited). Incorporated 29 October 1974.
21. Private document circulated to members.

22. Garret Fitzgerald, *Towards a New Ireland* (Charles Knight, 1972), p. 146 ff. In these pages Dr Fitzgerald deals specifically with issues raised by Northern Protestants at a Belfast meeting of the Movement. Eric Gallagher was present. Conor Cruise O'Brien, *States of Ireland* (Hutchinson, 1972), pp. 219–20.
23. Cecil Kerr, *Power To Love* (Christian Journals Ltd., Belfast, 1976), p. 7.
24. Cardinal L. J. Suenens and Dom Helder Camara, *Charismatic Renewal and Social Action* (Servant Books, 1979), Malines Document 3, pp. 87 f.
25. Tim Pat Coogan, *The IRA* (Fontana, 1980), pp. 496 ff.
26. Magill, August 1980.

CHAPTER 12

1. Rhona M. Fhields, an American psychologist, in her book *Society Under Siege. A Psychology of Northern Ireland* (Temple University Press, Philledlphia, 1976), uses the phrase 'psychological genocide' to describe the pressure brought in successive generations of 'British colonialism' to bear on the Irish people.
2. See above, ch. 1, n. 7.
3. E. Moxon-Browne, 'Attitudes Towards Religion in Northern Ireland', *PACE*, Summer/Autumn, 1980.
4. For example, at the end of 1980, a successful *modus vivendi* carefully built up between Unionist and SDLP councillors on the newly constituted District Council of Londonderry over a period of seven years, was jeopardized, if not ruptured, by the issue of playing Gaelic football, much of it on Sundays, in a predominantly Protestant part of the city.
5. M. W. Dewar, *Why Orangeism?* (Grand Orange Lodge of Ireland, Belfast, 1959), p. 23. With this quotation we may well contrast the sentiment of certain Orange songs, e.g. 'Dolly's Brae', quoted with evident relish by another clerical apologist for the Order, the Revd. John Brown, in Dewar, Brown, and Long, *Orangeism: A New Historical Appreciation* (Grand Lodge of Ireland, Belfast, 1967), p. 136. Its lines include:

> As fearlessly we charged on them, their terror it was great,
> Through rocks and whins, to save their skins, they beat a fast retreat . . .
> They prayed to Lady Mary, but their prayers were all in vain,
> For, in spite of all their Popish schemes, one hundred there were slain.

W. Peake, *A Collection of Orange and Protestant Songs* (Belfast, 1907), p. 67.
6. Dewar, *Why Orangeism?'* p. 23.
7. Barritt *et al.*, *Orange and Green*, p. 36.
8. Ibid.
9. Frank Wright, 'Protestant Ideology and Politics in Ulster', *European Journal of Sociology*, xiv (1973), 213–80; also published as a separate booklet.
10. See ch. 2.
11. Quoted by Liam de Paor, *Divided Ulster* (Penguin, 1970), p. 26.
12. Dewar, *Why Orangeism?*, p. 15.
13. Quoted by Whyte, *Church and State in Modern Ireland*, pp. 321 f. *Irish Independent* 19 January 1956.
14. *Studies*, Spring/Summer 1978.
15. *Republicanism, Loyalism and Pluralism in Ireland* (Presbyterian Church in Ireland, 1978). First published as three separate reports.
16. See pp. 110, 135, 170–1.
17. *Month*, March 1976.
18. Ibid., April 1974.
19. 'Ecumenism in Ireland Now: Problems and Hopes', *Irish Theological Quarterly*, January 1978.
20. ABC United States of America network programme, 16 September 1973. Taking part with presenter George Watson were William Cardinal Conway, Archbishop George Otto Simms, and the Right Revd. Dr John W. Orr (Moderator).
21. *The Visit*, p. 32.

Appendix I

Standing Committee to monitor and report on mixed marriages. (See ch. 9 on Ballymascanlon.) The report was a duplicated document circulated to the participating churches by the committee.

The 1977 report was an unusual document. It spelled out frankly both Catholic and Protestant grievances.

There were Catholic objections to the following: Protestant clergy interviewing the Catholic party before or without his/her talking with the priest. Protestant assurances that marriage in a Protestant church without Catholic dispensation is both lawful and valid. Protestant refusal or neglect to inform or refer in any way to the priest in cases of marriage in the Protestant church where the necessary dispensation has not been received.

There were also Protestant objections, e.g. Catholic insistence in requiring promises from the Protestant partner regarding the upbringing of children, a sense of injustice arising from Irish deviation from the norms in other hierarchies; Catholic insistence on information from the Protestant clergymen which imperils confidentiality when this is requested by the Catholic partner; the danger to spiritual development in the marriage when the priest or someone else insists that a marriage without dispensation is invalid (this type of pressure is driving growing numbers of young people to reject church ceremonies altogether); Roman Catholic requirements for the Protestant partner to accept claims over the marriage and family diminish his/her share of responsibility and spiritual freedom.

Appendix II

Political parties in Northern Ireland

OUP	The Official Unionist Party, which adopted the title 'Official' when rival unionist parties appeared. Leaders: Terence O'Neill to 1969, James Chichester-Clark 1969–71, Brian Faulkner 1971–4, Harry West 1974–9, James Molyneaux 1979–.
DUP	Democratic Unionist Party, founded 1972. Leader: the Revd. Ian Paisley.

VUP	Vanguard Unionist Party, 1972–6. Leader: William Craig. No longer active.
UUUC	United Ulster Unionist Council, an alliance of the above three parties to fight the UK elections of 1974, and the election for the 1975 Convention. No longer active.
UPNI	Unionist Party of Northern Ireland. founded by Brian Faulkner in 1974, when he lost the leadership of the Official Unionist Party. Leaders: Brian Faulkner 1974–6, Mrs Anne Dickson 1976–81. Disbanded October 1981.
UUUM	United Ulster Unionist Movement—that part of VUP which refused to join OUP when William Craig and other MPs were reconciled to it. Leader: Ernest Baird.
Alliance	A new party founded in 1970 on non-sectarian principles. Leader: Oliver Napier.
SDLP	Social Democratic and Labour Party, founded in 1970 by a combination of former nationalist and republican groups. Leaders: Gerard Fitt 1970–80, John Hume 1980–.
Republican Clubs	The political wing of the Official IRA. Holds a number of local Council seats.
Provisional Sinn Fein	The political wing of the Provisional IRA. It has so far contested no elections.
IRSP	Irish Republican Socialist Party. The political wing of the Irish National Liberation Army.

Appendix III

The office of Governor was instituted with the 1921 settlement. It had a ceremonial and public, though non-political, role. As representative of the monarch, the Governor officially opened the sessions of Parliament, presided over the Northern Ireland Privy Council and graced many important public functions. When visiting the Province, members of the royal family, the Prime Minister and the Leader of the Opposition normally were guests at Government House, Hillsborough, the Governor's official residence. The last holder of the office, Lord Grey of Naunton, while keeping strictly within the limits of his non-political role, had gained the confidence of many N.I. citizens. By his personal influence, he had done much to reduce the deterioration in relationships. Greater benefit could arguably have been derived by *all* sections from his considerable gifts of tact and insight. His departure was deeply regretted and his election in 1980 to the chancellorship of the NUU reflected the esteem in which he was held.

Bibliography

Abbott,W. M., SJ (ed.), *The Documents of Vatican Two*. (Geoffrey Chapman, 1966).

Barritt, D. P. and Carter, C. F., *The Northern Ireland Problem: A Study in Group Relations* (Oxford University Press, 1962).

Beckett, J. C., *The Making of Modern Ireland 1603–1923* (Faber & Faber, 1969).

Biggs-Davison, J., MP., *Catholics and the Union* (Ulster Unionist Party, undated).

Bleakley, D. W., *Peace in Ulster* (Mowbrays, 1972). *Faulkner, Conflict and Consent in Irish Politics* (Mowbrays, 1974). *Saidie Patterson, Irish Peace Maker* (Blackstaff, Belfast, 1980).

Boyd, Andrew, *Holy War in Belfast* (Anvil Books, Tralee, 1969).

Callaghan, James, *A House Divided. The Dilemma of Northern Ireland* (Collins, 1973).

Campbell, J. J., *Catholic Schools. A Survey of a Northern Ireland Problem* (Fallon's Educational Supply Company, Belfast, 1964?).

Coogan, Tim Pat, *The IRA* (Fontana, 1980).

Corkey, W., *Episode in the History of Protestant Ulster 1923–47* (William Dorman, Belfast, 1947).

Daly, Cahal B., *Violence in Ireland and the Christian Conscience* (Veritas, Dublin, 1973).

Daly, Cahal B. and Worrall, A. S., *Ballymascanlon* (Christian Journals Ltd., Belfast, and Veritas, Dublin, 1978).

Darby, J., *et al.*, *Education and Community in Northern Ireland: Schools Apart?* (New University of Ulster, 1977).

Deutsch, R., and Magowan, V., *Northern Ireland: A Chronology of Events* (Blackstaff, Belfast, 1974).

Devlin, Bernadette, *The Price of my Soul* (André Deutsch, 1969).

Dewar, M. W., *Why Orangeism?* (Grand Orange Lodge of Ireland, Belfast, 1959).

Dewar, M. W., Brown, J., and Long, S. E., *Orangeism. A New Historical Appreciation* (Grand Orange Lodge of Ireland, Belfast, 1967).

Egan, B., and McCormack, V., *Burntollet* (LRS Publishers, London, 1969).

Farrell, M., *Northern Ireland: The Orange State.* (Reprinted, Pluto Press, 1980).

Faul, D., and Murray, R., *Brutalities Dec. 1971–Feb. 1972* (Abbey, Cavan, 1972).
Whitelaw's Tribunals Nov. 1972–Jan. 1973 (Abbey, Cavan, 1973).
Faulkner, Brian, *Memoirs of a Statesman* (Weidenfeld & Nicolson, 1978).
Fhields, R.M., *Society under Siege. A psychology of Northern Ireland* (Temple University Press, Philadelphia, 1976).
Fisk, R., *The Point of No Return* (Times Books, André Deutsch, 1975).
Fitzgerald, G. M., *Towards a New Ireland* (Charles Knight, 1972).
Flackes, W. D., *Northern Ireland: A Political Directory* (Gill & Macmillan, Dublin, 1980).
Fraser, M., *Children In Conflict* (Secker & Warburg, 1973).
Gallagher, B., *Embers From the Fires of Ulster* (Christian Journals Ltd., Belfast, 1977).
Gray, T., *The Orange Order* (Bodley Head, 1972).
Grogan V., and Ryan, L., *Religious Freedom* (Sceptre Books, Dublin, 1967).
Harris, R., *Prejudice and Tolerance in Ulster* (Manchester University Press, 1972).
Hauser, R., *A Social Option* (published privately, 1975).
Hayes, M., *Community Relations and the Role of the Community Relations Commission* (Runnymede Trust, 1972).
Hurley, M., SJ, *Theology of Ecumenism* (Mercier Press, Cork, 1969).
(ed.), *John Wesley's Letter to a Roman Catholic* (Geoffrey Chapman, 1968).
Praying for Unity (The Furrow Trust, Gill & Son, Dublin, 1963).
Kee, R., *The Green Flag* (Weidenfeld & Nicolson, 1972).
Ireland (BBC Publications, 1981).
Kerr, C., *Power to Love* (Christian Journals Ltd., Belfast, 1976).
Lane, D. (ed.), *Ireland: Liberation and Theology* (Orbis Books, 1977).
Long, S. E., *Rather be an Ulsterman* (Slieve Croob Books, Belfast, 1972)
The Orange Institution (Grand Orange Lodge of Ireland, 1978).
Lyons, F. S. L., *Ireland Since the Famine* (Weidenfeld & Nicholson, 1971; Fontana, 1973).
The Burden of Our History (Queen's University of Belfast, 1979).
McAteer, F., *Won't You Sit Down and Listen?* (Derry Journal, 1972).
McCann, E., *War and an Irish Town* (First edn. Penguin, 1974; 2nd updated edn. Pluto, 1980).
McCreary, Alf., *Corrymeela, The Search for Peace* (Christian Journals Ltd., Belfast, 1975).
McKeown, C., *The Price of Peace* (McKeown, Belfast, 1976).
McNeilly, N., *Belfast Model Schools, 1857–1957* (Northern Publishing Office Belfast Ltd., 1957). *Exactly Fifty Years: Belfast Education Authority and Its Work, 1923–73* (Blackstaff, 1974).

MacStiofain, S., *Memories of a Revolutionary* (Gordon Cremonesi, 1975).

Magee, J., *Northern Ireland: Crisis and Conflict* (Routledge and Kegan Paul, 1973).

Marrinan, P., *Paisley—Man of Wrath* (Anvil Books, Tralee, 1973).

Moody, T. W., and Martin, F. X., *The Course of Irish History* (Mercier, Cork, 1967).

Murphy, Dervla, *A Place Apart* (Penguin, 1978).

Murphy, J. A., *Ireland in the Twentieth Century* (Gill & Macmillan, Dublin, 1975).

O'Brien, C. Cruise, *States of Ireland* (Hutchinson, 1972).

O'Donnell, E. E., *Northern Ireland Stereotypes* (College of Industrial Relations, Dublin, 1977).

O'Fiaich, Tomàs Cardinal, Introduction to *The Visit. Pope John Paul II in Ireland. A Historical Review* (Veritas/A. C. W., Dublin, 1979).

O'Neill, Terence, *Autobiography* (Hart-Davis, 1972).

de Paor, L., *Divided Ulster* (Penguin, 1970).

Patterson, M., *The Hungry Sheep of Ulster* (Platform Publications, Belfast, 1974).

Philbin, W. J., *Ireland's Problem* (published privately, 1974).

Probert, B., *Beyond Orange and Green* (Academy Press, 1978).

Robb, J. A. D., *New Ireland: Sell Out or Opportunity?* (published privately, 1972).

Rose, R., *Governing without Consensus* (Faber & Faber, 1971). *A Time of Choice* (Macmillan, 1976).

Smyth, W. Martin, *Stand Fast* (Orange Publications, 1974). *The Battle for Northern Ireland* (Grand Orange Lodge of Belfast, 1972).

Sockett, H. *et al.*, *Segregation in Education* (New University of Ulster, 1978).

Stewart, A. T. Q., *The Narrow Ground. Aspects of Ulster 1609–1969* (Faber & Faber, 1977).

Stewart, J., *Ulster DV* (Castle Press, Belfast, undated).

Suenens, L. J. Cardinal and Camara H., *Charismatic Renewal and Social Action* (Servant Books, 1979).

Sunday Times Insight Team, *Ulster* (Penguin, 1972).

Sweetman, R., *On our Knees: Ireland 1972.* (Pan, 1972).

Target, G. W., *Unholy Smoke* (Hodder and Stoughton, 1969).

Whyte, J. H., *Church and State in Modern Ireland* (Gill & Macmillan, Dublin, 1971; 2nd edn. 1980).

Worrall A. S. (ed.), *Who are we? What do we Believe?* (Christian Journals Ltd., Belfast, 1977).

Wright, F., 'Protestant Ideology and Politics in Ulster', *European Journal of Sociology*, xiv (1973), 213–80; also published as a separate booklet.

Church and Ecumenical Publications

CHURCH OF IRELAND

Elliott, E. P. M., *et al.*, *Issues in Ireland To-day* (Church of Ireland Gazette, 1980).
Matthews, Trevor, *Inter Group Conflicts* (Church of Ireland Gazette, 1980).
Role of the Church Committee, *People Are Not Pawns* (Church of Ireland, 1976).
   The Republic and Northern Ireland (Church of Ireland, 1980).
   Violence, Peace (Church of Ireland, 1980).

CHURCH OF ENGLAND

Ecclestone, G., and Elliott, E., *The Irish Problem and Ourselves* (Church Information Office, 1977).

METHODIST CHURCH IN IRELAND

Conference Statements, *A Call to the Methodist People* (Methodist Church, 1966).
   Relationships With the World Council of Churches and the Roman Catholic Church (Methodist Church, 1967).
   The Current Situation in Ireland (Methodist Church, 1979).
Jeffery, F., *Methodism and the Irish Situation* (Wesley Historical Society, 1973).
Gallagher, E., *A Better Way for Irish Protestants and Roman Catholics* (Methodist Mission Board, 1973).

PRESBYTERIAN CHURCH IN IRELAND

General Assembly Statements, *Republicanism, Loyalism and Pluralism in Ireland* (Presbyterian Church, 1978).
   Christians in a Situation of Conflict (Presbyterian Church, 1973).
   The Northern Ireland Situation, Numbers 3, 4, 5, 6 (Presbyterian Church, 1974, 1975, 1977, 1978).
   The Relation of the Presbyterian Church in Ireland to the Church of Rome (Presbyterian Church, 1970).

FREE PRESBYTERIAN CHURCH

Paisley, I. R. K., *Union with Rome* (Puritan Printing Company, undated).
   This We Will Maintain (Puritan Printing Company, undated).

RELIGIOUS SOCIETY OF FRIENDS

Barritt, D. P., *et al.*, *Orange and Green: Northern Ireland* (Northern Friends Peace Board, 1969).

ROMAN CATHOLIC CHURCH

Conway, William Cardinal, *et al.*, *Statements and Joint Statements* (published privately, 1972).

Irish Commission on Justice and Peace, *H-Block* (privately published, 1980).
Irish Episcopal Conference, *Irish Directory on Ecumenism* (Veritas Publications, Dublin, 1969).
　　　Directory on Ecumenism in Ireland (Veritas Publications, Dublin, 1976).
Justice, Love and Peace: Pastoral Letters of Irish Bishops, 1969–79 (Veritas Publications, Dublin, 1980).
Dallat, M., *et al.*, Aspects of Catholic Education (St. Joseph's College of Education, Belfast, 1971).

NON-SUBSCRIBING PRESBYTERIAN CHURCH

Wigmore-Beddoes, D. G., *Preaching to a Riot* (First Presbyterian Church, Belfast, 1971).

ECUMENICAL

Barkley, J., and Magee, J., *Irish History, Fact or Fiction?* (The Churches' Central Committee for Community Work, 1976).
Davis, R., *et al.*, *RISK: Hope Deferred*, vol. 10, No. 1 (World Council Churches, 1974).
Irish Council of Churches Advisory Forum on Human Rights, *The H-block Issue* (Irish Council of Churches, 1980).
National Pastoral Congress: Observers' Report (British Council of Churches, 1980).
Poyntz, S. G. (ed.), *Towards a United Church* (Tripartite Church Union Negotiating Committee, 1973).
Together with Youth (Christian Journals Ltd., Belfast, 1973).
Worrall, A. S. (ed.), *Violence in Ireland: Report to the Churches* (Christian Journals Ltd., Belfast, and Veritas Publications, Dublin, 1976 and 1977).

Political Parties, etc.

Fine Gael, *Ireland—Our Future Together* (1979).
Belfast Workers Research Unit, *The Churches in Northern Ireland* (1980).
Campaign for Social Justice, *The Mailed Fist* (1971).
Irish and British Communist Organization, *Ulster As It Is* (1973).
Irish Congress of Trade Unions, *Political Policy in Northern Ireland* (1972).
New Ulster Political Research Group, *Beyond the Religious Divide* (1979).
Provisional Sinn Fein, *Eire Nua, The Social and Economic Policy of Sinn Fein* (Sinn Fein, Dublin, 1971).
Social and Democratic Labour Party, *Towards a New Ireland* (1972).
Tara, *Ireland Forever* (undated).
Ulster Unionist Party, *Southern Ireland Church or State?* (1951).
　　　Peace Order and Good Government (1973).

Government Publications

Government of Northern Ireland, *Public Education in Northern Ireland* (HMSO, Belfast, 1970).
——,*The Future Structure of Teacher Education in Northern Ireland* (HMSO, Belfast, 1980).
——,Cameron Commission, *Disturbances in Northern Ireland* (Cmnd. 532, 1969).
——,Scarman Tribunal, *Violence and Civil Disturbances in Northern Ireland in 1969* (Cmnd. 566, 1972).
——,Northern Ireland Community Relations Commission, *First Annual Report* (1971).
Government of United Kingdom, *The Future of Northern Ireland* (Northern Ireland Office, 1972).
——,*The Government of Northern Ireland* (Cmnd. 7763, 1979).
——,*The Government of Northern Ireland* (Cmnd. 7950, 1980).
——,Northern Ireland (Central Office of Information, London, 1975).
——,Northern Ireland Constitutional Proposals (Cmnd. 5259, 1973).

Reports, Programmes, etc.

ABC Television, USA, 'Of God and Irishmen' (1973).
Greer, J. E., and McElhinney, E. P., *Teaching Religion in Ireland* (New University of Ulster, 1980).
Research and Development Unit of the Catholic Communications Centre of Ireland, *A Survey of Religious Practice, Attitudes and Belief in the Republic of Ireland, 1973–4* (1976).
Social Studies Conference, *The Conflict in Ireland. A Religious Dimension?* (Action Committee on Sectarianism, 1974).
Ulster Television, 'ULSTER The Economic Case' (1975).
——,'Faces of Violence' (1977).
Linder, R. D., *The Role of the Clergy in the Troubles in Northern Ireland 1968–76* (Kansas State University, 1980).

Newspapers, journals, etc.

DAILIES

Belfast Telegraph
Irish Independent, Dublin
Irish News, Belfast
Irish Press, Dublin
Irish Times, Dublin
News Letter, Belfast

WEEKLY, MONTHLY, AND OCCASIONAL
PUBLICATIONS

Administration, Dublin, vol. 2, No 4, 1972.
Community Forum, Northern Ireland Community Relations Commission

Community News, Northern Ireland Community Relations Commission
Corrymeela News, Corrymeela Community, Belfast
Fortnight, Belfast
Hibernia, Dublin
Magill, Dublin
PACE, Belfast
Protestant Telegraph, Belfast

RELIGIOUS PUBLICATIONS

Aquarius, Servite Priory, Benburb
Church of Ireland Gazette, Belfast
Doctrine and Life, Dominican Order, Dublin
The Furrow, Furrow Trust, Maynooth
Irish Theological Quarterly, Dublin
Methodist Newsletter, Belfast
The Month, Dublin
Presbyterian Herald, Belfast
The Revivalist, Belfast

Index

WITHDRAWN